THE WAR AT HOME

The War at Home

Perspectives on the Arkansas Experience during World War I

EDITED BY

MARK K. CHRIST

The University of Arkansas Press
Fayetteville
2020

ISBN: 978-1-68226-126-2
eISBN: 978-1-61075-685-3
DOI: https://doi.org/10.34053/christ2019.twah

24 23 22 21 20   5 4 3 2 1

Designed by Liz Lester

⊗ The paper used in this publication meets the
minimum requirements of the American National
Standard for Permanence of Paper for Printed
Library Materials Z39.48-1984.

Library of Congress Control Number: 2019947840

This collection is dedicated to
Homer W. Farra, Oscar Jones, Spencer Fox,
Maud Hines, William L. Sucha, Henry G. Carlson,
Gregory Bohn, Nina Byrom Stephenson, Leroy Johnston,
Walton Brooks, W. N. Gladson, Mary H. Spight,
and all of the soldiers and civilians who experienced
the War to End All Wars.

CONTENTS

PREFACE

Nearly 72,000 Arkansawyers, including more than 18,000 African American men, served in the U.S. military during World War I, and nearly 2,200 did not live to come home. To remember and honor them on the hundredth anniversary of the Great War, the Arkansas World War I Centennial Commemoration Committee was created in early 2016. Over the course of the next three years, the committee worked with people across the state to plan events to remember the events of 100 years ago. Of particular note was a partnership with the Arkansas Forestry Commission that saw a WWI Memorial Tree planted in each of Arkansas's seventy-five counties, with each planting sprinkled with soil from the Meuse-Argonne American Cemetery in France, where thousands of American doughboys are interred. To close out the commemoration, dozens of groups across the state participated in ringing bells eleven times on the eleventh hour of the eleventh day of the eleventh month of 2018—exactly 100 years after the guns finally went silent in Europe.

Among the mandates of the Arkansas World War I Centennial Commemoration Committee was a call to encourage new research into the events of World War I, and the group coordinated with the Old State House Museum in Little Rock to host a pair of seminars to explore the events and legacy of the Great War, the proceedings of which are collected in this volume. In the first seminar, committee chairman Shawn Fisher explored the nature of the South's involvement in the new war, Carl Drexler looked into how Arkansas ramped up its industrial base to support the war effort, Cherisse Jones-Branch examined the experiences of African Americans at home and abroad, and Elizabeth Griffin Hill looked at the ways in which Arkansas women participated in wartime activities. The second seminar included Tom DeBlack reporting on the horrific influenza episode of 1918, Jeannie Whayne analyzing the activities of women's suffragists during the war, committee vice-chairman Raymond Screws plotting the development of WWI's Camp Pike into today's Camp Robinson, Brian K. Mitchell studying the links between African American participation in WWI and the Elaine Race Riots of 1919, and Roger Pauly following Arkansas journalism from World War I to World War II.

In addition to the scholars who contributed their expertise to the seminars and this book, Georganne Sisco, Daniel Cockrell, and Leah Lambert worked with me, as a WWI Committee member, to develop the events. The Arkansas World War I Centennial Commemoration Committee strongly supported the seminars, particularly Shawn Fisher, Raymond Screws, Lisa Speer, Joel Lynch, Bill Wussick and Wendy Richter, and Angela Kubaiko of the Arkansas Historic Preservation Program provided crucial aid to these events as well as to the entire WWI commemoration. Thanks are also due to Ali Welky, whose editing skills are evident throughout this volume, and to postcard guru extraordinaire Ray Hanley, Bill Gatewood of the Old State House Museum, Elizabeth Freeman of the Arkansas State Archives (who truly went above and beyond for this project), Tim Nutt of the Historical Research Center, University of Arkansas for Medical Sciences, Rachel Whitaker of the Shiloh Museum of Ozark History, Sandra Taylor Smith of the North Little Rock History Commission, Geoffery Stark of the University of Arkansas Special Collections (who delved deep to find some obscure images), Nan Snow, and Mike Polston of the Central Arkansas Library System's Butler Center for Arkansas Studies. Thanks also to Mike Bieker, David Scott Cunningham, Jenny Vos, and Molly Rector of the University of Arkansas Press for shepherding this project through production.

Others helped in many ways both big and small, and their combined efforts are appreciated.

Mark K. Christ

THE WAR AT HOME

1 | Arkansas and the Great War

Southern Soldiers Fight for a National Victory

SHAWN FISHER

One hundred years ago, the world was engaged in a great combat, a "fiery trial" as President Woodrow Wilson called it. This war, Wilson said, was a "distressing and oppressive duty," but it was a war worth fighting, a war "for democracy, for the right of those who submit to authority to have a voice in their own governments, for the rights and liberties of small nations . . . for peace and safety to all nations and [to] make the world itself at last free."[1]

And yet, America's entrance into the Great War was met with over-whelmingly exuberance, even a lightheartedness. One Arkansas soldier, a draftee named Thomas Gibson of Judsonia, wrote home in August 1917, and perhaps exemplified America's national feeling of confidence at the outset of the war. Gibson told his mother, "One of my friends told me that the war would not last long. I asked him why and he said that his brother joined [the army] and that he was never known to hold a job more than two months."[2] This good-natured greeting of the Great War, however, was much contrasted with the feeling in Europe by 1917.

When the Great War began in Europe with the German invasion of Belgium on August 4, 1914, many blamed the immediate crisis on Bosnian separatists who assassinated Archduke Franz Ferdinand, the heir to the Austro-Hungarian Empire. However, the conflict had been brewing for many years. The origins of the war might sit squarely on the

| DOI: https://doi.org/10.34053/christ2019.twah.1

rise of the German state under Otto von Bismarck, whose demand for "blood and iron" marked a change in the diplomatic fortunes of Europe. But German aggression was met by equally bellicose French, English, and Russian maneuvering. The old Concert of Europe with its "spheres of influence" had given way to the unfettered lust of *Weltpolitik*——power politics played with one goal in mind: hegemony over all of Europe, and beyond. Emboldened by vast colonial resources and rapid industrialization, the great powers were capable of manufacturing prodigious amounts of war materiel. In short order, they cast aside their fear of continent-wide war and embraced a final showdown.

As much as anything else, the technologies of the era brought the nations into direct conflict. Waging war with battleships, submarines, trains, "wireless" radio communications, rapid-fire field artillery, airships, and even primitive airplanes promised a quick, decisive, and permanent end to war on the European continent. Never was a prediction more wrong. Within months, the continent was bogged down in trench warfare. The combat, far from quick and decisive, devolved into a bloody fight of attrition in which gains won yesterday were lost quickly tomorrow, only to be won and lost again and again.

In the United States, President Wilson hoped that if America entered the war, American fighting men would save France and Belgium, defeat the German military, and bring about his ultimate goal:——the end of war through the arbitration with the establishment of the League of Nations. The president asked Congress to approve a declaration of war in 1917, three years after the war began, for two primary reasons. First, the German navy's unrestricted submarine warfare continued to sink American ships despite the strident declarations of American nonbelligerency. Second, the British government had intercepted a telegram from German diplomat Arthur Zimmermann offering Mexico support if it invaded the United States. Another factor in Wilson's thinking was that the Russian government had collapsed and the tsar had been replaced with what at the time resembled a democratic government. Finally, in April, as the tide shifted toward war, Wilson intoned, "The day has come when America is privileged to spend her blood and her might for the principles that gave her birth and happiness and the peace which she has treasured. God helping her, she can do no other."[3]

It is a commonplace assertion that the Great War was the turning point of the modern world. Up until 1914, the arc of history—at least recent Western history—had bent toward progress, but after the war the world seemed broken, with all its faults and failings laid bare for inspection and derision. The noted military historian John Keegan stated that the First World War "destroyed the benevolent and optimistic culture of the European continent."[4] Certainly fascism and socialism took root during the war and after; certainly the war brought to Europe a cultural rot, a sort of intellectual gangrene that required an excision so massive that it left behind a quadriplegic. Winston Churchill said afterward that the war had left Europe in shambles: "the nations were broken . . . empires shattered . . . . Europe was ruined."[5]

The Great War crushed the dreams of the Progressive movement in the United States, too, whose advocates believed that with just the right social programs and institutions, a rising and inevitable utopia was at hand. One such advocate, Washington Gladden, wrote in his bestseller *Christianity and Socialism* in 1905 that "international wars are less common than they once were; their methods and implements have become so destructive that rulers shrink appalled from venturing upon them [and may make] war impossible, and to hasten the day of universal arbitration."[6]

Of course, the utopia they envisioned never existed, much less materialized, despite the *fin de siècle* optimism of the Progressives. Republicans in the Senate repudiated Wilson for the League of Nations and never approved the treaty. The last gasp of the Progressives was Prohibition; little need be mentioned of that failed social experiment. The "great crusade" which President Wilson and the nation embarked upon in 1917 was "the war to end all wars," but it became a corrupting fiasco. Just five years later, on September 18, 1922, Adolf Hitler, a decorated Great War corporal, said in a political rally in Munich that launched the rise of his National Socialist party: "It cannot be that two million Germans should have fallen in vain . . . . No, we do not pardon, we demand—vengeance!"[7]

That desire for revenge saw the whole continent swallowed up in yet another war, one which caused five times more deaths than the Great War. English poet Herbert Read, looking back at the whole bloody period of wars, wrote:

> Happy are those who can relieve
> suffering with prayer
> Happy those who can rely on God
> to see them through. They can wait patiently for the end.
> But we who have put our faith

in the goodness of man

and now see man's image debas'd

lower than the wolf or the hog—Where can we turn for consolation?[8]

The Great War did debase mankind to new lows. And it did usher in a new age of destruction. Hitler's vengeance was begat by the Great War and its technological progeny; the new death machines introduced during the Great War made Hitler's revenge easier still.

Each innovation of the war had its counterparts in all wars that came after: machine guns, tanks, combat aircraft, mobile radio, submarines, chemical warfare, flamethrowers, mortars, and so on. The Great War was the first great proving ground for just how far Western science and industry had truly come, or, perhaps, had sunk. As one historian put it, "The First World War inaugurated the manufacture of mass death that the Second [World War] brought to a pitiless consummation."[9]

The armies of the First World War were gigantic, and the U.S. forces were no exception. Within nineteen months, the U.S. Army grew from 107,641 Regular Army and 132,000 National Guard soldiers to nearly four million, and managed to send nearly two million to Europe in what was called the American Expeditionary Forces (AEF). This was a major undertaking. The U.S. military was small at the outset of the war and required many months of all-out effort to bring its divisions on line, struggling all the while to clothe and arm troops for the trench fighting in Europe. The army was inexperienced as well, mostly draftees and newly minted officers. By the time of the Armistice, however, there were forty-two American combat divisions in France.[10] Some men volunteered, some were drafted, but all fought, according to historian Edward A. Gutièrrez, "for honor, manhood, comrades, and adventure, but especially for duty."[11] Over 4.7 million Americans served in the military during World War I; some 61,000 Arkansans served in the various branches of the armed forces.[12]

Nationally, during the war years 1917–1918 there were 116,516 recorded deaths among U.S. service members. That was about 0.1% of the U.S. population at the time, with an average of 279 deaths each day. Actual combat deaths—rather than deaths from disease, accident, or natural causes—were much lower, with 48,000 dying of their wounds.[13] Of that number, 404 Arkansans were killed in combat. Over 224,000 American doughboys, of which there were some 1,751 Arkansans, were wounded in combat; according to the War Department, a merciful number, five out of six of them, returned to duty.[14]

Arkansans fought on the land, at sea, and in the skies to defend the United States and the people of France and Belgium—and in Wilson's estimation, "civilization itself."[15] Soldiers, sailors, and marines from Arkansas were involved in some of fiercest fighting of the war, including the first fight between American and German troops. When the war came to a close, at least twenty-six Arkansans earned the nation's second-highest honor, the Distinguished Service Cross; two soldiers—Field E. Kindley and Abe Short—won the medal twice (that is, with oak leaf cluster).[16] Field E. Kindley of Gravette, Arkansas, shot down eleven aircraft during his service in the 148th Aero Squadron, placing him number three behind the top U.S. ace, Eddie Rickenbacker; Sergeant Abe Short of Aurora, Arkansas, was honored for two different actions while serving in Company H, 38th Infantry.[17] Only 111 in the nation received Distinguished Service Cross with oak leaf cluster in WWI.[18]

A scourge far deadlier than combat was the Spanish flu. Some 40,000 U.S. fighting men died of pneumonia related to the flu during the war.[19] The Spanish flu killed some seventy-five million people worldwide over a period of about four years, and ranks as one of the most deadly disasters in history, natural or manmade. In Arkansas the statewide death toll is often cited as 7,000, but some doubt remains as to its accuracy, since rural death records were never systemically collected.[20] A total of 417 troops from Arkansas died from disease in the American Expeditionary Forces in France, and while no figures exist for the exact number taken by influenza, it is possible that 80% or more of that number died from the flu.[21]

By comparison, some 60,000 Arkansans served the Confederacy during the Civil War, and the state counted some 10,000 dead. Of course, those figures belie the great difference in population between 1860 and 1920—in fact, only 4% of the state population of 1.75 million served in the First World War; however, during the Civil War, of the white population of 325,000, some 20% served in some fashion.

From One War to Another

Clearly the numbers mentioned here reveal something important—specifically, that the Great War was significantly less intense for Arkansas than had been the Civil War. There are several reasons for this. First, America entered World War I late, three years late to be exact.

For most of this period, the Civil War and its aftermath loomed large in the minds of the Southerners, not the distant war in Europe.

In the South, the social event of the year for many decades was the reunion of the United Confederate Veterans. In 1911, the reunion was held in Little Rock and some 100,000 attended, which was a population approximately twice the size of the city at that time.[22] In 1913, there had been the "sheathing of the sabers" at the fiftieth anniversary of the battle of Gettysburg, with some 50,000 gray-bearded veterans gathering in Gettysburg over the July 4th weekend to camp in the field as two great armies; it was the largest reunion of Civil War soldiers of both sides.[23] There were parades and marching, singing and bands, fireworks and shooting matches, and even a movie was made of the event. The film depicted the grizzled survivors of the Army of the Potomac and the Army of Northern Virginia shaking hands for the camera, reaching across the stone wall at "the angle" in the center of the battlefield, where Pickett's Confederate division was demolished.[24]

President Woodrow Wilson gave the July 4th reunion address; he himself was a proud Virginian and member of the Sons of Confederate Veterans. He said, "We have found one another again as brothers and comrades in arms, enemies no longer, generous friends rather, our battles long past, the quarrel forgotten—except that we shall not forget the splendid valor."[25]

That new spirit of camaraderie accompanied a flurry of monument building across the South, led by the United Daughters of the Confederacy, which, though formed in 1896, by the time of WWI had 100,000 members.[26] Many of the monuments to the Confederacy were built during this era to honor the passing of a generation and to remind the South of its valor in defending what had developed as the Lost Cause mythology.

There are at least thirty-six Confederate monuments in Arkansas, many dated approximately to the fiftieth anniversary of the war. In addition, the UDC in Arkansas purchased what is now the Prairie Grove battlefield in 1917 for the grand price of $1,100. It intended to make the mansion there a museum, and reported that "grape shot and Minnie [sic] balls are ploughed up in quantities in surrounding fields."[27] The ladies of the UDC were looking back, and forward. The question seemed to be whether they and their sons had the grit of their Confederate forefathers.

Wilson's election as president was a significant marker for the old Confederates, too, as he was the first southern-born president elected to office since Zachary Taylor. Naturally, Wilson staffed his administration

President Woodrow Wilson gave the July 4th speech at the Gettysburg battle-field on the fiftieth anniversary of the battle in 1913. *Courtesy of the Library of Congress.*

Irl Vinson (left) and Voy Vinson (right) served as privates in Company D, 141st Machine Gun Battalion. They flank their grandfather, Jesse Roberts, a Confederate veteran. *Courtesy of Melissa Nesbitt, granddaughter of Irl Vinson.*

with Southern Democrats. His election was perceived by southerners as an effort at a national reconciliation. Wilson laid the groundwork for making the modern nation state as we know it, one where regional divisions were to take second place to so-called national priorities. In addition, as many parts of the South struggled to build a modern economy, Wilson and others worried that the nation was weakened by these "backward" economic regions. A focus on trying to reform the Southern economy was the cornerstone of his 1912 campaign speeches. Wilson focused on what he called *New Freedom*, the title of his 1913 book. These freedoms included limited government, lower tariffs, more equitable bank loans (especially for farmers), and business reform and regulation aimed at protecting consumers.[28]

Whatever Wilson might have intended, one set of statistics alone described what the war did to the South more than anything else. In 1896, cotton, Arkansas's number one agricultural product, was just 6 cents a pound; in 1910 it was 15.1 cents, in 1917 it reached 23.5 cents, and in 1920 it peaked at 33.9 cents.[29] The war, for whatever the cost in human lives and suffering, was an economic boon for Arkansas.

Nationally the greatest effort at North–South reconciliation came in June 4, 1914—106 years after the birth of Jefferson Davis—when a monument to the Confederacy was erected in Arlington National Cemetery with President Wilson in attendance.[30] This marked the first time that Confederates were buried at Arlington; the ceremony was attended by Union veterans belonging to their fraternal organization, the Grand Army of the Republic.

Wilson and his war were popular among the aging Confederate troops, too. In fact, their flagship publication *The Confederate Veteran*, which ran from 1893 to 1932, often published articles in support of the war effort. In 1918, the publication gave a boisterous endorsement of "President Wilson and his administration. . . . The United Confederate Veterans' Association, in convention assembled, desires to go on record before the world with reference to the great world war our country now is engaged in as heart and soul back of the Washington administration and one hundred per cent loyal to the colors."[31]

Governor Charles Hillman Brough of Arkansas, like many southern politicians of the day, spoke in support of the war at the twenty-eighth annual UCV convention in Tulsa in 1918. Brough held a doctorate from Johns Hopkins and often remarked about the honor of having Woodrow Wilson, now president, as a college lecturer.[32] Reared in Mississippi, Brough was a progressive in all things but race, and considered himself a true southerner, "to the manner born."[33] The salty old soldiers proclaimed after Brough's speech that "if [Pershing's] boys can't do it, call on us."[34]

In the *Confederate Veteran*, Rev. J. H. McNeilly appealed for support of the war with a uniquely southern twist. He carefully explains here the Confederate spirit of the Great War era:

1861-1917
THE AMERICAN SPIRIT

This postcard reflects an attitudinal shift as the aging Confederate veterans of the Civil War supported sending their grandsons to fight for the United States in World War I. *Courtesy of Ray Hanley.*

In these days of tragic import, with the world at war and men's highest ideals of justice, mercy, and truth threatened with utter overthrow, our sons are suddenly called to defend those ideals even unto death on the field of battle. In such a time the thoughts of the people are naturally and properly taken up with the urgent interests of the present, to the exclusion of the things of the past, however glorious they may be. In such a time the thoughts of the people are naturally and properly taken up with the urgent interests of the present, to the exclusion of the things of the past, however glorious they may be. And yet that past, with its memorable deeds, its patient sacrifices, its thrilling heroisms, sends forth the most inspiring call, the mightiest influence to stir the souls of succeeding generations to high and noble endeavor.

And when a people become forgetful of or indifferent to the grand spiritual forces and achievements of their past, that people has become sordid, selfish, degenerate, and incapable of great things. It is almost the only thing that can be said in favor of war, that it arouses men from the lusts of flesh and sense and shows them things worth dying for. . . . Every true American soldier should go into this war resolved to keep untarnished the name and fame of his ancestry by his own worthy deeds. This is especially true of those who are heirs of the traditions of the Confederate soldiers of 1861–65, in whose veins flows the blood of the men and women of that heroic period, and all the more because of the malignant and persistent efforts to misrepresent and dishonor the memory of those who stood for four years of dreadful conflict for their constitutional rights. The cause, origin, and course of that War Between the States, when truly recorded, will vindicate the Southern people as standing for liberty and justice.[35]

Through this lens, military service during the Great War was a means to honor the valor of Confederate veterans and a way to defend the Lost Cause. The "reunion" of the North and South at Gettysburg in 1913 was still ongoing in 1917, even if it represented a complex combination of surrender and combat.

The vital fighting "front" of the Great War as a means to battle for the Lost Cause was not in the hands of the United Confederate Veterans alone. The UDC "fought," too, namely in conducting war relief work. Mary B. Poppenheim, President General of the United Daughters of the Confederacy, urged her membership that "the hour for present-day patriotism has struck, and the U. D. C. have their opportunity to show that they are worthy daughters of the men and women of the sixties. In this crisis in our country's national life we must give our best and be worthy of our Confederate lineage."

One project that had passed at the national UDC conference was the plan for the various State beds in hospitals abroad to be dedicated "in memoriam" to Confederate leaders by the UDC. "In the meantime," Poppenheim preached, "continue your energies in behalf of the American Red Cross, preserving all records of work you do for it. Collect funds for your State hospital bed or ambulance equipment, as you may decide, and

Mary B. Poppenheim, President General of the United Daughters of the Confederacy, urged UDC members to support the World War I effort. *Courtesy of the Arkansas State Archives.*

have ready to be used when the general committee shall be able to give you definite and authentic information as how best to use these funds, and use your best efforts toward helpfulness in cantonment service. Every cantonment community knows the opportunities they have for woman's organized help in providing cheer and comfort for the young national soldiers temporarily in their midst."[36]

The UDC in Arkansas was busy. Members bought Liberty Bonds, handed out Bibles to hometown troops, and pinned medals on returning soldiers at Fort Roots.[37] The Arkansas Division of the UDC, in a report from its leader Mrs. Agnes Halliburton, also supported a bed in the American hospital in France, and their chosen leader was Patrick R. Cleburne, "Stonewall of the West." She said that "we hope our boys have a leader like Cleburne."[38] Reporting on their work in 1917 in support of the war, the Arkansas branch of the UDC implored, "Who will say the Daughters have not been loyal to their oath to President Wilson?"[39]

While the UCV and the UDC used their organizations and identity to fight for the Lost Cause by supporting the war effort, aiding recruiting, and providing war relief, the Sons of Confederate Veterans were also active. The SCV argued that their greatest contribution was education, namely about the U.S. government:

> The terrible holocaust which characterizes the present world war is testing, among other things, systems of government. . . . No people can hope to escape all effects of this volcano. . . . Therefore we Sons of Confederate Veterans turn with splendid zeal, stronger because of our sense of present greater responsibility and keener because our fathers offered their lives in defense of some of its principles now fundamental, to a renewed study of the fundamentals of American government."[40]

One such contribution to this study was to support the dissemination of Supreme Court rulings favorable to their states'-rights argument. They did so through the Chautauqua history series in an effort to, as they said, "make the occasion a high-class literary treat and an entertainment that will draw a crowd."[41] The tactic was to gather a large audience and simply read by "quoting literally and carefully the words of the court." People should follow up these readings, the SCV said, with "someone representing the UDC [who] should read some of our fine Southern poems, and the best musicians in the neighborhood should perform."[42] Arkansas chapters of the SCV were active in providing these Chautauqua history series across the state, thus doing their part in blending Confederate views with national service.

In many ways, what these organizations were doing was precisely what other civic organizations did during the war—they supported the war effort, just as all patriotic Americans were expected to do. However, they did so while forcefully articulating their uniquely Southern manifestation of patriotism, and in ways that buttressed their ideas about the Lost Cause.

The War at Home

Outside of the strictly Southern concerns about the war, another matter of utmost importance was popular support of the war in general. The U.S. government passed several laws during the period to clamp down on espionage and enemy propaganda. On April 13, 1917, President Wilson created the Committee on Public Information (CPI) to promote the war domestically while publicizing American war aims abroad. Under the leadership of a muckraking journalist named George Creel, the CPI recruited heavily from business, media, academia, and the art world. The CPI blended advertising techniques with a sophisticated understanding of human psychology, and its efforts represent the first time that a modern government disseminated propaganda on such a large scale. With such a coordinated program, displays of patriotism and calls to make sacrifices were common. Arkansas, for instance, obeyed the call to return wheat purchases, which were then used to feed troops and allies. In total, Arkansas reportedly returned "more than all the other States combined," some 126 train cars of wheat.[43]

One way to sell the war through propaganda was to go directly to the people. The CPI arranged a cadre of speakers to assail the American people with simple, effective speeches at a variety of venues. Theaters, music recitals, fairs, and other public gatherings were common subjects of four-minute speeches. In Arkansas, the State Council of Defense, chaired by Governor Brough, provided for the organization and support of the Four-Minute Men, of which Mr. H. L. Remmel of Little Rock was state chairman.[44] Each county in Arkansas had a council to serve as "the guardians of the patriotism and civilian morale of their counties" and had a Four-Minute Men committee.[45] In addition, the report cited "three hundred and seventy-five ministers as Four-Minute speakers" in Arkansas.[46] The men were trained and trusted to give the speeches written by CPI, and warned not to stray from the message. The impact of their speeches speaks for itself. One such speech, given all over Arkansas in 1917, went as follows:

> Ladies and Gentlemen:
> I have just received the information that there is a German spy among us—a German spy watching us.
> He is around, here somewhere, reporting upon you and me—sending reports about us to Berlin and telling the Germans just what we are doing with the Liberty Loan. From every section of the country these spies have been getting reports over to Potsdam—not general reports but details—where the loan is going well and where its success seems weak, and what people are saying in each community.
> For the German Government is worried about our great loan. Those Junkers fear its effect upon the German morale. They're raising a loan this month, too.

If the American people lend their billions now, one and all with a hip-hip-hurrah, it means that America is united and strong. While, if we lend our money half-heartedly, America seems weak and autocracy remains strong.

Money means everything now; it means quicker victory and therefore less bloodshed. We are in the war, and now Americans can have but one opinion, only one wish in the Liberty Loan.

Well, I hope these spies are getting their messages straight, letting Potsdam know that America is hurling back to the autocrats these answers:

For treachery here, attempted treachery in Mexico, treachery everywhere—one billion.

For murder of American women and children—one billion more.

For broken faith and promise to murder more Americans—billions and billions more.

And then we will add: In the world fight for Liberty, our share—billions and billions and billions and endless billions.

Do not let the German spy hear and report that you are a slacker.[47]

These sorts of efforts were not only effective at whipping Arkansans into a fury of patriotism, but also at ginning up long-standing feelings of anti-Catholicism and suspicion of the state's German Americans, which led to instances of violence and intimidation. On April 13, 1917, the sheriff of Logan County arrived at the Subiaco Abbey on a mission to destroy the abbey's radio. This was necessary, the monks learned, in order to prevent them from receiving messages directly from the Kaiser. Rumors also circulated that the monks had weapons and ammunition beneath the abbey.[48] In what can only be construed as a method of self-defense, five "prominent citizens of German origin" in Arkansas served on a committee "to spread patriotic education among [the] German-speaking population." The group published articles in *The Arkansas Echo*, a weekly German-language newspaper, which "rallied the German-speaking people [of Arkansas] to a loyal support of all war work."[49]

In fact, the first military operation of the Arkansas National Guard in WWI was to "find and destroy" a spy radio rumored to "somewhere in the Blue Mountains." After searching the area, Lieutenant Walter Hall and a small party of National Guardsmen found the station on the highest peak in the state, Mount Magazine. Rather than a secret wireless station, it was a forgotten and abandoned wooden derrick once used by the National Geodetic Survey.[50]

There was even a battle of sorts between the commanding officer of the First Regiment of the Arkansas National Guard and Governor Brough. The governor wanted to send troops from Camp Pike to Collegeville, near Bauxite, over concerns about the raising of a German flag in the community. A man there by the name of Hoffman said the flag would come down "over his dead body."[51] Colonel C. D. James, formerly regimental commander of the Arkansas National Guard and recently brought into federal service by President Wilson, refused to send troops, since the whole of the National Guard had been federalized. He informed the governor that he now took his orders only from his commanding officers in the U.S. Army. Deputies of the U.S. Marshals Service refused to respond to the situation in Collegeville, as they viewed the flying of the flag "in violation of no federal law." Residents of Bauxite, restless after the governmental delay, moved a posse to Collegeville but found that the offensive flag had disappeared, ending the crisis.[52]

Outside of winding up American jingoism with the Four-Minute Men, the CPI took immediate steps to limit damaging information. Invoking the threat of German propaganda, the CPI implemented "voluntary guidelines" for the news media and helped to pass the Espionage Act of 1917 and the Sedition Act of 1918. These actions resulted in a broad compliance with censorship requests from Wilson's administration. Newspaper editors and reporters from Arkansas's 300 newspapers, as well as military officers—who often acted as censors for their units—and the soldiers and civilians themselves all worked carefully to keep their correspondence and publications in compliance with the CPI's directives.[53]

Millions of soldiers wrote letters home during the war. Many of these, carefully screened by the military and then editors, were published in newspapers, including in many rural areas in Arkansas. Hundreds of these letters have been collected by Arkansas historian Mike Polston.[54] This collection is the largest depository of Arkansas WWI soldiers' letters and worthy of careful examination.

The War Abroad

Notably, one of the first Arkansans to reach the front was also probably the first American Expeditionary Forces officer to lead American troops in combat. William Heber McLaughlin hailed from

Lonoke County, where he farmed. He was a graduate of the University of Arkansas and would go on to be a state legislator.[55] As a lieutenant in France in November 1917, McLaughlin was wounded by shrapnel in the head while leading the first U.S. platoon to see combat in the war.

On November 2, 1917, the 16th Infantry Regiment relieved French troops on the front lines near Bathelemont in northeastern France, near Lorraine. McLaughlin was a platoon leader in F Company of the 16th Infantry Regiment, First Infantry Division. General Pershing had established that each regiment in the division would send one battalion at a time into the trenches for a ten-day rotation.

Early in the morning on November 3, 1917, just as the Americans were swapping positions in the trenches, they were hit by a German raiding party. An artillery "box" barrage hit first, isolating them from reinforcement. The German raiders then leapt into the tranches, and hard hand-to-hand fighting ensued in the darkness of the trenches. Three Americans died in this assault, the first of the war: Pvt. Merle Hay, Cpl. James Gresham, and Pvt. Thomas Enright. Gresham was shot in the head and nearly beheaded by a German knife across the throat. Five more were wounded, including McLaughlin. Eleven were taken prisoner, a whole squad, as the Germans fell back almost as quickly as they had attacked.[56]

These trench raids were mostly undertaken to gather intelligence, and the prisoners the Germans had taken meant it was a huge success. That is not how McLaughlin saw it. In his letter to his mother, McLaughlin said:

> Save all the papers about the first fight between the Americans and the Germans. It is my platoon that mixed [it up]. My men are rearing to get at them again, but I don't think there is a chance for a long, long time. You see in a war like this everybody has to have a chance, and when there are so many it is an awful long time between turns. I don't know what the American press is saying about it, but don't worry, we did wonderfully well when you consider the fact that they outnumbered us six to one.[57]

McLaughlin was promoted to captain and returned to the U.S. in the spring of 1918. He oversaw the training of soldiers before returning to Lonoke after the war. He died at age forty-nine in 1931, presumably from complications of his battle wounds.[58]

Lieutenant Grady H. Forgy of Mena wrote home in September 1918. His letter is a common example of the positive spin soldiers put on their situation. Forgy said in his letter:

I am now in a very nice place, about the best I have been in in France—one of the large base hospitals, in a very quaint and peaceful part of this country. I have a real bed to sleep on and it has sure enough white sheets. We have the best of food, and all the doctors, nurses and attendants do everything possible for the patients.

Why am I here? Well, you see, I got mixed up with a "Boche" shell, several of them, in fact, and I got hit on the left shin. It was just a small wound, tho, but I got a pretty bad case of shell shock. This was on July 31. I was pretty nervous for a week, but am almost well now and ready to go back. Oh; but that sure was some fight! We, all Americans whipped those damn Huns every time they would fight. We chased them until our own tongues were almost out. They tried all their devilish tricks on us, but could not get by with them.

We know now that the Hun is nothing to fear. He is yellow, and too low to let live. He will absolutely not fight hand to hand, and of all our wounded, I have not heard of a single man being hurt by a boche bayonet. It was all machine guns and artillery that we ran into, but we gained our objective anyway. Of course, we lost men, but I tell you truthfully we killed at least three or four to our one. My regiment had Prussian Guards in front of us, and they are Germany's best, but they are yellow too. They say the Americans are "Devil Dogs," and they hate us, but there is no love lost.[59]

In a similar way, Private Homer Grissom, in Company G of the 126th Infantry, wrote to his sister in Judsonia from a military hospital on Sept 18, 1918, saying:

I am well only I have lost two of my fingers. I was up at the Big Front helping run the Huns and they sent me a shell I could not dodge but I got plenty of them to pay for my fingers anyway . . . . I am in a good hospital. I have been here two weeks. I was wounded on the second of August. I guess you can read this. Some of it is written with my left hand as it is my right hand that is wounded and it is some difficult to write with it.[60]

Bill Waggoner of Lonoke County was elected to the Arkansas House of Representatives for the 1915 term, serving as temporary Speaker of the House during his second term. He also was elected to the Arkansas State Constitutional Convention, but he resigned upon accepting a

Bill Waggoner of Lonoke County resigned from the Arkansas General Assembly to accept a commission to serve as a second lieutenant during World War I. *Courtesy of Mike Polston.*

commission as a second lieutenant in the U.S. Army.[61] Waggoner invoked General William Tecumseh Sherman to explain his view of the war. Waggoner said:

> I never knew what war was like until I took part in this great battle. Sherman shouldn't have used such mild terms in describing it when he said "war is hell." For in his day they never used gas, machine guns, trench mortors [*sic*], high explosives, hand granades [*sic*], rifle granades [*sic*], tanks, air planes filled with bombs and every immaginable [sic] thing to destroy human life, if they had he would have used different language in describing war.[62]

As Arkansas soldiers shipped off to war they naturally took with them a southerner's outlook. One such young soldier, Herman Lane, was training as an officer and had this to say about his men:

> I was impressed from the beginning by the splendid type of manhood assembled here. They are a lively, well-appearing,

working bunch of men and represent the pick of the entire South. I can't describe what a mighty fighting force they would make if they remained in their respective companies as private soldiers such an assembly of physically perfect and well educated men cannot be pictured in one[']s imagination. One must see in order to comprehend the possibilities that lie in easy reach of our great country.[63]

One of the recurrent themes in these letters is the soldier expressing happiness with his lot. James Lankford of Judsonia wrote to his mother from Camp Merritt, New Jersey, on August 13, 1918, that "I could write this tablet full about my trip, but I haven't got time now."[64] Seeking to reassure his mother, he said, "I will get along all right wherever I am. So don't worry about me not getting along all right." He detailed all the gifts he had received from the Red Cross, such as "apples, pears, cigarettes, cards and gum." Like many other young men heading away from home on such an adventure, he was eager for the experience, saying, "We are only about 15 miles from New York City and if I can I am going up there soon as I can . . . cause I want to see all the world I can now."[65]

From Camp Beauregard, Louisiana, on November 30, 1917, three young men from Judsonia wrote to tell their hometown of "army life and how we like it."[66] Eager to explain their military service to the folks back home, the boys wrote that "when it rains we sit on our bunks by a big pine fire and tell of the past." "We all have a nice time," the men wrote, saying, "our mess kits are full of beef, beans, gravy, pudding, potatoes, peaches, apples, rice, tomatoes, bread and our cup filled with coffee." They were housed with eight men to the tent "with a stove, plenty of wood to keep a fire and electric lights . . . . When we retire at night we have a bunk, straw mattress and three blankets to rest our weary bones on. Our squad has received several boxes from home and friends for Thanksgiving and wish to thank you all for they certainly were appreciated."[67]

From Fort Brady, Michigan, on October 24, 1917, Private Glenn Cole wrote to his father, Rev. M. L. Cole. He stated in his letter that his camp near Sault Ste. Marie, Michigan, was "a nice little place" though it was "awful cold up here now. Colder than it ever gets in Arkansas." He was amazed by the Soo Locks, one of the most active waterways in the world, connecting Lake Superior to the other Great Lakes. Cole wrote that "you would be amazed at the stupendousness of the shipping which passes through the Locks. I was on guard last night and counted 115 ships, any one of which could carry Judsonia away at one load, then some."[68]

Cole related the seriousness of his job, stating that "you see all the shipping that goes through here is munitions and wheat, there [have] been one or two attempts to destroy the Locks by German suspects. The Guard is done under the same conditions, in regard to strictness, as if we were at the front. The battalion commander informed us that the punishment for sleeping on post was, to be a target for the firing squad."[69]

Cole felt this was "the hardest bit a soldier can do, walking a lonesome post in the most severe climate on earth. I believe I would as [like to] be in the first line trenches in France . . . but I am glad to . . . do some real soldiering." As sort of a postscript on his experience, Cole wrote that "there are a lot of deer up here and moose, too. Am going to get me one before winter is over."[70]

Like Glenn Cole, Foreman Kelley of Lonoke was also very aware of regional distinctions, telling his mother, "We have a fine bunch of boys in this company. Some were drafted and some enlisted. Our captain came from the south and not very far from my home and he takes a great pride and interest in the boys."[71]

Notably absent from these letters was talk about Dixie, Robert E. Lee, or Stonewall Jackson, Cleburne, or otherwise. This suggests that the Confederate view of fighting the Great War in defense of the Lost Cause was not much on these soldiers' minds. George Creel and the CPI, perhaps, had outdone the UDC and SCV.

In fact, some of the soldiers boasted not only of their pride in serving the nation, but in the service of all Americans. L. A. Girerd of DeWitt served at Camp Jackson in South Carolina. A member of a training depot, he did not deploy to France.[72] In January 1919 he wrote back home to explain what he was seeing as the war wound down:

> I am glad to know that the men who went across came back with a smile on their faces, and they said that the Germans were not hard to whip, after all, and that it is not—hard to go "over the top" as some think. The negroes are coming back also, and we can give them the same honor as the others, because they did their part in this war. There are several in the hospital here now with three wound-stripes on their sleeves, and they are proud of them. I think all have done their part in this terrible war, black and white, with or without uniforms, and that we are to be proud of the fact that we are living under the stars and stripes.[73]

Girerd's observation about the participation of the black troops is particularly important, as there were some 18,000 black veterans of the

Great War in Arkansas.[74] Due to the segregated army at that time, many of the 160,000 black troops that served in France were manual laborers; only about 40,000 were placed in combat units.[75] In most cases, no black troops served in the National Guard, as they were barred from it in the South—though there were exceptions, such as the famed 396th Infantry Regiment, the Harlem Hellfighters, in New York.[76]

Still, there were a few opportunities in the military for black soldiers —such as officer commissions. Douglas Robinson of Clarendon was the first black Arkansan commissioned as a second lieutenant.[77] Twelve other black Arkansans attended a ninety-day officers' training camp in Des Moines, Iowa, and gained a commission in the army. Though only one out of five black draftees served overseas, those who served in the AEF were proud to fight. Private William Brown of Helena wrote to his mother that "I am awful proud that I came over to France to serve my country for now that we have gone over the top we can go home with our chests stuck out like a peacock's about it."[78] Cliney Trammell from Magnolia wrote back that "we are here to do our best . . . . We have valiant soldiers who do not fear to die."[79] The suitcase of one black Pine Bluff soldier was labeled "I'm bound for France to give the Kaiser hell!"[80]

Black citizens also worked hard to contribute to the war effort. The Mosaic Templars of America in Arkansas donated more than $100,000 to the Liberty Loans, $50,000 of which was given by Scipio Jones of Little Rock to Secretary of the Treasury William Gibbs McAdoo upon his visit to Arkansas in 1917.[81] In addition, a push for racial reforms and a spirit of self-determinism slowly emerged during the war years, when National Association for the Advancement of Colored People (NAACP) chapters in Little Rock and Fort Smith were inaugurated in late 1918 and 1919.[82] Things were just ever so slightly looking up for Arkansas's black community.

But in 1919, whites attacked a peaceful black union assembly at a church in Phillips County near the settlement of Elaine. When blacks fired back, the county broke into open fighting and Governor Charles Brough called for troops to quell the unrest. The troops at Camp Pike had just returned from France and the governor, without a National Guard to call up, arranged a special train to speed the federal troops to Elaine. What followed, according to historian Kieran Taylor, "marked the bloodiest clash of a tumultuous year of racial violence and labor strife in the United States."[83]

The ensuing investigation by army officers alleged that many of those blacks involved in the riot were Great War veterans.[84] In fact, out of some

1,700 draftees in Phillips County, perhaps 1,200 were black.[85] This was a highly concentrated population of black veterans, to be sure, and one steeled by their war experience to resist racial oppression. As one local black leader put it, "We helped you fight the Germans, and are ready to help you fight the next fellows that get after you, but we want to be treated fairly."[86]

Of course, Elaine was not the only site of racial unrest in America in 1919; dozens of U.S. communities experienced violent racial strife in 1919, including Chicago and Baltimore. Violent labor disputes affected dozens of other cities during the so-called Red Summer. It is no coincidence that this occurred just as black troops were returning home after fighting overseas.[87] NAACP or no, blacks in Arkansas began to stand a little taller during the Great War, and were hitting back against racial injustice.

Conclusion

Arkansas's experience during the Great War cannot be easily summarized in a brief essay like this. The other authors in this volume will handily fill in the blanks left here. What we can say is that Arkansas rose to the call of the nation and worked hard to provide fighting men and materials for the war. That Arkansas would do so in its own unique way is without question. As doughboy L. A. Girerd said, "All have done their part in this terrible war, black and white, with or without uniforms, and . . . are to be proud of the fact that we are living under the stars and stripes."

2 | Arkansas's Women and the Great War

ELIZABETH GRIFFIN HILL

When the United States entered the Great War in Europe on April 6, 1917, women throughout the nation were called upon to step forward and contribute their homemaking skills to alleviate the critical needs of our own soldiers as well as those of our European allies, who had been at war since 1914. Although Arkansas's women of all ages, social classes, and races contributed to the efforts to meet the needs of the government and the military, one group of women was responsible for ensuring the success of the multifaceted endeavor. These women were already organized throughout Arkansas under the umbrella of the Arkansas Federation of Women's Clubs (AFWC).[1]

Middle-class women's roles had been evolving for several decades—particularly since the Industrial Revolution, which seemed to change numerous aspects of women's lives. In fact, the decades preceding World War I provided Arkansas's middle-class women with the training and preparation that enabled them to shoulder a great responsibility as the United States made an about-face and subsequently entered Europe's war and changed it into the world's war. During the war, however, women's responsibilities expanded from caring for their local communities to undertaking steps to meet the needs of the nation and its allies. And the shift from a local focus to a national perspective was apparently seamless.[2]

Just as Arkansas's white middle-class women were already reaching out to their communities for several decades before the war, African American middle-class women were taking advantage of economic and

| DOI: https://doi.org/10.34053/christ2019.twah.2

professional opportunities made available to them within the segrega-
tionist atmosphere in the state. Such opportunities included receiving
higher education at Branch Normal College (now the University of
Arkansas at Pine Bluff—UAPB), which was established in 1873 to train
African Americans to teach in Arkansas's segregated schools. And as
activists, the women chose to resist the status quo of segregation by working toward community self-sufficiency and economic independence.[3]

As an example of middle-class African American women's social
activism, a January 31, 1917, article in the *Arkansas Gazette* noted that
"Annie T. Strickland, J. Lillian Murphy, Jennie A. Johnson and Mary H.
Spight, representing the Federation of Colored Women's Clubs of
Arkansas, yesterday called on Governor [Charles H.] Brough to request
him to recommend that the legislature make an appropriation to establish
an industrial school for Negro boys."[4] The article noted that the organization had secured sixty partially improved acres in Jefferson County, which
the women planned to donate to the state for the use of the school.[5]

Throughout the war, African American women consistently contributed to women's campaigns and patriotic efforts. Because of the prevailing racial segregation of the time, however, the *Arkansas Gazette*'s
published invitation to African American women to attend training in
food conservation exemplifies their experiences during the war:

Colored Women Invited to attend
Arkansas Gazette's Free Cooking School

> Actuated to be of service to all the people of Little Rock and sur-
> rounding territory and to give the women as a whole the oppor-
> tunity to hear Mrs. Betty Wilson, Demonstrator, . . . the balcony
> of the Majestic Theater usually reserved for colored people will
> be open to colored women . . . . All are equally welcome. Come
> as a guest of the *Gazette*.[6]

Arkansas's African American women were expected to retain their separate spheres within society even as they participated in all aspects of the
organized women's work.

As both white and African American women were practicing their
own forms of activism, the home economics movement, which had
gradually been taking hold for several decades, came into its own just
three years before the war began. The federal Smith-Lever Act of 1914
authorized home demonstration work through the U.S. Department
of Agriculture's Cooperative Extension Service in participating states,

including Arkansas. The newly established program began in Arkansas in 1915 with seven counties taking up the work. The two intervening years prior to the United States' entry into the war seemed to provide sufficient time for the state's home demonstration program to mature enough to take a leading role in food conservation programs.[7]

In Arkansas, as in other southern states, the home demonstration work was segregated even though the program was under the auspices of a federal, executive-branch department. African American agents were employed to work with girls and women in counties in which the number of potential African American club members justified a separate agent. In counties with fewer African American women and girls, the white agent was responsible for the segregated work. The earliest agents were often recruited from within the ranks of school teachers. Later, home economics graduates of Arkansas's land-grant college in Fayetteville (now the University of Arkansas)—and its African American affiliate institution in Pine Bluff (now UAPB)—filled positions in individual counties with a goal to improve rural women's lives through advancing their gardening, canning, and cooking skills.[8]

The Woman's Committee of the Council of Defense for Arkansas

Arkansas housewives' cooperation was vital to any statewide conservation efforts. Although women worked independently to implement food-saving recommendations within their own homes, there was nothing haphazard or random about their contributions. The federal government had made sure of that as it authorized the Woman's Committee of the Council of National Defense ("the National Woman's Committee") in Washington DC. The Council of National Defense and its Woman's Committee directed the homefront war efforts in Arkansas as well as in the forty-seven other states that made up the United States at that time. In Arkansas, the Woman's Committee of the Council of Defense for Arkansas ("the Arkansas Woman's Committee") received and carried out the instructions from its superiors and in turn directed the work within each of the seventy-five counties. The third layer of hierarchy consisted of each county's own council of defense as well as the accompanying woman's committee. The organizational model was a tightly controlled pyramid. In Arkansas, however, African American women were not a part of the organizational pyramid.[9]

The Woman's Committee of the Council of Defense for Arkansas (the Arkansas Woman's Committee), served from July 1, 1917, to December 30, 1918. In addition, each county had its own Woman's Committee. *Courtesy of the Arkansas State Archives, Little Rock.*

The National Woman's Committee stated that its overriding purpose was to safeguard the moral and spiritual forces of the nation "so that those inner defenses of our national life may not be broken down in the period of the war."[10] Eventually, that rather ambiguous, all-encompassing purpose came to include the registration of women for general service; food production and conservation; industrial conditions concerning women and children; child education and welfare; education of women along all lines outside of the Red Cross service; and the maintenance of all existing social service agencies.[11] The National Woman's Committee sent detailed instructions for each state's women to follow. For the most part, however, women throughout Arkansas's counties interpreted the guidelines to meet specific local needs—not necessarily the ones targeted by the national committee.[12]

Less than three months after the United States entered the war, the Arkansas Woman's Committee assembled in Little Rock for the first time, on July 2, 1917. Members' first order of business was to appoint committee chairmen (as they were called at the time) for each of the seventy-five counties in order to conduct a food conservation campaign throughout the state. The national committee had prepared cards for women to sign, indicating their willingness to follow the federal government's guidelines for food conservation. The cards were created to ensure that women understood the importance of the work and would make a written commitment to the program. Throughout the war, women would be reminded of the importance of their vital—albeit mundane—contribution.[13]

In Arkansas, however, lack of communication, distrust of the government, and men's control over their wives' decision-making—not to mention cards that did not arrive on time—created obstacles during the first campaign, which was hurried and ultimately disappointing to organizers. During a second campaign, Arkansas's pastors, priests, and leaders of fraternal organizations insisted that men were to allow their wives to sign the cards. By December 1917, 55,000 Arkansas women had placed their signatures on the cards; in doing so, they assured the government of their participation.[14]

The Food Conservation Program

In fall 1917—in the midst of the second food conservation campaign—wheat was the first commodity shortage that home economists confronted in their newspaper columns. As they encouraged women to use only half the usual amount of flour in their baking, they offered recipes that incorporated substitutes such as soybean meal, sweet potatoes, peanuts, and cornmeal. Posters touting wheat conservation encouraged housewives to save the wheat for U.S. soldiers fighting in France. Other posters reminded the nation's women that children and babies in Europe were on the brink of starvation without the United States' help.[15]

The following recipe, published in the *Arkansas Gazette* in December 1917, went a step further than the usually recommended substitutions for half the flour. Instead, it combined mashed potatoes and cornmeal, with no mention of flour:

Potato Cornmeal Muffins

Two tablespoons fat, one tablespoon sugar, one egg, well beaten; one cup milk, one cup mashed potatoes, one cup cornmeal, four teaspoons baking powder and one teaspoon salt.

Mix in order given, bake 40 minutes in hot oven. This makes 12 muffins. They are delicious.[16]

Home demonstration agents led the way in vital food conservation efforts. These agents are shown in 1933 at what is now UA Pine Bluff. At least two of the agents —Mary L. Ray, left, and Lugenia Christmas, third from left—served during the Great War. *From RG 33, National Archives and Records Administration, Fort Worth, TX.*

By December 1917, meat had become the second commodity shortage. Initially, posters publicized the benefits of protein-laden fish, eggs, and beans. Home economists shared weekly menus that included few meat recipes other than stews and soups, which could be augmented with lots of vegetables (and stretched by adding water to the pot). By spring 1918, however, Arkansas's home demonstration program had hired a full-time specialist to teach women to make cottage cheese, a meat substitute packed with protein. A newspaper article touted cottage cheese recipes, such as the one below, which "a mere man"[17] would not recognize as such.[18]

Cottage-Cheese Loaf with Nuts

2 cups cottage cheese	1 T. fat
1 cup chopped nuts (see variations)	Salt, pepper
1 cup cold leftover cereal (any kind)	⅓ t. soda or more to neutralize acid
1 cup dry bread crumbs	Sage, poultry seasoning, or mixed herbs

| 2 T. chopped onion, or ½ t. | Worcestershire sauce, or |
| onion juice | kitchen bouquet if desired |

Mix all ingredients together thoroughly and bake in a buttered pan in a hot oven till top and sides are well browned over. Turn out on a hot platter. Serve with a brown or tomato sauce if desired.[19]

In July 1918—well past the beginning of the meat shortage—Mrs. Ruth Peck McLeod, a home economist, introduced soybeans as a war food in her weekly newspaper column. McLeod praised the soybean's high protein content as well as its high fat content. She offered several recipes, including the one below for soy bean (*sic.*) gumbo.

Soy Bean Gumbo

Five cups cooked beans, 2 green peppers, 1 cup brown rice, seasoning salt, paprika, celery salt, 3 cups bean stock, 6 tomatoes (or one No. 2 can), 1 onion.

Boil the brown rice for one hour and reserve the rice water. Cook the tomatoes, peppers, and onions until tender. Combine this mixture with the rice, rice water, and soy beans. Let simmer and serve.

Note: Carrots, okra, corn or any other vegetables may be used in this gumbo.[20]

Home economists provided little instruction regarding the reduction of fats—which included whole milk and butter. In September 1917, however, Herbert Hoover, the National Food Administrator at the time, asked that there be no sugar reduction in the making of preserves and jellies because the use of those items would reduce the amount of butter required for breads. Hoover's request verified the need to conserve fats. Also, in an article in the *Arkansas Gazette* titled "War Menus, Meatless Meals, Wheat Flour Substitutes," the author emphasized the use of skimmed milk (in lieu of whole milk) for making custards and creamed soups.[21]

During the summer fruit-canning season, women had no option but to preserve fruits with sugar substitutes, such as corn syrup, or by using only the sugar found in the fruit. As the months went by, McLeod offered other suggestions: boil the fruit pulp at least three times in jelly making; use the prune—a patriotic food—as a sugar saver and then save the pit to be crushed in making filters for gas masks. Prune recipes like this one abounded.

Stuffed Prunes

Steam one pound prunes and remove stones. Stuff part of the prunes, each with another prune, stuff other with chopped salted nuts or stuff with a mixture of one cup each raisins and walnuts and a few candied cherries. Another suggestion is to stuff prunes with stiff orange marmalade.[22]

McLeod also gave suggestions for creating concoctions from other fruits and nuts to satisfy a family's sweet tooth.[23]

Unlike in World War II, during which federally mandated rationing of commodities of all types was prevalent, conservation was mostly voluntary during the Great War. Because there were neither ration stamps nor penalties for not participating in conservation efforts, both positive and negative forms of rhetoric were used to convince women to conserve. As mentioned previously, propaganda posters often appealed to motherly instincts to help hungry European children; others appealed to the sense of patriotism as it reminded women to save the wheat or meat or sugar for the "boys"[24] in France who were experiencing the horrors of trench warfare.

Women's leaders and home economics professionals also employed various forms of rhetoric to spur Arkansas's women to accept the food conservation responsibilities that they alone could fulfill. Only two months into the war, for example, the editor of the *Woman's Home Companion* magazine waged a campaign against food waste by assuring women of the immense need to "starve the garbage pail."[25] In October 1917—following the unsuccessful first food conservation campaign—Mrs. C. E. Whitney, spokesperson for the Arkansas Woman's Committee, opined, "Our country has been wasteful and extravagant in the extreme. Luxuries had become necessities. There was an overabundance of many things and seemed to be no real necessity for rigid economy . . . . Both men and women drifted into extravagant and wasteful habits."[26]

In March 1918, dismayed by reports that women were not following her instructions to combine substitutes for half the flour in their baked goods, McLeod chastised her readers: "The victory will come to those who can hold out the longest, and food is the deciding factor in this case."[27] Four months later, on July 14, 1918, the Woman's Page of the *Arkansas Gazette* included a front-and-center article titled "Are You a Woman Slacker?"[28]

Despite the often negative rhetoric of Arkansas women's leaders, the Report of the Woman's Committee of the Council of Defense for

Home demonstration agents' contributions continued and even escalated during the twenty-year economic depression for Arkansas's rural families that began in 1920. *From RG 33, National Archives and Records Administration, Fort Worth, TX.*

By the 1930s, rural Arkansans depended on home demonstration agents and members to provide community training in vegetable and meat canning in order for families to survive the Great Depression. *From RG 33, National Archives and Records Administration, Fort Worth, TX.*

Arkansas, dated December 30, 1918, provided several pages of contributions from most of the seventy-five counties. Two counties' substantial paragraphs to report food conservation activities give a sampling of the work that was done by women throughout Arkansas:

Bradley County:

The chairman of Home Economics and Food Conservation was very active when we first felt the need to adhere to the call of the Food Administration. She, in connection with the county canning agent, conducted war cooking demonstrations in many places over the county, and for several weeks, once a week at the high school. War food recipes were carried in the papers during the entire period, and the clubs took up discussions on food conservation and substitutes, which proved beneficial. All clubs and missionary societies eliminated refreshments for the war period. War gardens were urged, and much interest manifested in every phase of food production and conservation. Eight hundred and twelve food conservation cards were signed.

Crawford County:

Through the home demonstration agent we organized the women of every community so that the food conservation work could be carried on. Early in the spring of 1918, every home made plans for a war garden. Under the supervision of the home demonstration agent a vast amount of food was conserved from these gardens. The Home Economics Club of Van Buren meets twice a month and talks over plans of conservation. Then we place in the window of some leading store food made from substitutes, and also we hand to the ladies recipes for the food exhibited. We went to the various communities and gave a demonstration in the use of substitutes. During the year 1918 our county conserved one car load of flour, fifteen thousand pounds of sugar per month, and sixty thousand pounds of meat. Gave out six thousand U.S. Food Leaflets on conservation of foods, and held twenty-nine demonstrations of food substitutes for flour, sugar and meat.[29]

The Arkansas Woman's Committee's county reports typically included contributions by white women only, unless annotated otherwise.

The American Red Cross Work

Although the Woman's Committee of the Council of National Defense shouldered the responsibility for education and encouragement of women in their vital food conservation efforts, another organization would be responsible for providing four million men with warm, knitted clothing; preparing intricate surgical bandages; and sewing clothing and other soft goods for medical hospitals on the front lines in Europe. The American Red Cross's mission was already well established within clearly defined limits. Specific goals already geared to the needs of the nation at war included helping to provide the troops with comforts and necessities while in the field, aiding them in transit, and assisting the Army Medical Corps in the care of the sick and wounded. Much of the hands-on work would be accomplished by the nation's women.[30]

Red Cross chapters had been conducting war work of various sorts since 1914; however, the United States' entry into the war produced a demand for supplies that "leaped hundredfold."[31] The Red Cross Woman's Bureau (the Woman's Bureau) was created in July 1917 primarily to direct the energy and eagerness-to-serve of the millions of wives, sisters, and mothers of members of the nation's military services.

The Woman's Bureau was faced with a herculean task as it worked to standardize the work of millions of women throughout the country. In Arkansas, every county had several workrooms staffed by carefully selected supervisors. The Woman's Bureau created patterns for women volunteers to cut out yard goods in order to sew hospital garments, surgeons' and nurses' operating gowns and masks, and hot water and ice bag covers. Eight large pattern companies cut the patterns, which could be purchased in retail outlets as well as in the workrooms.[32]

The Woman's Bureau's other immediate concern was the selection of twenty-three standard dressings, instructions of which were issued nationwide through two circulars. One described each dressing in detail, with diagrams; the second was for instructors. In her 1918 book *American Women and the World War*, author Ida Clyde Clarke compared the Woman's Bureau's massive responsibilities to those of a businessman who, "set to sink or swim, with the job of delivering hospital supplies to thousands of hospitals, and dependent on volunteer labor working part time, would have many times preferred to sink."[33]

Toward the end of summer 1917, during which Arkansas's women had sewn thousands of surgical bandages and hospital soft goods, word came from the Red Cross Commission in France to the Woman's Bureau

Red Cross canteens seemed to spring up along railroad lines as women worked together to provide coffee, sandwiches, and newspapers for military troops who stopped for breaks at stations along the route. *Courtesy of the UA Little Rock Center for Arkansas History and Culture.*

to report an imperative need for U.S. soldiers to have warm socks, sweaters, mufflers, and wristlets before Christmas. Quickly, the request, as well as standardized knitting instructions, found their way to Arkansas's newspapers and workrooms.[34]

By early December 1917, the hundreds of Red Cross workrooms in Arkansas's seventy-five counties were notified of the desperate need for 60,000 newly designed bandages for the hospitals on the front lines. In order to meet the immediate need, workrooms increased hours to include evening shifts.[35]

Although women followed food conservation guidelines in their own kitchens, much of the Red Cross work was done in workrooms, where women could work within an atmosphere of camaraderie and mutual support. Women who could not leave home were encouraged to knit and sew in their homes; but for many, the workrooms were therapeutic. One woman's sense of relief at working with others was printed in newspapers, "When [my son] gets on the ocean I think I'll have to come down here and work all day long to keep from worrying about him."[36]

In the final report of the Woman's Committee to the Council of Defense for Arkansas, several counties referred to Red Cross activities. Following are a few samples of those reports:

Clark County:

Hospital garments, 4,100; Mrs. A. Tims, Chairman
Surgical dressings, 16,576; Miss Gilberta Hari, Chairman
Refugee garments, 857; Mrs. L. C. Patterson, Chairman
Knitting, 2,532; Miss Kate Heard, Chairman
Home Service is assisting 130 families. Mrs. H. C. Anderson, Chairman

Jackson County:

A splendid lesson for those who did not register was the instance of a fine old lady who had a son in the war. The lady is totally blind, but she came to be registered, and made out a special card. She gave several hours each week to the Red Cross, made button holes and other work, and knitted between times.

Jefferson County:

The [Red Cross] canteen service has proven a great help and inspiration to the troops of soldiers passing through Pine Bluff.

Marion County:

The county registrar called upon the women of the community to furnish Red Cross box suppers to the men who would gather in April to listen to patriotic speeches on the Liberty Loan in the various townships. The boxes contained war bread, and the proceeds from the sales were used to buy supplies for the Red Cross working rooms.

Phillips County:

In the last Red Cross drive, the town being districted and the women sent out to solicit from women, they raised $4,648.

Washington County:

The Health and Recreation committee co-operated with the canteen committee of the Red Cross in providing a musical, an automobile ride, and box lunches for the departing selectives.[37]

Although African American women's contributions to the Red Cross work were not mentioned in the final report for Jefferson County, early on in the war the *Pine Bluff Daily Graphic* noted that African American community leaders anticipated that black women and girls would "devote much of their time to the work of sewing garments, preparing bandages and other necessary supplies, under direction and supervision of the leaders of the work among the white people."[38]

The Registration-for-Service Campaign

By January 1918, the Arkansas Woman's Committee was planning its second state-wide campaign. Now that the food conservation campaign had ended successfully, it was time to ask women throughout the state to sign cards indicating jobs they were already trained to fill or for which they were willing to be trained. Governor Brough set aside February 17 through 23 for Arkansas's campaign. Registrars' training began in early January; African American women were trained as registrars for their campaign.[39]

Prior to the event, 1,000 posters were distributed in each of the state's seventy-five counties. During the week, trained registrars set up booths in convenient places and made house-to-house canvassing visits when necessary. In preparation for the event, the *Pine Bluff Daily Graphic* announced that all white women would register at local banks and African American women would register at their schools. The article assured all women that they would never be drafted but would simply be asked to do their part at home. In Caddo Township (Clark County), African American pastors announced the locations and particulars of the registration booths for African American women.[40]

The complete report sent to Washington after the war showed that 43,000 Arkansas women had registered for service. Just about every chairman reported on the campaign as she completed her final report during December 1918. Although most simply gave the number of registrants, a few included narrative examples, which provide additional insights into the work in the counties:

> Sample County Reports:
> Registration-for-Service Campaign, February 1918
> Jackson County:
>
> During registration week, four-minute speeches were made each night at the moving picture theatres, and patriotic songs were sung. On two nights a special song entitled "Register" was sung.
>
> Jefferson County:
>
> 3,225 women registered. Many women did clerical work for exemption boards. Men and women worked together as a council.
>
> Logan County, Northern Division:
>
> Registered 600 women who volunteered for various kinds of ser-

Agricultural	Clerical	Domestic	Industrial	Training	Professional	Student	Public Service	Social Service	Red X & Allied Relief	Miscellaneous	Contributions

(T=Trained, U=Untrained)

Woman's Committee of Council of National Defense.   **Women's Organizations, State Council of Defense,**   DIVISION _____ UNIT _____

(Sign only one of these cards)

Name in full _Mrs. Arm, Jennie (Mrs.)_   Present occupation _Seamstress_
(Last Name) (First Name)

Address _Van Buren, Washington No._   By whom employed _____
(City or town) (No. and street or R. D. No.) Tel. No.

Age _45 yrs._   Married or single _Married_   Where employed _____

Color or race _Negro_   Country of birth _U. S. A._   References _____

Citizen: By birth _U. S._   By naturalization _____   Education (graduate or length of time attended):

Grammar _____ College (give name) _____

Persons dependent upon you, if any _1 boy for care_   High or private _High school_ Specialized training _____

Service offered (specify whether volunteer, expenses only, or paid) _Expenses Only_   Emergency service (specify whether volunteer, expenses only, or paid) _____

Time pledged for service _Spare time_   Will you go anywhere? _____ Home town only? _Yes_ In United States? _____

If training is wanted, specify line _____   Tuition paid or free _____   How soon can you start? _____

ENCIRCLE NUMBERS TO LEFT OF OCCUPATIONS IN WHICH YOU HAVE HAD EXPERIENCE OR TRAINING. UNDERLINE THOSE IN WHICH YOU WISH TO GIVE SERVICE.

I. Agricultural	Factory—Cont'd	85 Dentist	103 Publicity	VII. Social Service	Instruction—Cont'd.
1 Dairying	32 Cooking	86 Dietician	104 Statistician	130 Camp work	153 First aid
2 Farming	33 Housekeeping	87 Draftsman	105 Surgeon	131 Charities—Which?	154 Garments—Hospital
3 Fruit raising	34 Industries by home	88 Engineer	106 Teacher (subject):		Civilian
4 Gardening	35 Knitting (employ't)	Handicrafts:	Of adults	132 Club executive	
5 Poultry raising	36 Laundress	89 Metals	Of children	133 District nursing	IX. Miscellaneous
6 Stock raising	37 Practical nurse	90 Textiles	VI. Public Service	134 Hospital	170 Unoccupied Woman
II. Clerical	38 Trained attendant	91 Woods	110 Inspector	135 Industrial welfare	171 _____
10 Accountant	39 Seamstress	92 Journalist	111 Institutional mgr.	136 Investigator	X. Contributions
11 Bookkeeper	40 Waitress	93 Laboratory worker	112 Mail carrier	137 Playgrounds	A. Ambulance
12 Cashier	III. Industrial		113 Police patrol	138 Protective assoc'n	B. Driver for car
13 Clerical work (gen.)	50 Baker	94 Languages (foreign):	114 Postmistress	Recreational:	C. Duplicating mach.
14 Filing	51 Boarding house	Read well	115 Signaling	139 Dancing	D. Funds
15 Office assistant	52 Buyer		116 Telegraphy	140 Music	E. Home for convalescent hospital
16 Office manager	53 Camp		117 Wireless	141 Reading aloud	
17 Private secretary	54 Institutional	Speak well	118 Telephone	142 Relief visiting	F. Hospital
18 Typewriter	55 Dressmaker	95 Lawyer	Transportation:	143 Settlement	G. Laboratory
19 Shipping clerk	Factory	96 Lecturer	119 Aviatrix	144 Social clubs	H. Motor boat
20 Stenographer	56 Needle trades	97 Librarian	120 Horse	VIII. Red Cross & Allied Relief	I. Motor car
III. Domestic	57 Food trades	98 Musician	121 Motor car	Instruction:	J. Typewriter
30 Care of children	58 Leather trades	99 Osteopath	122 Motor cycle	150 Surgical dressings	K. Share home with widow or children
31 Cleaning	59 Hat trades	100 Pharmacist	123 Power boat	151 Dietetics	L. _____
	60 Metal trades	101 Photographer	124 Railroad	152 Elementary hyg.	
	61 Munitions	102 Physician			
	62 Paper and printing				
	63 Wood trades				
	64 Textiles				
	65 Forewoman				
	66 Inspector				
	67 Janitress (cleaner)				
	68 Laundry operative				
	69 Manager				
	70 Manicure and hairdr'r				
	71 Messenger				
	72 Milliner				
	73 Retail dealer				
	74 Restaurant				
	75 Saleswoman				
	76 Waitress				
	V. Professional				
	80 Actress				
	81 Architect				
	82 Artist				
	83 Author				
	84 Chemist				

Mrs. Jennie McArn, an African American resident of Van Buren, asked for expenses only as she volunteered to work as a seamstress. The reverse of her card indicated that she was the mother of three sons, two of whom were in military service in France. *Courtesy of the Arkansas State Archives, Little Rock.*

vice, including aviation, motor truck driving, telegraphy, nursing, and expert farming (graduates of our agricultural college).

Miller County:

925 women registered during house-to-house canvass, 71 of this number signing to go wherever the government wanted them to go, 61 to go anywhere in the United States.[41]

Crawford County reported that in Van Buren, 736 white women and fifty-three African American women completed registration-for-service cards. While the reports tell of patriotism and willingness to sacrifice, they also provide evidence of women's distrust and fear of the federal government. Reports from eight counties alluded to mistrust, German propaganda, and fear of being subject to the draft, as well as fear of being forced to vote. Once again, as was noted during the food conservation campaign, many men refused to allow their wives to sign any government paper.[42]

Working for Children's Improved Health and Education

During the war, the National Woman's Committee continued the emphasis on young children's health that had begun with the Children's Bureau of the U.S. Department of Labor. Preschool children and babies' health and well-being were prioritized under the broader concern for overall children's health and education. The importance of the work was encapsulated in the national goal of 300,000 babies' lives projected to be saved during Children's Year, March 1918 through March 1919. Arkansas's quota was to save the lives of 2,170 babies.[43]

To begin the campaign, the Arkansas Woman's Committee's Child Conservation committee sent out to county organizations information concerning prenatal care, birth registration, infant feeding, and food for children. Next were campaigns to weigh and measure children younger than six years of age.[44] Although most counties did not elaborate on their child welfare work other than to provide numbers of children served, a few counties provided enlightening details of their work:

Crawford County:

We have examined and weighed 592 children under six years of age. In Van Buren this work was accomplished at a central location, and great thanks are due the women's clubs of the city, who so cheerfully and loyally assisted us in making this campaign a splendid success. Graduate nurses were in charge, and at stated hours lectures were given by nurses and local physicians.

Miller County:

Greatest task and one most perfectly executed: the registering of children of the county, ages one to six. Child Welfare committee spared nothing to make this work a success. Out of the 2,000 names given to the committee as an estimate of the children of registering age by the county superintendent of schools, committee registered, weighed and examined 1,951. At the same time the committee in charge of birth registration reported birth certificates for 487 white children and 200 Negro children in Texarkana, Arkansas; in the rural districts, 277 white children and 248 Negroes.

Washington County:

Child Welfare work was pushed by the county unit. Features of

During February 1918, 43,000 Arkansas women signed registration-for-service cards. Mrs. Harriet Euler of Uniontown, Crawford County, volunteered as a practical nurse and may have been called upon to provide nursing care during the Spanish influenza epidemic that fall. *Courtesy of the Arkansas State Archives, Little Rock.*

the work have been health exhibits, lectures on the care of children, child nutrition, and social and moral conditions. A steady campaign was waged in many towns in the county to have every child under six years of age weighed and measured, and birth registration was encouraged by the distribution of window cards to register babies. Charts and posters were used throughout the county for exhibition in rural schools. Efforts were made to establish free clinics and to secure a visiting nurse.[45]

Improved education and school attendance made up the second emphasis within the National Woman's Committee's wartime program to improve children's health and education and was already a major concern within Arkansas. By 1910, a disconcerting 40% of Arkansas's schoolchildren were employed—mostly in agriculture—and the state's seventy-six accredited high schools produced a mere 300 graduates annually.[46] An article in the March 1918 *Educational News Bulletin*, which discussed the problem of child labor in Arkansas, averred that "[t]he biggest thing a boy or girl can do for his country, right now, is to go to school every day. That is his 'bit' and the most effective assistance he can render humanity."[47]

As a result, during the latter months of the war, Arkansas's women were tasked with the dual responsibility of working toward improved education as well as improved school attendance. There was little evidence, however, that rural women attempted to follow guidelines from Washington to confront parents of truant students. The report from Johnson County (below) was an exception.

Bradley County:

The chairman had a shower of suitable pictures for school rooms, after a delightful program at the Mothers' Club on the subject, and she, with a committee of ladies, took them to the schools. A few talks were given the children on "Books for the Children to Read," "How to Know a Good Picture," and "Care of the Teeth."

Johnson County:

Education chairman is investigating the child attendance of schools, urging those not attending to attend, and pushing the movement of better attendance, better educated teachers, more intelligent patriotism and war work.[48]

In a letter dated November 13, 1918—two days after the Armistice—the National Woman's Committee was optimistic about the delayed "Back-to-School Drive," noting that the displacement of temporary laborers by returning soldiers would provide "a clinching argument for a drive to withdraw all children from industry to the protecting and developing influence of the school-house."[49]

Arkansas's Women in Industry

Although Arkansas's women were making major contributions to the war effort, they were also experiencing changes for women brought about by the war, particularly in employment matters. As the number of single women who worked outside of the home before marriage had risen from 20% in 1850 to 50% by 1900, women were already a fixture within the nation's workforce by the time of the war.[50] And as the state Women in Industry department of the Arkansas Woman's Committee became functional, it was tasked with ensuring appropriate working conditions for women.

Mary H. McCabe was the state chairman of the department; early on, Governor Brough appointed her as Secretary of Minimum Wage and Maximum Hour for Arkansas. McCabe and her department worked to ensure enforcement of the Minimum Wage and Maximum Hour Law throughout the state. The department's inspections resulted in findings and awards to women employed in factories, restaurants and hotels, retail stores, laundries, and telephone companies.[51] In her final report, McCabe noted:

> The demand for the Minimum Wage and Maximum Hour Law is an expression of awakened social conscience of the people of Arkansas. Thinking men and women are everywhere realizing the individual and social menace of the low wage, and demanding that it be made possible for able-bodied, willing women to earn their living by their day's work.[52]

In spite of McCabe's unrealistic evaluation of changes in attitudes at the time toward women's wages, telephone operators in Fort Smith and Little Rock[53] went on strike against Southwestern Bell Telephone Company during fall 1917.[54] For both groups of women, the strikes combined demands for higher wages with demands that discharged employees be reinstated. Nationally, according to historian Philip S. Foner, longtime telephone operators were striking for higher wages as they realized that women in newly filled wartime manufacturing positions were receiving higher pay.[55]

In Little Rock, as the number of operators to be employed increased dramatically with the creation of Camp Pike—which eventually housed 50,000 to 60,000 military trainees—experienced operators seemed well positioned to bargain for increased wages. As the strikers and Southwestern Bell communicated with each other and the public through paid newspaper advertisements, however, an already-impressive benefits package for the women became public knowledge. For example, the telephone company touted extra pay for evening work, car fare when working two shifts, and an in-house restaurant at minimal cost to the women. The company provided a room where the operators could rest and read, accompanied by a graduate nurse to look after their needs while at work and to visit the homes of women who were ill in order to provide medical attention.[56]

In its response, however, the International Brotherhood of Electrical Workers No. 47A, commonly known as the Telephone Operators' Union, stressed that a wage increase was the women's foremost concern:

This photograph of operators at work in the Little Rock Telephone Building in 1915 gives no indication of the upheaval to take place among the women employees during fall 1917. *Courtesy of the Arkansas State Archives, Little Rock.*

The highest authorities in this nation say: "Practically all findings of minimum wage commissions and boards in the United States agree that the woman who does not receive help from her family cannot live decently on less than $8.00 per week."

We challenge the company to furnish a statement showing the percentage of girls who are paid $8.00 per week or less —a living wage or less. Our best information indicates that 70 percent of telephone operators receive less than a living wage. Strikebreakers are being paid $18.50 to $16.50 and hotel expenses.[57]

On November 14, 1917, Southwestern Bell countered that its 166 operators—Little Rock women rather than outsiders—received an average salary of $9.43 per week (six-day week, eight-hour day), which did not include an anniversary payment that was also given at certain levels. The actual salaries included forty-four operators who earned $8.00 or less, with trainees gradually earning $8.00 per week in their thirteenth month of employment. Senior operators earned $10.50 per week, with monitors, supervisors, and assistant chief operators earning $12.00 to $20.00 per week.[58]

Also on November 14, following violence on the grounds of the Southwestern Bell building four days earlier, the company served notice that—as a result of the mediation failure—it would file an injunction against union representatives and certain individuals "to restrain them in any way from interfering with the business of the company."[59] On November 25, a newspaper article reported that—earlier in the week—Southwestern Bell's representatives had assured the forty-nine striking telephone operators that the decision as to whether they were rehired would be decided by the operators who did not strike. In the meantime, the striking operators had agreed to waive their demand for reinstatement of eleven discharged employees, as the state labor commissioner and city officials were to find jobs for them elsewhere.[60] In the article, which was published under the umbrella heading "News of the Labor World," the newspaper opined that Southwestern Bell's decision to permit the present working force to decide "makes settlement of the difficulty more remote than before."[61] Following the November 25 article, central Arkansas's newspapers were virtually silent as to the dispute.

However, a January 4 article in the *Arkansas Gazette* titled "No Action on Strike," which was also in the "News of the Labor World" section, noted: "A report was read concerning the number of operators still out of work and their financial condition but no definite action was taken concerning the strike at the meeting of the Central Trades Council last night."[62] Although newspaper coverage was sparse and inconclusive going forward, the January 4 article made clear that organized labor in Little Rock likely did not intend to support the telephone operators by going on a sympathetic strike.

In Fort Smith, however, organized labor took an opposite approach to the telephone operators' situation by calling a general strike on December 8, 1917. According to a December 9 article in the *Arkansas Gazette*, "The strike is the result of the Southwestern Bell Telephone Company refusing to settle with the operators who have been on a strike since September 19."[63] The general strike created havoc throughout the city as citizens were faced with living without power and light. On December 15, the *Arkansas Democrat* reported that "[a]ll crafts that joined the general strike, which was settled yesterday, were at work today."[64]

The Fort Smith telephone operators' strike was settled on December 26, 1917, and sixty-three operators returned to work. The disposition of two operators—whose discharges had been a point of contention—was left to the local manager. The agreement was that wages

Striking Fort Smith operators were rescued by organized labor, which called a
general strike that created
havoc within the city. In
Little Rock, however,
Southwestern Bell sought
an injunction against the
women and sympathetic
strikers in November
1917. Six weeks later, a
newspaper article indi-
cated that organized labor
likely would not support
the operators. *From the
Arkansas Democrat.*

PHONE COMPANY TO SEEK INJUNCTION

Will Ask That Strikers Be Restrained From Picketing and Other Actions.

ARBITRATION A FAILURE

Neither Side Will Yield on Matter of Reinstating 11 Girls Who Were Discharged.

and working hours would be threshed out by a federal mediator.[65] At that time, according to the article, a similar settlement for the Little Rock operators was anticipated. Instead, newspapers remained virtually silent on the subject—other than advertisements for telephone operator positions, which ran almost daily.

The newspapers' silence regarding the Little Rock strike was broken on May 25, 1918, however, in an article reporting a political candidate's speech. "In his speech last night at Liberty Hall, Prosecuting Attorney M. E. Dunaway, candidate for Congress against Congressman H. M. Jacoway, . . . also attacked the Southwestern Bell Telephone Company for what he termed its attitude in organizing against the girl strikers."[66]

The fall 1917 strikes by white female telephone operators in Little Rock and Fort Smith against Southwestern Bell Telephone Company were followed a few months later, in late May 1918, as Local No. 36 of the International Laundry Workers' Union began strikes at all seven laundries in the city for higher wages. Much like the white telephone operators in Little Rock—who went on strike during a time of greatly expanded need for their services related to the creation of the Camp Pike cantonment—the primarily African American women of the union[67] were the exclusive providers of laundry support to 75,000 men at three nearby military establishments.[68] Unlike the telephone operators, however, the laundry workers' grievances were referred to the National War Labor Board (NWLB) in September 1918. The women received a favorable award on November 9.[69]

Author Elizabeth Haiken noted that the NWLB representatives found that several aspects of the women's case fit well with the board's agenda, including "recognition of workers' right to a living wage, the maintenance of pre-war conditions of labor relations, and the payment of equal pay for equal work, regardless of the workers' race or gender."[70] Haiken noted that the laundresses received a favorable award because their working conditions and standard of living—which had never been adequate—had deteriorated as the cost of living in Little Rock had increased during the war. In addition, Local 36's activities received particular attention because of the emphasis throughout the nation on maintaining stability in work related to the war effort.[71]

Despite the strength that its name evoked, however, the NWLB did not have the power of enforcement, and several of the laundry owners eventually attempted to evade compliance. With the ending of the war in late 1918, the NWLB lost even its persuasive advantage and informed the workers that they were on their own. During its sixteen months of operation, however, the NWLB considered 1,250 cases and made 500 awards.[72]

With the ending of the war, business owners in Little Rock as well as throughout the nation became increasingly hostile toward workers. In Little Rock, a well-organized open-shop drive was launched. With support from local labor and trade organizations, however, the women of Local 36 established their own laundry, which provided them with steady and fairly well-compensated employment.[73]

The Nineteenth Amendment and the Spanish Influenza Pandemic

As revealed above, some Arkansas women's experience, expertise, and contributions to the war effort did not provide sufficient bargaining tools in their quests for higher wages. On the other hand, Arkansas women's life-saving aid—particularly through their food conservation efforts, vital sewing and knitting in Red Cross workrooms, and service during the great flu pandemic—contributed to the amplification of middle-class women's call for woman suffrage.

Arkansas's women, however, were not of one accord regarding

> The Citizens' Co-operative Laundry, which is being engineered by the officials of the Little Rock Trades and Labor Council, changed the work-day from nine hours to eight hours and placed all inexperienced workers who were getting less than the minimum wage up to that pay, and rated all other workers correspondingly, the first day they took charge of the plant. The old City Steam Laundry is now owned and operated by the Citizens' Co-operative Laundry on a strictly union basis.
>
> In May 1918, International Laundry Workers' Local No. 36 struck all seven laundries in the city. The primarily African American women received a favorable award from the National War Labor Board. Later—with support from local labor organizations—the Citizens' Co-operative Laundry was established. *From the* Arkansas Gazette.

suffrage. County reports noted women's refusals to sign food-conservation or registration-for-service cards because of fear that they might be forced to vote. Women also voiced their distrust of the government and fear of being drafted into Red Cross or military service. As author J. Blake Perkins noted, "In Arkansas, particularly in the vast number of rural communities across the state, many citizens even by 1917 remained either staunchly opposed to or unconvinced and apathetic about the U.S. government's decision to involve the nation abroad in the Great War."[74] Lack of information and adequate communication, in combination with isolation from the outside world, likely added to women's prevailing suspicion and fear.

Despite some Arkansas women's concerns and fears about the suffrage, however, women's significant contributions during the war gave momentum to the movement and no doubt had a positive impact on men and governments. Although there were other deciding factors—including the realization that other countries had already given the suffrage to their women—the timing of the approval of the Nineteenth Amendment was positively affected by women's wartime efforts. And Arkansas's suffragists were well aware of this prevailing truth. In December 1917, Florence B. Cotnam, chairman of Arkansas's Equal Suffrage Central Committee,

African American nurses stand in front of the Great Southern Fraternal Hospital in Little Rock, c. 1920. In July 1918, the National Association for Colored Women, meeting in Denver, adopted a resolution asking the War Department "to assign 2,000 colored nurses for hospital duty in the war zone to care for wounded negro (*sic.*) soldiers." *Courtesy of the Butler Center for Arkansas Studies, Central Arkansas Library System, Little Rock.*

wrote an open letter in the *Arkansas Gazette*, calling 1918 a time of great opportunity for women activists. Her reasoning was simple: "[O]ur country never needed us as it does now."[75] As their final contribution during the war—no matter individual women's motivations—Arkansas's women came through for the citizens of their state in combatting one of the great pandemics of history.

In late September 1917, the *Arkansas Gazette* reported that "[p]recautionary measures to prevent the spreading of 'bad colds,' which might prove to be Spanish influenza, have been adopted at Camp Pike, and many individual units have been quarantined as a result of the rapid spread of the disease."[76] Ten days later, on October 6, the *Arkansas Gazette* reported that 13,000 cases of Spanish influenza had been identified at the military base.[77]

On October 5, as the disease rapidly spread throughout the state, the Arkansas Woman's Committee was called upon to help struggling families, college students, and young men in the barracks of the Student Army Training Corps.[78] In Little Rock, the county home demonstration agent, assisted by five field agents who were not able to do their work because of the quarantine, organized a so-called "diet kitchen" and got it up and running in a few days.[79] Later, Little Rock women—through the efforts of the Council of Defense and other organizations—took over the entire responsibility of providing supplies and delivering food to over 2,000 central Arkansans.[80]

Similar contributions were recounted throughout Arkansas as most of the state's sixty-eight home demonstration kitchens were converted into diet kitchens. Women were able to provide services in smaller towns and rural communities, in cooperation with the home economics department of each county council of defense. Miller County reported that during the influenza epidemic, members of the woman's committee, through the church societies, "did splendid work in making and delivering soup free from the government kitchen to the sick."[81]

Women who had signed up for nursing duties during the registration-for-service campaigns were also called upon to provide care to the numerous victims of the flu. Several counties' experiences are recounted below:

Clark County:

During the influenza epidemic all those who registered for practical nursing were called for, and a number who could leave their homes responded to the call and helped care for the sick.

Faulkner County:

On October 5, 7:00 a.m., an emergency call came from Dr. G. D. Huddleston, for volunteer nurses to be used in an influenza epidemic at the SATC [Student Army Training Corps] barracks and Hendrix College. Immediately we went over the registration cards and secured about 158 names. The women of Conway responded nobly, and out of about 400 cases we only lost two of the boys.

Hempstead County:

The rural woman was given every assistance during the influenza

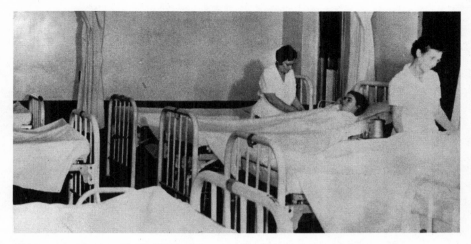

On October 25, 1918, Dr. C. W. Garrison, state health officer, appealed for nurses to serve where needed throughout the state as the deadly Spanish influenza spread. These women provided nursing care to University of Arkansas students. *Picture Collection NO. 1189, Special Collections, University of Arkansas Libraries.*

epidemic, and nursing and caring for children when they were ill was the special work of the committee.

Pulaski County:

Council of Jewish Women assisted in notifying by telephone 200 volunteer practical nurses, rather women who registered for practical nurses, endeavoring to get them to volunteer their services during the influenza epidemic. This necessitated constant telephoning from 9:00 a.m. to 5:00 p.m., and over 30 women responded.[82]

After the War

Documents from the American Red Cross Collection, recently processed by the Butler Center for Arkansas Studies, provide a stunning realization of the way that life moved on after the all-absorbing Great War ended: "In October [1920] we decided to have a section in the Armistice Day Parade, and World War I began to take its place as a memory in our lives with the exception of the men in the Veterans Hospital (whose lives will always be in touch with the Red Cross.)"[83]

With the ending of the war, there was suddenly a surplus of food and other commodities, coupled with various complicating factors that created a devastating economic depression for farm families by the early 1920s. Because much of Arkansas's manufacturing was tied to agriculture, the state lost 60% of its manufacturing companies between 1919 and 1921, i.e., 16,000 jobs. Although businesses recovered fairly well toward the end of the decade because of utility companies' efforts, agriculture could not overcome its losses, which were complicated by a years-long drought. As a result of the farm crisis, farm families were reduced once again to poverty; thus, many moved into larger cities or out of state.[84]

During the 1920s, home demonstration agents' reports alluded to hunger among children. In Saline County, the agent noted, "Greatest needs were the needs of the children. Many showed evidence of malnutrition."[85] In the aftermath of the Great Flood of 1927, the white agent in Phillips County reported that "the Health Unit Nurse and I visited the school weighing them and giving health talks to all the children from the Primary to the High School, every two weeks, and after weighing the children, and checking up on them, we found 70 that were undernourished and underweight."[86] And Arkansas's rural home demonstration members took up the work as they provided hot bowls of soup and crackers at lunch time for school children during the coldest months of Arkansas's winters.[87]

Also during the 1920s, the state's organized women—who were the officers and leaders of the Arkansas Woman's Committee during the war—returned to what they did best: lobbying the state and national legislatures for social issues, particularly the needs of children. At its biennial state convention in Little Rock, November 17–19, 1920, the Arkansas Federation of Women's Clubs seemed to pick back up where it had left off before the war, with its particular focus on lobbying for improved health for young children.[88]

At the AFWC's convention, one children's health bill before the U.S. Congress was of note. The Sheppard-Towner Act would go on to provide for the protection of maternity and infancy and supply a method of cooperation between the government of the United States and the state of Arkansas.[89] During the 1922 state convention at Blytheville, the organization resolved that "our club women sponsor and take special interest in nutrition classes in schools and that we encourage the movement to put into every county a full time health organization."[90]

During the 1919–1920 biennium, the legislature made a strong effort toward improved education as over 31% of the state's budget went to public schools and universities. Statistical abstracts provided by the United States Bureau of the Census show some of the results, with the number of high schools increasing from 163 in 1916 to 209 in 1924. Even more impressive is the fact that the number of high school students increased from 4,725 in 1916 to 12,968 in 1924.[91] However, as the tax base was cut with the depression of the 1920s, legislators struggled to find enough funding to maintain schools at the level they had reached by 1920.[92]

Resistance to consolidation of rural schools was of major concern to education reformers in Arkansas as well as other southern states during the 1920s. By 1930, however, every southern state had established, to some degree, a form of consolidation. Reformers assured rural people that the emptying of the one-room schoolhouse, so dear to each community, would enhance country life, advance farm prosperity, and ensure that young people would not be forced to move to cities to seek opportunity.[93] Despite Arkansans' opposition to the ideas espoused in such rhetoric, perhaps the gradually increasing number of school days per year and the growth in the number of high schools and high school students provided some consolation to Arkansas's reformers amid the ongoing struggles.

Significantly, the 1920s brought changes for Arkansas's women, who were joining women throughout the nation in making plans to enter or continue in the workforce after marriage. Connie J. Bonslagel, state home demonstration agent, noted in 1929 that eight young home demonstration agents had resigned to be married, with two or three having no intention of staying throughout the year when they came to the position. On the other hand, a 1928 listing of agents included ten for whom the term "Mrs." preceded the first name, indicating that the married women had apparently been grandfathered in with the U.S. Department of Agriculture policy change.[94] According to historian Carl Degler, as the Depression deepened, married women whose husbands had jobs were often denied employment or let go on the "plausible, though clearly illiberal"[95] grounds that men needed work more than married women did.[96]

For local Red Cross chapters, the change in focus after the war was dramatic and emphasized how quickly Arkansans' daily lives changed and their collective memory moved on. In January 1919, county offices received orders to "stack needles" and call in all outstanding work to be shipped by January 31. The hospital committee soon received instructions to discontinue making hospital garments and confine the work to refugee clothing instead. By 1922, the Little Rock office's home services section had by far the heaviest load.[97]

Although the Red Cross continued to provide Christmas boxes to disabled soldiers, by 1927 the focus was on alleviating the effects of devastating tornadoes and floods throughout the state. The Pulaski County office provided telling details of its work with refugees of the Great Flood of 1927: "Families are housed on the state fairgrounds in tents. Sanitary units are formed and in the six months that follow we try to relieve starvation, homelessness and nakedness and prevent and treat malaria and pellagra."[98]

In her annual narrative report for 1927, Carrie W. Moore, African American home demonstration agent in Phillips County, reported that the first refugees came by boatload at midnight. After three days, more than 1,000 were housed in the Eliza Miller High School in West Helena as well as in churches in the area. Upon the refugees' arrival, 1,000 cups of soup were served to them at Moore's direction, along with dry clothing provided by the Red Cross.[99]

The 1927 flood occurred amid two decades of drought, devastation, and hardship for Arkansas's people. The Cooperative Extension Service's home demonstration clubs were at the forefront of the fight against starvation, just as they had been during the Great War and the Spanish influenza pandemic. In 1934, the usually reticent state agent paid the women—both African American and white—a rare compliment:

> Because of the general poverty and because of the large numbers of unemployed families who are being moved into the country, the thrifty farm families find themselves with an unaccustomed responsibility in taking care of the needy. Home demonstration clubs are doing much social, economic, and educational welfare work. Where they are, they teach the newcomers to garden and can. Where they prove unteachable, club women can for them; many demonstrators [include] one or more hundred quarts for charity in their budgets.[100]

Just as the home demonstration program painted a picture of starving families and great need within rural communities, the Pulaski County chapter of the American Red Cross described similar conditions throughout the state's most populous county. Its 1930 report spoke of training workers in order "to prevent, as far as possible, the pauperization of our people."[101]

3 | Gearing Up Over Here for "Over There"

Manufacturing in Arkansas during World War I

CARL G. DREXLER

American entry into World War I presented the country and its military with significant challenges. Amid early-war isolationist sentiment, President Woodrow Wilson had resisted building up the U.S. military over prewar levels, meaning that mobilization for the conflict had to be done quickly and in many different areas at once. Recruitment efforts exploded, prewar militias were nationalized into the National Guard, and production of military goods was rapidly expanded to clothe and equip an expeditionary force that more than quadrupled the size of the peacetime army.

All the states played a role in mobilization, but this chapter focuses on Arkansas's part. In what proved to be the first experience the world had with what Captain B. H. Liddell Hart[1] termed "mechanical warfare," Arkansas and its people worked to support the conflict through several different production activities. The ways in which Arkansans came together in this effort brought about changes in the state that endured long after the war.

This chapter deals with mobilization, but more specifically on manufacturing, which is here understood to include several things. Here, "manufacturing" can be taken to mean items for the war produced in Arkansas

| DOI: https://doi.org/10.34053/christ2019.twah.3

factories. Also under consideration is Arkansas's place in wartime manufacturing on a nationwide scale through the production of unique and necessary raw materials that fed industries outside of the Natural State. What follows, then, is a look into how the state geared up "over here" to prepare to send Arkansans and other American soldiers "Over There."

American Manufacturing in World War I: Organizing for Conflict

America's entry into the Great War signaled a new kind of organization for mobilization. Previous wars, including the Indian Wars and Spanish-American War, were small enough that American involvement could be handled largely by government arsenals. The Civil War offered a different challenge, one that was met by a mixture of centralized production and procurement, but with a lot of independence at the state level, particularly in the South. The First World War, however, came at a time when "scientific" approaches to management and organization were extremely popular among capitalists and middle management, and there was great emphasis placed on nationwide preparation for the conflict based upon sound scientific principles.[2]

THE COMMITTEE FOR INDUSTRIAL PREPAREDNESS

The United States did not enter the war until 1917, but it had plans in place. Beginning as early as 1915, clerks in several federal offices compiled lists of industrial facilities that either already produced military equipment or could be quickly retooled to make military goods in the event of a declaration of war. Though numerous, these efforts lacked comprehensiveness. In April 1916, the U.S. Navy took steps to make a thorough and detailed survey. Under the auspices of the Naval Consultation Board, headed by Thomas Edison, the Committee on Industrial Preparedness (CIP) set up a structure for gathering information quickly and across many fields. The CIP established subcommittees in each state composed of five members, drawn from the American Society of Civil Engineers, American Institute of Mining Engineers, American Society of Mechanical Engineers, American Institute of Electrical Engineers, and American Chemical Society, all professional organizations for fields deemed crucial to a war effort. These state subcommittees would survey their professional society members around the state for information about their firms and ideas about how they might contribute to mobilization.

In Arkansas, the state chapter consisted of chemist J. B. Rather, mechanical engineer B. N. Wilson, electrical engineer W. N. Gladson, civil engineer C. H. Miller, and mining engineer J. R. Fordyce. Of these, Rather, Gladson, and Wilson taught at the University of Arkansas, while Fordyce and Miller ran private firms based in Little Rock.[3]

THE COUNCIL OF NATIONAL DEFENSE

In the summer of 1916, as the French and Germans vied for control of Verdun, the U.S. Congress approved the Council of National Defense (CND), an organization that would bring together military, political, scientific, and business leaders to prepare the country for war. The CND was to be a body with expansive powers that would, over the course of the war, centralize administration of the country's war-oriented economy. At the war's inception, President Wilson stated that "the country is best prepared for war when thoroughly prepared for peace," and that "from an economic point of view, there is now very little difference between the machinery required for commercial efficiency and that required for military purpose." Not only did this represent a giant step toward involvement in the war, it heralded, as historian Paul Koistinen[4] writes, the onset of what Dwight Eisenhower would later describe as the military-industrial complex, melding commercial-industrial realms with those of the armed forces. Though traditionally associated with the Cold War and more recent years, the military-industrial complex was formed in the early years of World War I.

The CND gained wider powers in October 1916, when President Wilson created the National Defense Advisory Commission (NACD) to the Council of National Defense. Where the CND itself set large-scale policy, the National Defense Advisory Commission worked to articulate that policy at the local level. One of the roles it took on was the data-collecting task of the CIP[5]. It is important to note that much of the impetus for forming the CND and its NACD came from industry, not from the military. Business leaders whose efforts were focused on rational plant management and routinization of industrial practices doubted the ability of the U.S. military to mobilize in the event of war, and they took steps to get those preparations underway. The U.S. government went along with the plan, making funds available for war industries long before America became involved in the conflict. The NACD continued its work until early 1918, when it was upgraded into the War Industries Board, which had more powerful government backing and the ability to coordinate transportation, orders, and finished goods.[6]

STATE COUNCILS OF DEFENSE

To support the CND, states formed state committees of defense, which then coordinated with county and community committees of defense. So, from the federal level down to community levels, manufacturing and war-related production were highly organized and hierarchical. Government, society, and military at all levels were integrated through this system to an extent not seen before in American history. Arkansas's State Council of Defense first met in May 1917 and soon was very active in two different efforts: food production and fuel production.

The State Council of Defense also took on three efforts that were deemed crucial to developing a workforce capable of fueling wartime industry and preparing the country for postwar advancement: public health, college attendance, and the creation of a home guard. This last effort supplanted police and militia called into service and was headed by Confederate veteran J. R. Gibbons.

It should also be noted that, in addition to coordinating production and manufacturing, the committees of defense, at all levels, also dealt with "public morale." This meant both education and policing. On the education front, the committees of defense made available to local communities speakers who delivered prepared lectures on the reason for American involvement in the conflict, the importance of working long hours, the perceived dangers of unions, and other topics deemed important to manufacturing and the war effort more generally.[7] In terms of policing, people reported to committees of defense when they observed talk, meetings, and writings considered disloyal to the American cause.

Arkansas Manufacturing
and the War Industries Board

The state, county, and community councils of defense all played roles in local production and small-scale manufacturing, in addition to serving as "thought police" and public information bureaus. They were not, however, the only appendage of the Council of National Defense that was active in wartime manufacturing, and other organizations arguably had bigger, if less locally inflected parts to play. Chief among these was the War Industries Board (WIB). The Food Administration, the Fuel Administration, and the WIB were the three major subdivisions of the CND. While the Food Administration coordinated food production for both local consumption and overseas export and the Fuel Administration occupied itself with everything from home heating to coal mining for the U.S. Navy, the WIB managed all the manufacturing for the military. Its role in creating markets for materials, setting prices for commodities, and even managing shipping and order fulfillment made it very influential during the war.

To understand how Arkansas fit into the WIB's manufacturing efforts, it helps to separate out two areas of work. First, providing raw materials for use in production facilities elsewhere is a key part of Arkansas's manufacturing history. Second, the production of goods inside the state was also significant in furnishing our doughboys with the needed equipment and supplies.

For a typical American soldier, much of his kit could be made with Arkansas products. His khaki-colored uniform would consist of woolen trousers and tunic, often lined with cotton or furnished with cotton accessories. Leather belts, boots, gloves, and equipment cases were mounted with brass or iron hardware, all of which were produced to some extent in Arkansas during the war. Steel helmets were a new phenomenon during the war, and the Americans copied the pattern from the English. New pieces of equipment, from airplanes to tanks to gas masks, were also required by the two million American men sent to Europe. These men also needed food, bandages, reading material, tents, stretchers, and a host of other items. Finally, each foot soldier carried a rifle that, while not made in Arkansas, might well have had a stock carved from Arkansas hardwoods or fired bullets propelled by gunpowder that used Arkansas cellulose fibers.

Most of those basics were made in the United States, but not all. Most of the Americans' tanks came from France, and though we were working at fielding our own airplanes, many American fliers piloted British planes into combat. The British and French also made many of the artillery pieces the American military used overseas, drawing on their years of experience in the shell-blasted trenches of the Western Front.[8] Weaponry rapidly evolved and advanced during the war, allowing others to buy or borrow some of the more advanced systems from those who already had experience with them under fire.

Importantly, American manufacturing processes were in operation, or at least being geared up, well before our actual involvement in the war in 1917. Though the start of the war in Europe in 1914 created a brief economic downturn, the demand from Allied nations for food, raw materials, and some finished products quickly created a minor economic boom in the United States. Though the government attempted to quell public uneasiness about involvement in the war through officially restricting mobilization, industry benefited greatly even before 1917. From 1915 on, our farmers and industrialists reaped large rewards by selling to France and Britain, meaning that when the United States entered the war, the economy had already at least partially transitioned to a war footing, and the ensuing wartime production was more of an expansion in certain areas than a complete revolution in production.

Fueling Manufacturing Nationwide: Raw Material Production in Arkansas during the Great War

Our state has long been one focused on the growth and harvesting of natural resources, rather than on industrial production. Arkansas will never be accused of being a Rust Belt state like those of the Northeast and mid-Atlantic. So, it follows that manufacturing in Arkansas during the war featured the production of raw materials for manufacturing facilities elsewhere. These resources most significantly include cotton and timber, but mining and other endeavors factor into this discussion.

Producing these raw materials was, in part, directed by the state's prewar economic and political structures. Particularly in the years between 1915 and 1917, when the American business world became deeply involved in the European conflict before the country itself joined in, the economy adjusted to the needs of global conflict, and Arkansas's industries were borne along with this sea change.[9] Wartime production was also influenced by state, county, and community councils of defense, which worked to increase production in all of the following sectors. They helped coordinate the logistics of production, exhorted people to work longer hours, and sought to identify those who harbored misgivings about the conflict or did not, for whatever reason, feel like doing what society felt was their part.[10]

FORESTRY PRODUCTS

The war increased demand for forest products. Before American involvement, sales to France and England created a small boom in demand. Both of those countries either lacked manpower, as their lumbermen were in service, or lacked access to forests sufficient to their needs. France, in particular, suffered from its forests in the east becoming battlefields or being occupied by German soldiers. America's declaration of war and move toward mobilization increased demand.

Any army of the period needed timber to construct barracks, hospitals, training camps, administrative facilities, and arsenals to prepare for war. In-theater, men needed supports for dugout shelters, duckboards to keep their feet out of the mire, and fence posts to support barbed wire. Food and equipment, including ammunition, went forward in wooden boxes, crates, and barrels. Oil and gasoline to supply wooden-framed airplanes shipped in wooden barrels. Gun barrels, needed by millions of foot soldiers, required hardwood stocks. In an era before synthetic materials were widely available, wood was the versatile medium used to produce much of what armies lived in and carried with them.

Arkansas's timber stands helped answer the need. Timber resources accounted for 51.4% of the value of all manufactured good in the state in 1914, making it Arkansas's largest manufacturing industry. The state was sixth nationwide in the value of forest products produced in 1919, ahead of all southern states save Louisiana and Mississippi.[11] Arkansas significantly out-produced the northern lumbering states of Michigan, Wisconsin, and Minnesota. Most of that production centered in the cutting and milling of yellow pine and cypress, which grew in all corners of the state. These woods were used extensively in construction and container production.

The state also led the way in hardwood production. Arkansas was one of the major producers of species such as oak, red gum, hickory, elm, ash, and cottonwood. These had more specific purposes than yellow pine and cypress, including the milling of rifle stocks and production of field instruments used extensively by the Allies. These were usually shipped out of state to arsenals in need of raw materials, as Arkansas did not produce many firearms during the conflict.

The state did, however, lead the way in the production of wood veneers and both tight and slack cooperage, both of which had military applications. Veneers were used to cover cheaper wood in making furniture and other fashionable items, such as desks and file cabinets used by a growing force of military clerks and officials. "Tight and slack cooperage" is industry-speak for barrels meant to hold liquids and solids, respectively. The Factoria Addition on Little Rock's east side was home to a number of barrel factories and veneer plants in the years before the war, and their production undoubtedly converted over to items needed by the military. With timber being such a large industry in Arkansas, both at the time of the war and continuing down to today, it is no surprise that one of the state's major contributions to the war effort was through the production of forest products.[12]

Demand for wood was not solely for military consumption, however. The Fuel Administration, one of the arms of the Council of National Defense, sought to limit consumption of coal and natural gas among civilians, keeping it free to be used by the military and the railroads, who needed it for high-temperature fires in smelters, furnaces, and factories. In their stead, the Fuel Administration, represented in Arkansas by Harvey Couch, encouraged the burning of wood as a heating and cooking fuel throughout the duration of the war.[13] Indeed, across the country, the Fuel Administration worked to limit domestic consumption of fossil fuels in favor of wood-fired heating and cooking.

The demand for wood during the war frustrated the U.S. Census Bureau's attempt to characterize the long-term health of the industry in its decennial accounting, which was compiled in 1919.[14] Arkansas looms large in its efforts, however, as the state's important place within the timber industry before the war meant that it was well situated to be a significant contributor during the conflict.

COTTON BYPRODUCTS

Cotton byproducts were Arkansas's second-largest manufacturing sector, next to timber, in 1914. Cotton gins across the South produced bales of cotton that could be shipped off to make an innumerable array of goods, some military and some civilian. Besides the pure cotton, which was considered an agricultural product and not a manufactured one, gins put out a large quantity of cottonseed and "linters," the little strands of cotton left on a seed after ginning. These were of some industrial use.

The seeds, for instance, could either be saved for the next year's crop, or could be crushed for their oil, which was found in the late nineteenth century to be usable in cooking. If you have a tub of Crisco in your kitchen, you are using crystallized cottonseed oil[15]. The crushed seed would also be sold in cakes to be fed to cattle. Little of the gin product of the era was left to rot in the fields as in previous generations.

The humble linter was also worth something, though not in an industry you might expect. Smokeless gunpowder involves a number of ingredients, one of which is cellulose, basically plant material that can be very finely crushed and can burn very rapidly. Arms manufacturers found that, when removed from the seed and baled, cotton linters could be treated with several chemicals and used as cellulose for smokeless powder production. This gave a very important military role to a very small waste product from the ginning operation.

Arkansas cotton gins baled and shipped linters to munitions plants across the country throughout the war. To list just a few instances, the Warren Cotton Oil & Manufacturing Company, in Bradley County, shipped 1,500 bales of linters, which required sixty-five train cars, to Memphis in 1916 alone. Pine Bluff, in that same year, saw thirty-seven cars' worth of linters leave its yards, headed to Rhode Island for use in munitions plants.[16] This industrial necessity, though just simple wisps of fiber attached to a tiny seed, was crucial to the American war effort, and it was one of the major contributions Arkansas made.

MINING

Resources obtained through mining were less important than timber and cotton, but they still were crucial to the military and represent the diversity of materials provided by the state and its workers. Arkansas was thirty-seventh of the forty-eight states that made up the United States at the time in terms of mining output in 1919, with proceeds amounting to around $8.2 million. This marked an actual decline in the importance of mining to the state's economy over the preceding ten years. Still, much of what was mined went to the war. The major portion of Arkansas's mining output, about 63% of the total, focused on bituminous coal mined in the northern Ouachita Mountains. Boone, Scott, Franklin, and Logan Counties were major producers within the state. As mentioned above, coal was crucial for war industries in the east and for the railroad that moved goods and soldiers to the places they needed to be.[17]

Bauxite mining, in Pulaski and Saline Counties, was second in importance to coal, though the production was sufficient to make Arkansas the leading supplier of bauxite in the country. Bauxite is the primary ore from which aluminum is extracted, a significant fact considering that the Great

War was the first conflict in which aluminum was widely used. Canteens, mess tins, and insignia were all elements of the common soldier's kit that were made of aluminum. The light-but-strong metal also went into bicycles, automobiles, and aircraft.

A few other metals, such as copper, zinc, antimony, and manganese, were mined in Boone, Sevier, Washington, Yell, Montgomery, and Pike Counties during the war years. These were valuable to the war effort either as primary components of uniform and equipment pieces, or as alloying agents added to some other metal to produce desired qualities, such as hardness or workability.[18]

Although iron ore was very important to the war effort, it was not widely mined in Arkansas. There was some iron ore mining around Eureka Springs and in Howard County, but the net result of this paled in comparison to the ore production of states like Pennsylvania, Ohio, and Indiana, all of which produced over 100,000 tons of ore per year. The census bureau reported Arkansas's yield only in the ignominious "all other states" category.[19]

While production of iron ore was low, there were some efforts made at developing processing facilities. Both Nashville and Hot Springs attracted business concerns interested in starting furnaces and bloomeries to create pig iron, but it is unclear how successful these endeavors were during the war. Texarkana was known to have been successful in iron processing, as its furnaces were active throughout the conflict, but the ore processed there came primarily out of the red dirt of northeastern Texas, and it is, therefore, not so much an Arkansas product.

LEATHER

Leather represented another manufacturing sector in Arkansas during the war. In the years before nylon, the American soldier wore a leather belt, sported leather boots, had a leather brim on his cap, had leather gloves, used leather equipment cases, and had a host of other leather goods issued to him by the military. The advent of the air service placed new demands on leather manufacturers, as fliers needed straps to hold their gear on and often wore suits of lined leather to keep them warm in the air. This voracious appetite for animal skins soon translated into a nationwide leather shortage, which affected both the supply available to our own troops and that sought by Allied powers to clothe and equip their own soldiers.

The Morning Star Zinc Mine at Rush in Marion County saw high production during World War I. *Courtesy of the Butler Center for Arkansas Studies, Central Arkansas Library System, Little Rock.*

Though Arkansas was not one of the top leather producers at the time[20] (being twenty-ninth nationwide), the nationwide leather shortage drove up prices and encouraged production. To help increase the supply available to the military, the Arkansas State Council of Defense sparked several legislative changes. First, it pushed through a ban on the consumption of veal. This was meant to both increase the supply of beef and ensure that full-grown hides were available for sale to the military. Second, the State Council set out regulations for keeping stock out of railroad rights-of-way, particularly inside city limits. This was done in hopes of keeping the animals off the tracks and thereby reducing the amount of leather and meat lost to cow–train collisions. Owners were also encouraged to build fences to keep their stock off the rails. While this measure invokes somewhat gruesome mental images, and may seem like a strange thing to focus a statewide policy on, it was far from a small problem at the time. In August 1918 alone, 166 head of cattle were struck by trains on Arkansas railroads, so conservation measures stood to measurably increase the amount of leather and beef available for the war effort.[21]

FOOD FOR OVER HERE AND OVER THERE

While Arkansas's rural, agricultural economy contributed to manufacturing, producing raw materials for others' use, for 88% of Arkansans, business meant farming, which meant food production, something not captured in Great War tabulations on manufacturing and industrial activities.[22] Yet, Arkansas farmers worked very hard to produce for the state, the rest of the country, the military overseas, and the Allies.

As was the case with other industries, disruptions to British and French society interfered with their own food production networks early in the war. This created a small boom in agriculture for the United States in 1915 and 1916, as overseas sales skyrocketed. Farmers enjoyed higher prices for their produce, though the demands of feeding Europe, and, after 1917, the U.S. Army, stretched their abilities.

Under the auspices of the Council of National Defense's Food Administration, food production increased, particularly wheat needed for bread. That production was administered on the county level by specially appointed bureaucrats who worked to minimize wastage and coordinate growing, harvesting, and milling. Those who did their part had a placard to that effect posted on their mailbox or fencepost, letting the neighbors know they had contributed to the war effort.[23]

The State Council also oversaw rice production. Volunteers for service were of such number that the rice harvest in eastern Arkansas was threatened, so the State Council worked to bring in laborers from elsewhere in the state. Once the crop was in, the usual practice of polishing the rice was curtailed due to lack of hands. While unpolished rice was deemed less desirable, it was a cost- and time-saving measure.[24] It was later found that unpolished rice cut down on beriberi, a neurological disease linked to a vitamin deficiency, so the war-sparked change produced nutritional benefit.

Besides coordinating production, the State Council worked on other measures focused on economy and restraint in consumption. People were encouraged to plant their own kitchen gardens, freeing commercial produce for exportation, and farmers were encouraged to donate proceeds from a portion of their produce to buying war bonds and otherwise raising money for the military. This latter program was so successful that it was implemented nationwide by war's end.

The Little Rock Picric Acid Plant

While much of Arkansas's involvement in wartime manufacturing related to the production of raw materials, the state had one major wartime industrial facility: a plant that produced picric acid. Arkansas's report on its activities during the war identified four major war facilities in the state: Camp Pike, Eberts Field, the Aviation Warehouse, and the Little Rock Picric Acid Plant. (One wonders why Fort Roots did not make the list.) Camp Pike trained thousands of soldiers for service on the Western Front. Eberts Field prepared others for the Army Air Corps. The Aviation Warehouse, located in Little Rock, stockpiled and shipped airplane parts to airfields across the country, from the Southwest to Florida. The Little Rock Picric Acid plant stands apart in that it was the only one that was a manufacturing facility. It presents us with a unique aspect of Arkansas's involvement in the Great War that temporarily changed the way Arkansans thought about the economic future of their state.

PICRIC ACID IN THE GREAT WAR

Picric acid is not watery liquid we often think of acids as being. Rather, it is a thick, honey-like, yellowish fluid or crystal. It was very valuable during the war from a military standpoint because it is an extremely powerful high explosive; it is even more destructive than TNT. It began to replace black powder in artillery shells starting in the 1890s, and, as such, was one of the factors in making the battlefields of the First World War so incredibly dangerous and battle scarred.[25]

Though it is extremely destructive, picric acid is also stable enough that it can, unlike nitroglycerin, be trusted explode only when intended (at least in the vast majority of cases). It is largely insensitive to shock and vibration, and will generally detonate only when acted upon by a fuze or other source of fire. Picric acid could be put in an artillery shell and fired without it going off in the cannon barrel, killing friendly troops. Yet, down range, when a fuze initiated it, it would reliably produce massive amounts of destruction.

Beyond these attributes, it had the added bonus of being the basis for chloropicrin, a chemical warfare agent. Chloropicrin is a gas, lethal in its own right, that is absorbable through the skin. Those exposed to it would, at minimum, become sick to their stomach. Both sides used chloropicrin as a lethal gas and as a "mask breaker." Some of the more lethal gases, such as phosgene, could be blocked by German gas masks, but chloropicrin, by acting on the skin, could get around the mask. The affected soldier would be compelled to remove his gas mask, lest he drown in his own vomit. With the mask off, he could not avoid inhaling the other gases, which would then kill him. Chloropicrin that did not affect soldiers outright might settle on equipment or food, thereby poisoning enemy soldiers later on. As the base for this gas, picric acid was a very valuable substance, one that Americans used ourselves but also sold in great quantities to the French army.[26]

Picric acid does have some significant drawbacks, however, which is why it is not in service now, while the less-powerful TNT is a near-universal explosive of choice. First, picric acid remains stable so long as it remains fluid. When it dehydrates, it forms into a salt-like substance, the individual crystals of which can explode when crushed or heavily shaken. This makes dehydrated picric acid extremely dangerous to handle, much less ship or store. Those salts form very rapidly when picric acid contacts metal, meaning that iron artillery shells had to be given an interior coating before being loaded, an extra step that was expensive in time and resources, and any kind of manufacturing flaw could present risk to munitions workers, armorers, and gun crews.

There were a few cases of picric acid plants in England blowing up during the war, killing scores of workers. On this side of the Atlantic, an accident at Halifax, Nova Scotia, occurred on December 6, 1917, when the French *S.S. Mont-Blanc*, loaded with picric acid, collided with the Norwegian vessel *Imo*. The resulting explosion measured approximately 2.9 kilotons and was the most powerful explosion in human history until the advent of the atomic bomb. It killed nearly 2,000 people and destroyed the Halifax shipping docks.

Picric acid was found to have some therapeutic qualities, however, and sometimes appeared in first aid kits as a burn dressing. Lamentably, over time, as the picric acid dried out, those kits became very dangerous, and there was a period in the 1970s when fire departments and bomb squads fanned out across Arkansas, collecting old first aid kids and destroying them. These still pop up occasionally on eBay or in second-hand shops[27].

OPENING THE LITTLE ROCK PICRIC ACID PLANT

When the Great War began, only one government entity and a handful of private firms in the United States manufactured picric acid. These supplied the small demands of the U.S. military along with the much greater requirements of Allied forces, notably the French and English. The German spring offensive of 1918 spurred demand from all sectors, and the U.S. government decided that the country needed to produce more picric acid. As a result, the War Industries Board announced that it would let contracts for three new picric acid facilities, attracting bids from across the country.[28] Three cities—Memphis, Tennessee; Louisville, Kentucky; and Little Rock—emerged as top contenders for one of those contracts.[29]

Little Rock's bid won. This victory was due largely to the efforts of George Firmin and Ed Cornish of the Little Rock Board of Commerce. They offered the military cheap land, rail connections, and some existing buildings in a city blessed by a temperate climate and possessing relatively weak labor unions. Plus, they believed that Arkansas could furnish the 2,000 construction workers and 4,000 munitions workers the plant would require.[30]

Citizens celebrated in the streets of Little Rock on May 21, 1918, hailing the good news. They saw the $10 million facility as both an immediate boon to the economy and the beginning of a new chapter in Arkansas's economic history. The state, they felt, would go from a wholly agricultural economy to one that included significant industrial production, as well.[31]

The place chosen for the facility was an area known as the Factoria Addition, now the site of Bill and Hillary Clinton National Airport and the adjoining Bankhead Drive exit along Interstate 440 in southeastern Little Rock. This was the focus of Central Arkansas's industrial development before the war, and the presence of existing plants, which could be converted to military use, factored into the success of the city's bid. In the early 1910s, Factoria housed several woodworking plants, focused on making barrels and veneers, along with a cannery that churned out hominy and canned vegetables. Rail lines connected it with Argenta (what is now North Little Rock), and Factoria was set to be the hub of Arkansas's new manufacturing horizon, according to the boosters' stories in the *Arkansas Democrat* and *Daily Arkansas Gazette*.

Work began on the picric acid plant with great zeal, as orders were placed for building materials within days of the announcement of the contract. Approximately 400,000 board feet of lumber came in, along with 600,000 bricks, glass, iron, and myriad other construction materials.[32] The companies brought in to build and operate the facility, Pratt Engineering and the Everly M. Davis Chemical Company, hired construction workers by the hundreds. These men came either out of Little Rock, which provided a convenient commuter workforce, or from farther afield, and took up residence in the bunkhouses and dining halls constructed at the facility. Ads for plant workers were in the papers as soon as mid-June, and newspaper stories indicate that munition and construction workers labored next to each other throughout the war. By the Armistice, construction was 90% complete and the plant was operating at 50% of its planned maximum.[33]

OPERATING THE LITTLE ROCK PICRIC ACID PLANT

There are no depictions of the plant in period newspapers, but there are a few pictures of the sister facility at Brunswick, Georgia, which was larger, built by other hands, and never went into operation. What we do have is a 1921 depiction of the closed plant drawn from the Sanborn Fire Insurance Maps. For those not familiar with these, the Sanborn Fire Insurance Company, as its name suggests, offered fire insurance, and therefore had a business need to know where buildings were, what they looked like, and what they were made of. To aid their business, they produced a series of very useful maps for cities across the United States, noting the footprint, standing height, and construction materials for buildings. Fortunately, the 1921 Little Rock set includes the picric acid plant.[34]

When we look at the map, we see the facility at its most complete and can read the production process, ingredients required, and articulations with the national war effort inscribed on the landscape. As far as ingredients, the thing that set picric acid apart from other high explosives of the period was its use of phenol. Phenol is a crystalline substance distilled from coal tar, itself a byproduct of breaking coal into coke and coal gas. Also known as "carbolic acid" or "coal-oil acid," phenol was discovered in the nineteenth century and used as an antiseptic by Joseph Lister before other properties were discovered. In the late nineteenth century, Hermann Sprengel found one of those other properties, noting that, if treated with nitric and sulfuric acids, it would produce a powerful explosive. This was trinitrophenol, or picric acid.[35] At the Little Rock facility, phenol came from a coal oil refinery built in the northeastern corner of the facility. It was surrounded by several boilers and storage tanks.

The nitric and sulfuric acid required to produce picric acid from phenol were both manufactured on site. The sulfuric acid building lay on the eastern edge of the plant, and was a two-story wood-framed building clad with metal sheeting. A shed housing several sulfur burners stood immediately to the east. Production of sulfuric acid involved the reduction of sulfur in those burners before it was rendered into an acid in the sulfuric plant. That acid was then used both in the production of nitric acid and in the finished product, picric acid.

The nitric acid building sat east of the sulfuric building, and it consisted of a production room, storage tanks, furnaces, and a storage building. Producing nitric acid required sodium nitrate, which was only available from Chile at the start of the war. By war's end, the government had opened nitrogen fixation plants, the first two in our history, at Sheffield and Muscle Shoals, Alabama.[36] Whether it was sailed in from Chile or brought by rail from Alabama, Little Rock munitions workers treated sodium nitrate with sulfuric acid to produce nitric acid.

With phenol, nitric acid, and sulfuric acid all produced on-site, the plant had what it needed to make picric acid. The different elements were likely combined in the concentration building. This process started with sulfuric acid, which would be loaded into a large lead-lined sulfonation tank, into which workers would lower a quantity of solid phenol. A steam coil running through the sulfonator would keep the mixture at a constant temperature as an agitator mixed the two steadily over a period of eighteen to twenty-four hours. This solution was then cut with water to cool and dilute it before being mixed with a solution of nitric and sulfuric acid. This last combination produces a lot of heat, and the mixture had to be carefully monitored lest the solution melt. Monitoring involved adding water to keep the solution under 120 degrees centigrade.[37] This process consumed up to 500,000 gallons of fresh water per day.[38]

Picric acid crystals formed as the mixture cooled at the end of this last stage. The slurry of crystals and water was finally centrifuged to lower the moisture content to a desired point. The material could then be packed (using non-sparking wooden tools) and shipped to a munitions plant, where it could be loaded into shells[39].

The maps show that the plant buildings were all surrounded by fire hydrants connected to a one-foot-diameter water pipe, underscoring the concerns staff had for the safety of the facility. Also, most of the buildings were plumbed and electrified, something few Arkansas residences could boast in 1918. That power came from the power station constructed north of the main plant. By 1921, this appears as an Arkansas Power and Light facility.

Railroad lines crosscut the entire facility, coming into the plant from the northwest. These connected the plant with Little Rock and Argenta (North Little Rock), bringing in raw materials, carrying out finished

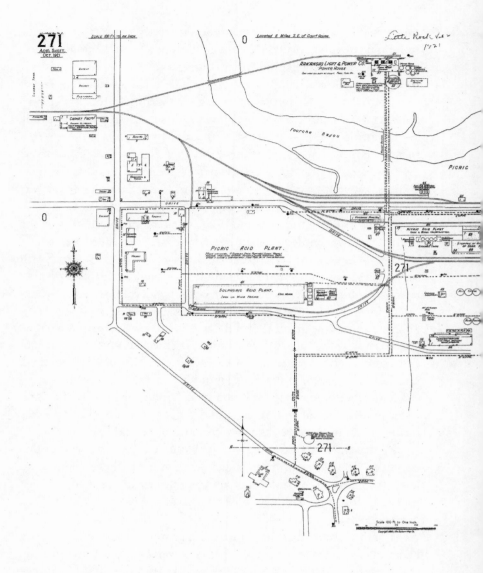

This 1921 Sanborn Fire Insurance Company map shows the extent of the picric
acid plant in eastern Little Rock. *Image published with permission of ProQuest LLC
as part of its Digital Sanborn Maps web product. Further reproduction is prohibited
without permission. Inquiries may be made to: ProQuest, P.O. Box 1346, Ann Arbor, MI
48106 USA. Telephone +1 734 997 4111.*

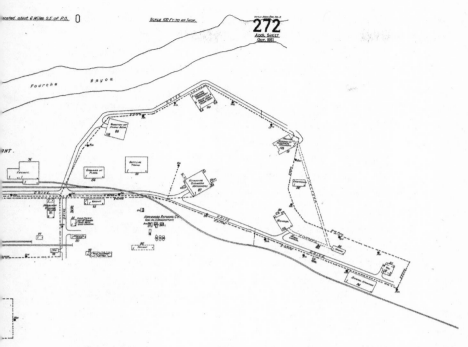

product, and serving as a commuter line for workers living in Little Rock. In Little Rock, those rail lines connected with the Missouri Southern railroad, which would carry the picric acid to arsenals elsewhere.

LIFE AROUND THE PICRIC ACID PLANT

What the Sanborn maps do not show is the community that began to form around the picric acid plant. This community survives today as the Cherry Acres area, to the north, and a community once known as Picron, to the south. Though Cherry Acres is still a neighborhood in Little Rock, Picron has been enveloped by College Station, though both Google and Zillow maintain geographic coordinates for it. Despite its now-modest presence, Picron was once set to be a major new residential area some thought could grow to rival Little Rock.

Both Picron and Cherry Acres formed to house workers at the Picric Acid Plant. Though there was some housing to be had at the plant itself, workers, particularly those with families, wanted something more, and land speculators quickly gobbled up the surrounding landscape. Lots went on sale, and construction firms built dozens of family homes. Lots were big enough to have a house along with a garden and even enough space for some cows, chickens, and pigs. More than simple homes, these amounted to small urban farmsteads.[40]

This bucolic imagery masked a few realities about life and work at the plant. First, work there was quite dangerous. The workers produced a high explosive made of a petroleum derivative and two harsh acids, so the potential for grievous workplace injuries was ever present. Noxious fumes and chemical burns were common, and the early twentieth century was not known as a paragon of workplace safety. Second, those hazards went beyond the obvious forms of exposure. The crystals from the plant could settle on clothing, hair, and skin, often turning the workers a pale shade of yellow. Period documents use the term "canaries" to refer to workers in picric acid plants.

Adding to the health risks were the dangers of inhaling the gaseous form of the acid (which was basically a chemical warfare agent), or getting the acid itself on one's skin. The chemical would travel through the bloodstream and sicken the exposed person. No document for the Little Rock plant shows this, but fatalities for exposure at other facilities were known during this period. Women working in picric acid plants in the United Kingdom were even reported giving birth to babies with yellow skin.

Not all dangers were chemical. To keep the plant going, the plant soon had its own police force, wearing gray military-style uniforms and every piece of law enforcement gear available at the time. One paper even suggested that the force was equal in size and formidability to the Little Rock Police Department. While that may be a bit of hyperbole, it should be remembered that a large work force was needed to build the plant, and a larger one was required to staff it, so a major industrial facility focused on producing a military commodity during wartime was likely to require a significant security force. The few existing accounts of plant workers at the Brunswick, Georgia, plant suggest that the police force served the company and the government first, and it cultivated a reputation for being hard on workers and compelling labor in unsafe conditions.[41]

STAFFING THE PLANT

We don't know to what extent these dangers deterred workers, but we do know that the plant was constantly plagued by an unexpected shortage of hands. Ads for workers went out as soon as the plant was announced, but getting together the 4,000 workers that the plant required appears to have been a constant nightmare for state and plant officials. The first calls went out for workers from around Little Rock. As these proved inefficient, the net was cast a little wider. Ads for workers appear in newspapers from Jonesboro to Texarkana by mid-1918.

More-drastic measures were soon needed. Little Rock staged at least one volunteer day, on which thousands of men from the city went to the plant to offer up a day's work. The city also contemplated a work draft, and even went so far as to identify job categories deemed "non-essential" that would be closed by the city police to compel those engaged in those trades to go work in the plant. Chauffeurs, bowling lane operators, barbers, tobacconists, florists, dance instructors, elevator operators, and soft drink manufacturers were among those deemed subject to labor drafts.[42]

Ultimately, the answer for this shortage appears to have come from farther afield. The newly founded Department of Labor opened an office of the U.S. Employment Service in the Old Post Office on Markham Street, in downtown Little Rock. From there, administrators scoured the state for workers, but they settled on the idea of shipping in workers from the distant reaches of the fledgling American empire. In mid-1918, the first of two waves of Puerto Rican workers, hired from fields in the Caribbean by the U.S. Employment Service, arrived in Little Rock. Of the first wave, workers were split between the Little Rock Picric Acid Plant and Camp Pike. The second wave, numbering about 1,500 workers, was sent only to the plant.

The appearance of the Puerto Rican workers opens a unique window onto Arkansas's Hispanic heritage. Clearly, by this point in the war, the picric acid plant, a major portion of Arkansas's industrial contribution to the war effort, was not going to be a success without these workers. Yet, they received little preparation for coming to Arkansas to work in the plant.

In October 1918, the citizens of Little Rock staged a clothing drive specifically aimed at equipping the Puerto Rican workers.[43] Apparently, most had been brought to Arkansas in the sandals and light linen clothing common to agricultural workers in the Caribbean. They were not prepared to be working around dangerous chemicals, and were utterly unequipped to endure the abnormally cold winter of 1918. Unsurprisingly, many wanted to return to Puerto Rico. Most stayed, however, and became part of the social fabric of the plant. They even participated in talent shows and other social functions put on by the plant staff to raise funds for the war.

The Puerto Rican staff stuck it out through the winter and the unsafe conditions, and unfortunately shared in another grave situation that struck in the fall of 1918. The great influenza epidemic of 1918 hit the plant while it was still in operation, and while there were some early hopes that the workers could be effectively quarantined, eventually the flu arrived. Dozens of workers fell ill, and at least sixty-six Puerto Ricans died during the outbreak. Visitors to Calvary Cemetery, in southern Little Rock, can today visit a memorial to the islanders who passed away while working at the plant.

CLOSING THE LITTLE ROCK PICRIC ACID PLANT

Unlike its sister facility in Brunswick, Georgia, the Little Rock plant did start producing picric acid before the war ended, and it manufactured a significant quantity of it, though hard numbers are lacking.[44] The mere fact that Arkansans managed to go from the bidding process to a functioning munitions plant within the space of seven months is a remarkable achievement. It was, however, short lived.

The world rejoiced when the belligerents signed the Armistice on November 11, 1918. Soldiers from all over the world, including Arkansas, would be heading home. Newspaper accounts indicate that amidst the joy, some at the plant felt pangs of anxiety. Would the plant remain in operation, now that the war was over? Many hoped that, since the Little Rock plant was the only operational government-owned picric acid plant, the military might opt to keep it open.

The army dashed those hopes when it suspended production that December. Having decided to shift to TNT for its high explosive of choice, and no longer needing to supply France and Britain, the U.S. military had no more need for picric acid. Rumors surfaced that some company might step in to take over the nitric and sulfuric acid buildings, using them to make industrial chemicals, but none of those panned out.

Eventually, the facility was sold at auction for $750,000, a fraction of the $7,000,000 originally spent on the plant. The winning bidder was Harvey Couch, former fuel administrator and owner of the Arkansas Power and Light Company. Couch was really interested in buying the power station, and he broke up most of the other buildings, selling off the lead-linings from the acid tanks and other fittings for the buildings. A few small businesses moved into some of the smaller plant buildings, but there is no indication that the main buildings were ever reoccupied. Over the next few decades, the footprint of the plant faded from Little Rock maps as building after building winked out of existence.

A stone cenotaph was placed at Little Rock's Calvary Cemetery in memory of the many people from Puerto Rico who died while working at the Little Rock picric acid facility. *Courtesy of Mark K. Christ.*

Manufacturing, Production, and Social Control

It is important that we ask what kinds of effects mobilization for World War I brought to Arkansas. The early twentieth century was a period noted for its contestations over workers' rights, workplace safety, distribution of wealth, and the roles and powers of different economic classes, the social impacts of manufacturing played a part in this. It was also a time when "scientific" principles of workplace management were all the rage among the managerial classes, with Taylorism much in vogue. How those trends articulated with wartime manufacturing offers another dimension of this period.

LABOR RELATIONS

Despite government and social pressure on citizens to work under any conditions, the manufacturing sector in Arkansas was not without its tribulations during the First World War. This reflected a nationwide trend by which the demands of industrial production for the war effort and the loss of men to military service gave great power to organized labor and workers individually. Workers had a nearly unprecedented ability to press for living wages and some share of control of their working lives.

As historian Elizabeth Haiken has admirably covered, the women of International Laundry Workers' Union Local No. 36, of Little Rock, successfully went on strike in late 1918. Arguing for a pay increase from $7.50 per week to $9.00 per week, the laundresses (who were mostly African American) brought the seven major Little Rock laundries to a standstill. While one does not typically think of a laundry as being a crucial battleground in the history of labor relations, consider the context. The seven major laundries in Little Rock served the Little Rock Picric Acid Plant, Fort Roots, and Camp Pike, which together represented about 75,000 people. Keeping those people clean and healthy involved a supply of fresh clothing and linens, so having the city's laundries taken off line hindered military preparedness. So crucial was the labor of the washerwomen that the National War Labor Board intervened almost immediately, siding with the striking workers.[45]

Organized labor involved more than laundries, of course. Nationwide, the American Federation of Labor (AFL) and Industrial Workers of the World (IWW) sought to improve conditions for lumbermen, miners, factory workers, and workers in myriad other industries. Of the two, the AFL seemed to focus more on labor issues, while the IWW opposed the war and the development of a war-oriented industrial machine. Local branches of the AFL, such as the Pine Bluff chapter, went so far as to publicly distance themselves from the IWW, which was routinely blamed for everything from aiding draft resistance to burning fields and timber stands in hopes of crippling America's war effort.

During the war, membership in the IWW often meant arrest. With the IWW playing a hand in violent labor disputes in Oklahoma, Arizona, and Oregon, being caught in Arkansas with an IWW card or even IWW literature became grounds for official scrutiny. Several workers at Camp Pike were arrested and dismissed for membership in the IWW.

In September 1917, four men were arrested in Stuttgart and charged with being members of the organization, and locals believed they were agitating plantation laborers to demand higher wages for working the rice fields. Two of the men were known to be from Arkansas—one from Fordyce and one from Stuttgart. That night, a group of fifty farmers took them from the jail and marched them to the city limits. They then whipped them, applied tar and feathers, and expelled them from the region, threatening to hold a "neck tie" party if they returned. As there were several instances of IWW officials being lynched during the war, these were far from idle threats.

The government and press worked hard to connect organized labor with draft resistance and German influence, both of which authorities sought to stamp out. They found ready assistance with the state, county, and community committees on national defense. As part of the role of these organizations was to monitor the public for expressions of disloyalty and dissatisfaction, they became appendages to law enforcement officials, turning in those who showed signs of dissent. Beyond that, community councils of defense were to "apply the last of [local] public condemnation to those who gave aid and comfort to the enemy through failure to give their time, money, or labor to the cause of the nation."

As a result, Arkansans were routinely brought up on charges. For instance, in June 1918, Little Rock barber Charley White was charged with sedition for once suggesting that "a boy who had worked at the [picric acid] plant had not received his wages." William Daniels faced similar charges a few weeks later when he supposedly defamed the government for not paying him his wages. Fred Carroll, aged nineteen, was charged with sedition the following month. In October, Patsy Pailes, headed to work at the picric acid plant, told a coworker that it was foolish for people to subscribe to the Liberty Loan because "the big mucks in Washington will get the money." He was arrested for sedition.[46] These individual prosecutions, just a few examples, served to undercut the ability of individuals and groups, including labor organizations, to voice dissent for the militarization of the economy and the country's involvement in the war. This climate also blunted the ability of labor organizations locally to push for greater safeguards for workers, in terms of both pay and day-to-day safety.

For the picric acid plant, those dangers were many. The destruction of several plants in the United Kingdom and the massive destruction in Halifax, Nova Scotia, caused by picric acid were well-covered in the paper, and the workers in the plant would have known they lived under constant risk of something going catastrophically wrong. One man, W. Clarence Woodward of Faulkner County, died by falling from scaffolding at the plant. Working around strong acids, often without safety clothing, added another layer of danger. Despite the serious risks, the militarization of both government and civilian life during the war made it harder for organized labor to work for safer conditions.

Work hazards may have taken human form, as well. Depositions given by Puerto Rican laborers at the sister plant in Brunswick, Georgia, paint a stark picture of conditions. One of these workers, Rafael Marchán, alleged that foremen beat workers, made them work long hours for which they were not compensated, and committed other outrages against them with the support of the local police force. As Picron had a well-staffed and equipped police force, it seems possible that the organization of labor at the plant included some level of violence and coercion. Certainly, that would be consistent with the period.[47]

Wartime Manufacturing and the Postwar Years

The period of World War I and the years immediately following is a fascinating one, both nationally and here in Arkansas. The people of this state worked hard to contribute to the war effort, and they produced substantial quantities of the things America needed to defeat Germany and its allies. It was a period of great complexity and possibility.

Many traces of that time remain with us today. Most obvious is the combination of our military and our economy known as the military-industrial complex. Today, Arkansas manufacturers produce rocket propellants, grenades, small arms ammunition, machinery, flares, chaff, explosives, missile guidance systems, loading systems for munitions of all kinds, and many more products of war. In 2016 alone, defense contracts netted Arkansas $176,826,284.[48] Though massively expanded during the Cold War, that system was born of the Great War.

The war remains with us in other ways. When the Little Rock Picric Acid Plant closed and Harvey Couch of Columbia County purchased it, primarily for the power station that he used to connect Little Rock and Pine Bluff in what became the state's first electrical grid. This was one of the core elements of Couch's company, Arkansas Power and Light, which endures today as part of Entergy Corporation, supplying power to nearly 700,000 Arkansans.

By and large, however, a state whose largest industries were agricultural was not likely to be changed drastically by such a short war. The soldiers returned to their farms, and we continued to be a state focused on growing things for decades after. The promise of a new industrial age did not, in most instances, pan out.

The Little Rock Picric Acid Plant, for instance, did not last a year after the Armistice. The government chose not to retain any stockpiles of picric acid after the war. As a result, it classified some 11,875,000 pounds of the stuff as surplus.[49] It was given to the U.S. Department of Agriculture, which trained farmers how to use it to remove stumps. Over time, the plant's buildings were stripped of useable materials and the eastern half of the site became a bauxite quarry in the 1950s. Today, Interstate 440 cuts through the northern portion of it, and the remaining western half is now the Holiday Inn Express at Bankhead Drive. Its effacement from the landscape is complete.

The only place we can find its legacy is the still-scarred landscape of northern France and Belgium, where shells from the war, including those filled with Arkansas picric acid, pop up by the thousands every year in what is known as the "Iron Harvest." It may take another 500 years to render the entire area safe. Unfortunately, this is one of the long-lasting legacies of Arkansas's manufacturing sector during the Great War.

4 | "Fighting, Protesting, and Organizing"

African Americans in World War I Arkansas

CHERISSE JONES-BRANCH

When discussing World War I Arkansas, African American achievements and struggles have often been overlooked and relegated to the margins of history. Their stories, however, reveal much about the complexity and contours of black life in the state when the United States officially entered the war in April 1917. Black men entered military service to extend democracy in foreign lands, and African Americans in Arkansas supported the war effort through various means. However, all black Arkansans engaged in a constant struggle to make the world "safe for democracy" as they worked for the realization of full citizenship in their home country. They skillfully employed the language of patriotism, loyalty, and democracy as the United States became embroiled in an international war. As they did so, they fervently believed that they would then gain access to the rights and privileges to which they were fully entitled as Americans.

Like their white counterparts, African American men in Arkansas served in the military during World War I. A cursory search of Ancestry.com revels much about their civilian lives in Arkansas. Many were professional men. Harvey Cincinnatus Ray, for example, was twenty-eight years old when he filled out his registration card. Ray was born in Bunceton,

| DOI: https://doi.org/10.34053/christ2019.twah.4

Missouri, in 1889. He was a former faculty member at Langston A&M University in Oklahoma, and a graduate of Lincoln Institute in Jefferson City, Missouri. In 1915, he became the first federally appointed African American U.S. Extension Service agent in Arkansas.[1] Ray worked for the Arkansas Agricultural Cooperative Extension Service until his retirement in 1955. He was also the father of Gloria Ray Karlmark, one of the nine African American students (known as the Little Rock Nine) who integrated Little Rock Central High School in 1957.[2]

Being an African American soldier in the South during Jim Crow segregation was a precarious situation to find oneself in. Stereotypes abounded about African American soldiers' mental and physical capacity for war. Many thought they would be too fearful and cowardly to be brave soldiers. Others believed they should serve in the military as long as legal segregation was maintained within the realm of the military. Some southern whites in particular feared changes to the racial status quo and were threatened by the presence of African American men wearing military uniforms and carrying weapons. But black Arkansas men clamored to serve their country. In Little Rock, by June 1917, 1,691 black men out of 5,200 men total had registered for war service.[3] Indeed, by the end of the war, 17,544 black Arkansas men were inducted into military service. At least one source asserts that they made up 30.4 percent of those registered in Arkansas and 34.6 percent of those inducted into military service.[4]

As African American men registered for military service, black ministers used their pulpits to inspire their sense of patriotism. Draft officials even encouraged ministers to utilize sermons to explain the registration and draft. In Pine Bluff in June 1917, for instance, black and white ministers gathered at the Young Men's Christian Association to learn more about the system from the local sheriff. A Pine Bluff planter, J. M. Gracie, also sent black ministers who sharecropped on his land to attend the gathering.[5]

Black registration was further supported by Arkansas's black and white leaders. Governor Charles H. Brough was confident that black men would serve and that, in fact, "he had never heard of the negro traitor" and was confident that he never would.[6] African American educator H. C. Yerger from Hope in Hempstead County assured whites of black loyalty, particularly after concerns that Germans were encouraging them to revolt against the U.S. government. Yerger had been born in Hempstead County in 1861 and educated at Philander Smith College

Corporal Mitchell Chaney of Magnolia was one of thousands of African American soldiers from Arkansas who served in France during World War I. *Courtesy of the Butler Center for Arkansas Studies, Central Arkansas Library System, Little Rock.*

in Little Rock, Boston University, and Virginia's Hampton Institute. He began a fifty-year teaching career in Hempstead County in 1886.[7] To alleviate white concerns about black loyalty Yerger asserted:

> They may as well be singing psalms to a dead horse. Anyone with any reflection cannot doubt the loyalty of the negro to the government. . . . There are thousands of negroes in Arkansas and the South today who are willing to offer their lives as a sacrifice to protect this country against any foreign power. . . . I was born and reared in the South and have lived in Arkansas all my life. I have been in public service for 33 years and I know my

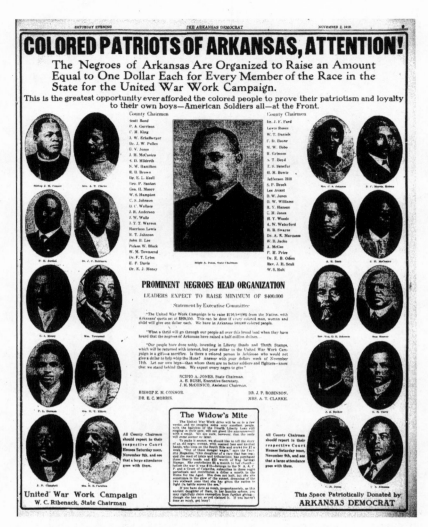

Prominent Arkansas African American leaders called on black Arkansans to donate funds to support the war effort. Arkansas Democrat, *November 2, 1918.*

people. Though they have their race prejudices as other people, yet I know there are things they will not do. They will not rob banks or trains, fly aeroplanes nor run submarines, neither will they commit treason. . . . I am now in the fifty-sixth year of my life and I believe in peace with all mankind, but if it becomes necessary I do hereby offer myself to my state to go to the front and help see to it that "Old Glory" will not rail in the dust.[8]

Arkansas's black educational institutions also helped recruit black men to serve in the U.S. Army. In one example, Branch Normal College, known today as the University of Arkansas at Pine Bluff (UAPB), signed a government contract with the Committee on Education and Special Training to train 2,400 soldiers for army mechanical trades. Barracks were built at the institution, which had four army officers in addition to its fourteen-member faculty.[9] By June 15, 1918, Branch Normal College had enrolled 120 men who trained as carpenters, blacksmiths, and mechanics.[10]

Among Arkansas leaders' concerns, regardless of race, was making recreational activities and facilities available for soldiers. Throughout the South and most of the nation, segregation prevailed and African American soldiers were prohibited from accessing the resources available to white soldiers. When they sought recreational activities, they looked to Little Rock's segregated Young Men's Christian Association, or YMCA. In 1918, black soldiers who were about to be transferred partook of an "entertaining program," which started with the singing of "My Country, 'Tis of Thee." The program included such activities as song and joke contests, and a watermelon-eating competition for which there were cash prizes.[11]

At a time when many Americans had to be convinced to support an international war, African Americans had even more reason for doubt because of their daily struggles with racial discrimination and political and economic marginalization. Additionally, frequent complaints to the War Department revealed the poor treatment black soldiers endured from white officers who physically assaulted them and referred to them by such racist names as "nigger," "coon," and "darkey." These reports, along with unequal conditions in camps and discrimination in the application of the draft law, prompted Secretary of War Newton Baker to declare that "the War Department will brook no discrimination, based on race or color." While this was difficult to enforce, in at least once instance a white officer in Arkansas was punished for treating black soldiers unfairly. In 1918, Captain Eugene C. Rowan of the 162nd Depot Brigade, headquartered at Camp Pike in North Little Rock, was charged with "willful disobedience of the orders of a superior officer." This was the first case in which racism resulted in the War Department taking action against a white officer. Rowan was charged with refusing to obey an order from the brigade commander to call a formation because the troop included black and white soldiers. A Georgia native who had lived in Mississippi,

Rowan argued that his decision was "in keeping with his own personal feelings" and that he did not want to give an order that would "compel white men to 'lower their self-respect'" by essentially forcing them to stand in close proximity to African American soldiers. He was subsequently dismissed and court-martialed. The army tribunal's judgment was upheld by the War Department.[12]

Despite the Rowan case, racial discrimination within the military continued unabashedly. Black military personnel were critical to help boost morale among African Americans by delivering reports about their countrymen's service both domestically and abroad. In 1918, Elroy W. Willis, a black sailor, talked about African American soldiers in France at Little Rock's New Taborian Temple, which had been built between 1916 and 1918 for the Knights and Daughters of Tabor, a black fraternal organization.[13] Willis, who had just returned from France, had previously talked to fifty black soldiers in Hot Springs before they left for Camp Pike. In both cases, Willis particularly emphasized the praise heaped upon black soldiers by their superior officers.[14] While most of these officers were likely white, some black Arkansas men attended a ninety-day officer training camp in Des Moines, Iowa, as part the Seventeenth Provisional Training Regiment. On October 15, 1917, they were commissioned as officers.[15] Some of the officers included First Lieutenants William H. Clarke from Helena and Frank L. Drye from Little Rock, who were then sent to Camp Dodge in Johnston, Iowa, and Camp Grant in Rockford, Illinois.[16]

However, very few black soldiers actually became officers. In fact, most of them labored at jobs during the war that usually differed very little from their civilian occupations. They were expected to perform physical labor for white landowners, much like many of them probably did before the war. Indeed, historian Randy Finley has noted that "black soldiers faced the double standard of being given inferior jobs yet always being expected to perform those tasks super-humanly."[17] In November 1918, black soldiers were contracted to rebuild a levee in Chicot County that had been damaged by a flood in 1916. The federal and state governments, Camp Pike's leadership, and the Chicot County officials who had requested black soldiers as laborers were complicit in this arrangement. Arkansas's governor Charles H. Brough had received a letter from the adjutant general in Washington DC. that authorized Colonel Charles Miller, Camp Pike's commandant, to grant a twenty-day extension for one hundred African American soldiers to work on the project.

This unidentified African American soldier was among the many recruits who trained at Camp Pike. *Courtesy of the Butler Center for Arkansas Studies, Central Arkansas Library System, Little Rock.*

Additional to physical labor, in July 1918, black soldiers who were part of a "camp sanitary squad" were used as bait in the effort to combat mosquitos at Camp Pike. As an article from the *Arkansas Democrat* reported, "Has no one ever noticed a negro soldier standing like a statue on a street corner at Camp Pike, with shirt sleeves rolled up above the elbows and a glass bottle in his hand?" In this experiment, black soldiers stood at one of sixty-eight designated spots in or near the camp for fifteen minutes every Friday night until a mosquito landed on their arms. They then covered it with a glass tube containing a wad of cotton saturated with chloroform. The specimen was then placed in a pillbox and taken back to headquarters. Black soldiers were expected to report if they heard any mosquitos "singing their war song in that locality" and performed this labor while white non-commission officers on horseback "checked up on the men to see that none are missing or laying down on the job."[18]

The Politics of Race in Arkansas

In Arkansas, political struggles further informed African Americans' understanding of a war "to make the world safe for democracy." Before America became involved in World War I, black Arkansans were purged from the Arkansas Republican Party, to which many had been loyal since Reconstruction. In the late nineteenth and early twentieth centuries, African Americans, also known as "black and tan Republicans," were increasingly marginalized by the all-white faction of the southern Republican Party. Known as the "lily-white movement," this was southern white Republicans' attempt to limit African Americans' voting power. As a result, some African Americans abandoned the Republican Party over the course of the twentieth century.[19]

However, not all blacks left the Republican Party, and in Arkansas in particular African Americans fought to maintain their visibility within the state organization. In 1914, however, the Arkansas Republican Party voted to become "lily white." An article in the June 1914 issue of the *Daily Arkansas Gazette* titled "Lily Whites Bar 'Man and Brother'" reported the following:

> Without advance notice and scarcely a world of apology, the white majority in the Pulaski County Republican Central Committee, at a meeting held yesterday at the Chamber of Commerce, deprived of representation the Republican negroes of the county. Negroes will no longer be giving representation in the party organization of the county nor will they be allowed even a voice in the selection of the party's candidates. All they may do in the future is blindly vote the ticket or seek suffrage expression with some other party.[20]

Black Republicans, however, fought the attempts to exclude them even as some urged caution. After white Republicans voted 159 to 123 to remove black candidates, it was stated that "the announcement of the outcome of the vote caused much uproar among the negroes and several of them leaped to their feet." Black Republican chairman John E. Bush, one of the wealthiest African Americans in Arkansas and the cofounder

John Bush, chairman
of Arkansas's African
American Republicans,
fought efforts to exclude
black candidates during
WWI. *"John Bush,"
ASA_Photo_G5565_002,
Arkansas State Archives,
Little Rock.*

of Mosaic Templars of America, quieted them and decided that they would not take any action at that time. However, they immediately began to organize and called for a July 6 county convention at the Mosaic Temple on Ninth Street and Broadway in the heart of Little Rock's black community at the same time that white Republicans planned to meet. Both groups claimed to be the regular Republican convention.[21]

Despite their increased marginalization, African Americans remained loyal to the Arkansas Republican Party throughout the World War I years and beyond. For example, in 1920, after the "lily-white movement" took hold, black Republicans met in Little Rock at the same time that white Republicans were meeting in Russellville to elect delegates for the national convention in Chicago.[22] Black Republicans further adopted a resolution denouncing the congressional Republican convention's endorsement of "lily whitism" and branded its members a "band of political marauders" and "human leeches." Conversely, they commended white Republicans who had refused to participate in removing African Americans from the party.[23]

Black Women in World War I Arkansas

While they have rarely been fully appreciated as active participants in World War I, black women also served their country and their state in various capacities during the war. Like white women, black Arkansas women's duties on the homefront were often extensions of their labors and activism within their communities. In April 1917, shortly after the United States entered the war, members of the Arkansas Association of Colored Women held a "patriotic meeting" at a church in Hope to "arouse the negro women in their duty in the country's crisis," and urged them to "cooperate with men in time of war economy in cooking and dressing and in raising good gardens." One black woman, Dora Hamilton, also known as "Aunt Dora," gave a speech pleading with her colleagues for the "absolute loyalty of her race to the country." Aunt Dora further declared that she had seven sons and that she was "ready to lead them all to the defense of her home and country." During this meeting members planned a public flag-raising ceremony to be followed by another patriotic meeting at the local segregated school.[24]

Elizabeth Griffin Hill has written about how white women's social and community activism before and during World War I occurred under the auspices of the Arkansas Federation of Women's Clubs.[25] Indeed, the organization even had its own page in the *Arkansas Gazette* on which its activities were chronicled every Sunday. While black women did not enjoy this privilege, mining the *Arkansas Gazette* among other newspapers reveals much about their activism during war years. Established in 1905, the Arkansas Association of Colored Women (AACW) consisted of black women leaders engaged in patriotic work, even as they also continued to push for reforms that were most important to their communities.[26] Affiliated with the National Association of Colored Women (NACW), established in 1896, the AACW adopted the national association's motto "Lifting as We Climb," which reflected black women's understanding of their obligation to engage in uplift activism in African American communities throughout Arkansas.[27]

Among their concerns was the establishment of an industrial school for African American boys. In January 1917, AACW representatives met with Governor Brough and asked him to recommend that the legislature appropriate funds to build the school on sixty acres of land the organization had purchased in Jefferson County.[28] This was a very important issue for black women, who were deeply concerned about African American juvenile offenders who were often sent to the penitentiary with convicted criminals. They continued to push for an industrial school until one was built in 1923.[29]

Black women used their organizational affiliations to confront racism and racial stereotyping. In November 1917, they protested the showing of D. W. Griffith's silent film *The Birth of a Nation* at Little Rock's Kempner Theatre. The film, based on Thomas Dixon's novel *The Clansman*, was released in February 1915 and portrayed African Americans as unintelligent, uneducable, and sexually aggressive. Black women presented a petition signed by twenty-five club representatives to Little Rock mayor Charles E. Taylor and the Board of Censors.[30] Their efforts, unfortunately, were to no avail.

While fighting racism was an ongoing pursuit, black women embraced wartime initiatives by registering to work at civilian jobs to help ease labor shortages. Black fraternal organizations encouraged African Americans to respond to their country's call to register. The Masons, for instance, participated in a two-hour meeting, singing and hearing patriotic songs and speeches at their lodge in Pine Bluff. They were then urged "to do their part for the successes of the Army in this world contest with the enemies of world democracy."[31] Accordingly, registration for black women was held at the Mosaic Templars building in Little Rock.[32] Indeed, black women from all over the state registered for war work with the Arkansas Council of Defense's Woman's Committee and participated in food conservation programs.[33] They were often encouraged to do so by local businesses. In Camden, for instance, black women registered at a booth at the Ouachita Drug Company.[34]

Indeed, the aforementioned Mosaic Templars building was the most logical place to organize black Arkansans. Prominent African Americans led the state's efforts to organize blacks to raise approximately $400,000 for the United War Work Campaign. Featured on an entire page in the November 1918 issue of the *Arkansas Democrat*, the executive committee, led by well-known black attorney Scipio Africanus Jones, employed patriotic language with a subtext containing the expectation of appreciation and improved conditions for African Americans in Arkansas and throughout the nation after the war. He stated:

> The United War Work Campaign is to raise $170,500,000 from the Nation, with Arkansas' quota set at $869,550. This can be done if every colored man, woman and child will give one dollar each. We have in Arkansas 500,000 colored people. . . . What a thrill will go through our people all over this broad

Little Rock attorney Scipio Africanus Jones urged blacks to contribute to the war effort with an expectation of improved conditions for African Americans in Arkansas after the war. *"Scipio Africanus Jones at desk," ASA_Photo_PS16_05, Arkansas State Archives, Little Rock.*

land when they have heard that the negroes of Arkansas have raised a half-million dollars. . . . Is there a colored person in Arkansas who would not give a dollar to help whip the Huns? Let our own boys—than whom there are no better soldiers and fighters—know that we stand behind them. We expect every negro to give.[35]

While men like Jones and A. E. Bush, son of Mosaic Templars of America founder John E. Bush, were the state chairman and secretary of the executive committee, respectively, black women like Henrietta E. Carolina, a leader in the AACW and the Daughters of Tabor, were among its members as well.[36]

But not all black women were members of Arkansas's black middle and upper classes. Many of them were poorly paid domestic and agricultural laborers who jumped at better employment opportunities in Arkansas's limited industrial sector. In 1917, the Pulaski County

Cooperage Company became the first industry in the state to employ women "in the heavy manual labor formerly done by men or boys."[37] Nine black women were hired and paid one dollar and fifty cents to two dollars per day. They reportedly liked working for the company because it was "better than housework."[38] In 1918, black women were hired as common laborers in Missouri Pacific "shops" to replace men who had gone into military service.[39] In the same year, black women were hired to assume jobs formerly held by men at the C. P. Wilson stave mill and the J. M. Piel and Brother Hoop Mill in Lake Village in Chicot County. The Wilson mill hired twenty black women, while the Piel mill only hired ten. And they were expected to wear overalls at a time when most women would not have even worn pants. While they were certainly paid less than black men and white women, it was more than they had earned in their former occupations.[40]

Black women were among the lowest-paid wage workers but that did not mean that they passively accepted gender and racial discrimination. Indeed, they often fought back. In September 1918, black laundresses protested their poor pay and claimed that their employers failed to recognize the International Laundry Workers' Union to which they belonged, and called on them to pay the twelve-dollar-per-week minimum wage. They demanded that laundry working conditions be regularly inspected by Laundry Workers' Union agents. Black laundresses' complaints were investigated by National War Labor Board representatives to whom they testified about the laundries' lack of heat and the difficulty of standing on concrete floors. A total of 450 workers were affected by these conditions, 350 of whom were women. Black women made up sixty-five percent of all of these workers.[41] Managers of the Little Rock Laundry, Imperial Laundry, and Frank's Steam Laundry argued that ten dollars per week was sufficient for wages. They further objected to closed or unionized shops. The managers preferred to deal with workers individually and claimed that they had had no trouble from their workers before the union was organized.[42] It is not clear how or if this matter was resolved. What is evident, however, is that black women understood the value of their labor, particularly during the World War I years and, when necessary, did not hesitate to demand what they rightfully deserved.

Black women were further expected to increase their agricultural labor during the war, as men were increasingly unavailable. In June 1918, for instance, W. T. McKell, a county farm demonstrator employed by the Arkansas Agricultural Extension Service, and J. A. Blackford, who was in charge of the Federal Employment Bureau in Arkansas, traveled throughout Craighead County in the northeastern corner of the state registering black women "for the purpose of hoeing cotton in this vicinity" and considered this "necessary work . . . owing to the fact that so many of the farmer boys have been and are being called to the colors."[43]

White landowners in the Arkansas Delta were additionally concerned about black women who refused to continue sharecropping because they received government allotments from their male relatives who had been drafted. Planters repeatedly contacted the Department of Labor about needing black women and children to pick cotton. There were indeed great concerns about decreasing control over black labor in the rural South. Uncontrolled and financially independent black labor was considered dangerous. In fact, a Department of Labor representative asserted that "some steps should be taken to use the idle negro women and children of Little Rock, Pine Bluff, and other cities of the State. The department has observed that these women have absolutely quit work as soon as they began to receive the government allowances. If the evil continues to grow it may be necessary for the government to take some steps to break it up, even though it may be the discontinuance of this $30 allowance."[44]

In order to retain a workforce during the war years, planters conspired with local councils of defense to issue a "Work or Fight" order, which allowed them to use vagrancy laws to draft black men who were not, according to historian Nan Woodruff, "engaged in employment essential to the war." In some communities, they attempted to apply these orders to black women, who, because of their gender, were not under the jurisdiction of draft boards.[45] In Pine Bluff, the Chamber of Commerce started a movement to expand the "Work or Fight" order to include women. In September 1918, its board of directors unanimously adopted a resolution to make the order applicable to women. White planters who attended the meeting complained that hundreds of black women refused to perform agricultural or domestic labor and that their "disinclination to work has caused quite a hardship on a number of large plantations that depend upon the negro women to pick the cotton."[46] Despite their complaints however, black women's contributions to the war effort were considerable.

In addition to their industrial and agricultural labor, black women assisted the war effort through the American Red Cross. The Red Cross had long existed, but it was called upon to perform such wartime duties as providing troops with "comforts and necessities" while they were stateside

Negroes Help Red Cross.

Pine Bluff, April 18.—(Special.)—The negro women have organized a sewing unit of the Red Cross, at the Grand Masonic temple, with the following well-known negro women in charge: Alice O'Bryant, chairman; Hampton Lewis, secretary; Dora Adair, teacher of domestic science at Branch Normal College, captain. Forty-five women have enrolled and began work in the sewing room Wednesday.

This article recounts efforts of African American women in Pine Bluff to support Red Cross efforts. Arkansas Democrat, *April 18, 1918.*

or in the field overseas.[47] In Arkansas, as elsewhere around the nation, the Red Cross and the Arkansas Women's Committee established sewing rooms for women to construct such items as "hospital supplies, knitted socks, sweaters, and wristlets, for 'the boys.'"[48] Because Jim Crow laws regulated the times in which they lived, black women did their part for "the boys" in segregated units. In Pine Bluff, for instance, black women organized a sewing unit at the Grand Masonic temple and enrolled forty-five women.[49] Pine Bluff mayor Simon Bloom also allowed black women to use the city chamber and sewing machines from the city's schools.[50] And in Fourche in Perry County, black women who had knitted for the Red Cross were reported as having done "excellent work."[51]

Black women further served as Red Cross and local nurses. According to Elizabeth Griffin Hill, by November 1917, there arose an increased need for trained nurses. The U.S. Army's War Department began a campaign to enlist graduate nurses in the Army Nurses Corps. Qualified nurses were called upon to serve in the U.S. military or in the American Red Cross military nurse corps. In Arkansas, local Red Cross chapters began to train women in basic nursing skills.[52] Among the known black Arkansas Red Cross nurses was Maud Hines, who served from 1917 to 1918.[53]

A recruiting station was set up for African American women on Ninth and Broadway Streets in Little Rock in response to the federal government's call for 25,000 student nurses to take the place of trained nurses who were sent overseas. The station enrolled black women

Maud Hines served as a Red Cross nurse in Arkansas in 1917 and 1918. *"Maud Hines," ASA_ Photo_G5565_33, Arkansas State Archives, Little Rock.*

between the ages of nineteen and twenty-five. Applicants had to produce a health and dental certificate. They further were required to "be of good moral character and possess some education."[54] Little Rock educator Carrie Still Shepperson was in charge of the station. Born in Georgia in 1872, Shepperson moved to Little Rock in 1895 after the death of her first husband and taught at the predominantly African American Union and Capitol Hill Schools and at Mifflin Wistar Gibbs High School. Shepperson, who died in 1927, was the mother of composer and musician William Grant Still Jr.[55]

Indeed, some of the women who trained under Shepperson's direction were called upon for their services. In November 1918, black nurses were called to assist ill African Americans who were employed by the Picric Acid Plant, a government-run facility in Picron, Arkansas, located four miles southeast of Little Rock.[56] The plant, which the federal government built in Arkansas in May 1918, had reported more than 100 cases of influenza and had requested two graduate nurses and several practical nurses.[57]

When the nation was called upon to buy bonds and stamps to support the war effort, most African Americans and their organizations leaped at the opportunity to do their share. The Mosaic Templars of America purchased $50,000 in Liberty Bonds after a visit from Secretary of the Treasury William Gibbs McAdoo in 1917.[58] In 1918, the Ministers' Council of the Little Rock district of the African Methodist Episcopal church declared, "We must stand by our country in the purchase of war savings stamps." In addition, the council planned to support an African American pastor and social workers at Camp Pike to aid black soldiers.[59] Also in 1918, black women, members of the H. H. of Ruth, Number 171, a fraternal organization, purchased a $50 Liberty Bond from Citizens Bank, in Osceola in Mississippi County.[60] In Newport in Jackson County, African American planter Pickens Black was a member of a "War Savings Stamp Limit Club" and personally purchased $1,000 worth of stamps.[61]

Finally, during this same year, the National Women's Liberty Loan Committee (NWLLC) announced that the National Association of Colored Women had embarked upon a campaign during the fourth Liberty Loan to raise funds among black club women in Louisiana, Arkansas, Texas, and other southern states.[62] Indeed, the Arkansas committee of the NWLLC was led by none other than the governor's wife, Anne Wade Roark Brough. In September 1918, she addressed black women at the First Missionary Baptist Church on Seventh and Gaines Streets in Little Rock at what was reported as the "largest organization of negro women for any of the war work campaigns" to encourage African American participation in Liberty Loan drives.[63] Black women took the initiative to organize themselves for loan campaigns in meetings at the aforementioned church, where more than 250 women gathered, and at Shorter College, an African American institution in North Little Rock, where it was reported that "interest among the negro workers is increasing daily."[64]

African Americans were additionally encouraged to purchase bonds by powerful local white elites. In Rison in Cleveland County, prominent lumberman and planter C. K. Elliot, along with other white businessmen, attended a meeting at a local black church and utilized the following biblical story to scare and manipulate African Americans into purchasing Liberty Bonds:

> He told of how Pharaoh delivered the children of Egypt from bondage, and how the death angel passed over the homes where the stain of blood was noticed on the door. He then compared that incident to the present time by stating that unless we bought Liberty bonds, thus placing a sign over our door, our homes would not be missed by the death angel and that we would be placed in bondage by the German government.[65]

After Elliot's address, fourteen $50 bonds were sold to African Americans who had attended the meeting.[66]

After the War

When the war ended in 1919, returning black Arkansas soldiers, like soldiers all around the nation, were generally welcomed home as heroes. In Hot Springs in Garland County, black soldiers marched to Whittington Park, where they were officially recognized for their service by the city's mayor, J. W. McClendon, and greeted by their families and local black leaders. Their return was celebrated with a program featuring a ball game and a dance.[67] African American soldiers' were also heralded during a picnic and reunion in Conway in Faulkner County.[68]

Despite their brave and heroic service, however, black soldiers returned to a country deeply entrenched and invested in maintaining the racial status quo. Black soldiers returning to Arkansas learned that Democratic representative Thaddeus Caraway had introduced a bill to keep African Americans from enlisting in the army or navy to "prevent race trouble." This was an attempt, more appropriately, to placate white fears of blacks' rightful expectation of increased access to the benefits of full citizenship after their military service. This bill would have discharged African Americans in the military within sixty days and would have kept any of them from receiving appointments to the nation's naval and military academies.[69] Concurrently, Caraway proposed a bill to prohibit interracial marriage.[70]

The presence of black soldiers and increased African American assertiveness generally frightened and infuriated many white Americans, who in turn responded violently. In September 1919, Clinton Briggs, a recently discharged soldier who had served in France, was lynched in Star City in Lincoln County after he allegedly "made indecent proposals to Miss Ollie Bailey," the eighteen-year-old daughter of J. M. Bailey, a prominent Lincoln County planter. Briggs was held captive by approximately thirty men and was shot while being taken to a tree to be hanged. The coroner determined that his death resulted from "gunshot wounds inflicted by persons unknown," a commonly used refrain when black men were murdered by white mobs. Briggs was the second African American to be lynched near Star City for allegedly assaulting a white woman.[71]

The most notable incident occurred in 1919 in Elaine, Arkansas, when black farmers in Phillips County challenged economic and racial oppression by organizing the Progressive Farmers' and Household Union of America (PFHUA). On September 30, 1919, PFHUA members gathered at an African American church in Hoop Spur to discuss suing their landlords for their fair share of what historian Nan Woodruff described as "the largest cotton crop in southern history."[72] During the meeting, a shootout ensued between union members and Phillips County law enforcement officers. A Missouri Pacific railroad employee was killed and another white man was wounded.[73] In October 1919, as hundreds of angry and armed whites descended on Phillips County from other parts of the state and Mississippi, Arkansas governor Charles H. Brough dispatched 500 U.S. Army troops from Camp Pike to quell what many mainstream newspapers called an "insurrection."[74] Hundreds of black men were arrested, and black men, women and children were killed by U.S. Army troops and others. In the end, twelve men were accused of murder and put on trial in the aftermath of what became known as the Elaine Race Riot, more appropriately called a "massacre." It was not until 1925 and due to the notable skills of black attorney Scipio Jones that the last of the men were finally released. Yet the impact of white fear and anger on postwar black assertiveness lingered for decades afterward.[75]

Conclusion

During World War I, black men served in the American military both stateside and overseas. And black women supported them on the homefront by becoming nurses, registering to perform important wartime work, and utilizing their organizational affiliations to press for much needed social, political, and economic reform. They all rightfully expected their patriotism and loyalty to be rewarded at the war's end. Unfortunately, the reality of being black in America, and particularly in the South and Arkansas, proved recalcitrant to change during or after World War I. Indeed, the racial violence that occurred in its aftermath reinforced some whites' commitment to maintaining inequality and injustice.

But, despite this, black Arkansans overwhelmingly and patriotically supported their nation during the Great War. As they did so, however, they challenged America to "make the world safe for democracy," both domestically and internationally. And they challenged the nation and the state to uphold their democratic promise by fighting, protesting, and organizing in subsequent decades.

5 | "To Carry Forward the Training Program"

Camp Pike in the Great War
and the Legacy of the Post

RAYMOND D. SCREWS

When the United States entered the Great War in 1917, many young men joined the military to fight the Germans on European soil. However, it was not enough, and President Woodrow Wilson implemented the draft to bolster the American numbers in the service. Whether these men were volunteers or part of the conscription, they were sent to one of the many military training posts throughout the country.

One such man was James Harris Atkinson, who most assuredly possessed the same anxiety as most young men before shipping off to camp to train for the great endeavor in Europe. Atkinson, who was no slacker (a derogatory term given to those young men who refused to join the military during World War I), became a well-known Arkansas historian. Arkansas historian Mike Polston wrote an article about Atkinson that focused on some of his letters while he trained at Camp Pike, located just north of Little Rock. But Atkinson, who was teaching school, also kept a diary, in which he expressed his excitement and apprehension about going off to military service. "Good by [sic] diary," Atkinson wrote. "It may be for a long, long time. I am leaving for Little Rock tomorrow. I am ordered to report to my local board at 8 a.m. Friday to be sent to Camp

| DOI: https://doi.org/10.34053/christ2019.twah.5

Pike." Atkinson also expressed relief that he finally gained the opportunity to serve. "It seems my time has really come at last. I have made three efforts to enter training camp. I have been rejected in the draft one time. I was ordered to go to Jackson Barracks . . . but my school board [would not give me] my release until after the close of school." He continued: "I am entirely reconciled to whatever fate awaits me. What does one life count for in this great struggle!"[1] Although the young Atkinson never fought in Europe, as the war ended before he could mobilize, like so many American men, he anticipated helping the cause for his country.

To some degree, Atkinson understood the sacrifice that awaited, which included the change in his life and the effect it would have on his family. "I have enjoyed these days at home and I wish they could be more," he wrote. But Atkinson also lamented, "I do not mind the war but I do mind my father and mother worrying about me. Oh God!" "I can go," he assured himself, "knowing that I am needed at home less than I have been at other times." "One chapter of my life is closed," he wrote, with understanding.[2]

Such was the plight of men all over the United States after the country declared war on Germany on April 6, 1917. But in order to train these young men, the United States needed military reservations. Almost immediately after the United States declared war, the Board of Commerce for Little Rock became involved in the pursuit of an army training facility. It is conceivable that the U.S. entry into the Great War was anticipated by the organization; only nine days after Congress voted to enter the war, the Board of Commerce sent a representative, George Firmin, to meet with General John J. Pershing. Then the board created a Military Affairs Committee in an attempt to win a post in the Little Rock area. The committee met on a daily basis and at times the meetings stretched from mid-morning to the end of the work day.[3]

After the Firmin meeting with General Pershing, the Board of Commerce submitted its application for a training cantonment. Then the board, led by the Military Affairs Committee, began the process to locate a site for the post. It did not take long to discover land north of the Arkansas River in an area located near Argenta (now North Little Rock) and close to Fort Roots, which overlooked the river. The U.S. Army had three basic issues with the location selected by the Little Rock Board of Commerce. With the possibility of thousands of training soldiers, an adequate water supply was needed. In addition, the site lacked railroad access to not only bring in troops but construction supplies as well. Finally, the selected site, which was in a fairly underdeveloped area of Pulaski County, contained wetlands that harbored malaria-carrying mosquitos.[4]

While the Board of Commerce was in the process of securing a post, the Firmin/Pershing meeting levied another benefit. Fort Roots saw improvements that included a road from Pike Road in Argenta to the fort.[5] Meanwhile, the board addressed the issues with the proposed training site. An underground stream was located in Argenta that might supply the cantonment with the 2.5 million gallons of water daily that was demanded by the army. Other water sources continued to be sought after construction began, but the well in Argenta satisfied the requirement at that time. The Missouri Pacific Railroad agreed to build a spur to the post in just three weeks after given the go-ahead. And, finally, the Board of Commerce worked with the state health department and together they devised a plan to eradicate mosquitoes.[6]

One can imagine that the Little Rock business leaders, who made up the membership of the Board of Commerce, believed it was beneficial to construct a military training post in the area, and not just for patriotic reasons. As businessmen, they could see the economic advantage that a cantonment might create, possibly for years to come. As historian David Sesser wrote, area businesses and elected officials knew that building a military reservation in the Little Rock vicinity would be an "economic boon."[7] This was especially true after members read items in the newspaper such as one about Brigadier General Lloyd England, the respected Adjutant General of the Arkansas National Guard, who indicated that it was the opinion of many leaders in Washington DC that the war could take years to end.[8] War is war, and business is business, and so many times in history they go hand in hand.

Of course, patriotism also played a role among the political and business leaders in Little Rock. In the first sentence of his book about Camp Robinson (as Camp Pike was later renamed), Arkansas historian Ray Hanley wrote, "Arkansas, from its pre-statehood pioneer days, has always been among the quickest to answer the nation's call in times of war."[9] That can be debated, especially when it comes to the Civil War, but those were an entirely different set of circumstances. Regardless, Little Rock had competition to win the new cantonment in the western region of the American South. Other communities vying for the privilege of building a military training cantonment were Alexandria and Shreveport, Louisiana, and Hattiesburg and Holly Springs, Mississippi, and Little Rock had competition from within Arkansas from Fort Smith.[10]

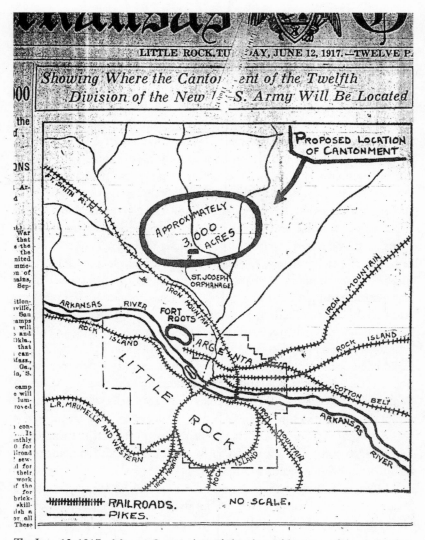

The June 12, 1917, *Arkansas Gazette* showed the planned location of the new military cantonment north of the Arkansas River.

As new training cantonment sites were considered in April, May, and June, Germany spread anti-American propaganda in Mexico.[11] This was a concern because the United States had just been involved in an incident along the Mexican border. Tensions were still high between the two countries when the United States declared war on Germany. The need to get training camps built quickly was paramount. In the meantime, while Little Rock waited for the decision on the location of the post, the army decided that soldiers from Arkansas and Louisiana would train at the new cantonment as part of the Twelfth Division.[12] Very quickly, the states of Mississippi and Alabama were included.

In early May, it was reported that General Pershing would soon visit Fort Roots and presumably tour the Little Rock site for the divisional training camp. The *Arkansas Gazette* wrote that the general's visit would have a "potent effect" on placing the reservation in the central Arkansans location.[13] Optimism was in the air as the *Gazette* reported later in May that "the official inspection of Little Rock for the army concentration camp of the twelfth district was made yesterday, and the fate of Little Rock's hopes are in the hands of the Army Board of Inquiry." But Generals Pershing and Leonard Wood were not part of that group, and in fact had not yet visited, although it was continually reported that General Wood could be in Little Rock soon. Nonetheless, the paper explained, "chances in favor of success" are good. Those who made up the Board of Inquiry included Colonel George Howell of the U.S. Engineers in Little Rock, Colonel J. H. Clayton of the Medical Corps stationed at Fort Roots, and Captain William T. Merry of the Reserve Officers Corps. The board left for Shreveport the next day. The final report was to be reviewed by General Wood.[14]

It might appear that the Little Rock site held an advantage over the other five sites because Howell was in Little Rock, and that might be true. However, the addition of Colonel Clayton could have balanced out the advantage since it was reported that some officers at Fort Roots were not in favor of locating another military post in the area.[15] But it seems that the opposition came later in the summer. The Board of Commerce of Little Rock worked hard during the selection process to secure the cantonment. For the Board of Inquiry, the Military Affairs Committee of the Board of Commerce created a "comprehensive summary" of qualifications about the site that they had been developing for weeks. "I believe the results of our canvass of the city's resources is one with which none of the other cities can compete," explained George Firmin, who along with his assistants compiled the statistics for the summary report. It was thought, at that point, that the post would be built to accommodate 28,000 men.[16] The Little Rock Board of Commerce, led by Firmin, had all of its ducks in a row.

Although there were no official announcements throughout May,

Little Rock was clearly the leader to win the divisional post. The Pine Bluff Chamber of Commerce threw its hat in the ring of support for Little Rock. But this was to be expected since that city is close enough to Arkansas's capital city to benefit economically from a post in the area. George Firmin said, "This action by Pine Bluff is deeply appreciated by us, and it shows a spirit of co-operation that should mean much to us. The help of Pine Bluff will go far, and we will not forget it."[17] There was no such incentive for Pine Bluff to support fellow Arkansas city Fort Smith. Not that it made much difference, because by the end of May, it was believed that Fort Smith only had a slim chance of being awarded the cantonment.[18] However, the first of June found a new threat to Little Rock. Memphis entered the competition, and that city could be a formidable opponent for the Little Rock Board of Commerce.[19]

On June 2, the same day that Memphis entered the race, it was reported that the other sites originally in competition for the military reservation had been eliminated from the contest. The *Arkansas Gazette* reported, "All Little Rock's qualifications have proved acceptable to the Army Board that made the inspection . . . and the single consideration of artillery range is the only thing that has delayed a decision." That one issue is why Memphis and possibly two other sites east of the Mississippi River were considered.[20] But the Little Rock Board of Commerce was prepared. During the first week of June, representatives from Little Rock made a report to the War Department that demonstrated the city's advantages for the cantonment.[21] And the board continued to be industrious.

The first week of June was a busy one for the Little Rock Board of Commerce and its Military Affairs Committee. The board raised $233,000 in an attempt to secure the post. These funds would be used for a water system to the site as well as a railroad spur line if Little Rock won.[22] In addition, the board attempted to get General Wood to Little Rock to inspect the cantonment site. But the general did not arrive, as he had supposedly been delayed when a large log blocked the railroad track along the Chattanooga and Birmingham route of the Alabama Great Southern on which the general was traveling. No one was hurt, it was reported, but General Wood did not show up in Little Rock.[23] If indeed the report was true, was Memphis behind the shenanigans? It is probably not so because they would have been risking the lives of many, including General Wood. More probable is that the log was an act of nature, if it was there at all.

After General Wood was presented with the report, the Board of

Inquiry was ordered to inspect the Fort Smith site, which supposedly was already eliminated from consideration.[24] If this report caused consternation among the Little Rock leaders, it did not last long, as the city was awarded the cantonment the very next day, on June 11, 1917. The telegram received by the Little Rock Board of Commerce president, W. B. Smith, read: "The lady wins, congratulations." The site selected was five miles north of Little Rock and covered 3,000 acres. Arkansas congressman H. M. Jacoway sent a telegram stating that the "Fight for cantonments for Little Rock has been won. Department just made decision."[25] Before this time, the state had one only military post, and that was Fort Logan Roots, located just a stone's throw from the new post. Fort Roots was built in the 1890s and replaced the Little Rock Arsenal.[26]

On the day Little Rock was awarded the Twelfth Division cantonment, across the sea, the British had some success in the week-long Battle of Messines against the entrenched Germans, located on the Western Front in Belgium. In America, the Cardinals defeated the Phillies in fifteen innings.[27] And, along with these events, central Arkansas entered World War I.

The Little Rock area was not the only one to join the effort to win the Great War. In fact, thirty-two new military training posts were constructed in 1917. Sixteen of them were built for the U.S. Army, and sixteen more to train National Guard soldiers. The Little Rock post was a U.S. Army training cantonment. And these new training facilities were needed. In 1919, Leonard P. Ayres wrote, "To carry forward the training program, shelter was constructed in a few months for 1,800,000 men."[28] In the Southeastern Department of the U.S. Army, Little Rock was a late selection, as nine of the twelve sites were already chosen by the end of May.[29] The first three of the cantonments of the Southeastern District to begin construction were in Atlanta; Augusta, Georgia; and Columbia, South Carolina.[30] Little Rock was not far behind, however, and by the end of June, construction of the site north of the Arkansas River began. By the first week of September, cantonments built throughout the country could house 430,000 men and soon rose to 770,000, which averaged about 48,000 men for each post.[31]

It was estimated that the Little Rock post would cost $3.5 million to build and also bring in a payroll to the city of $2.5 million per month. The *Gazette* explained, "The work incidental to the construction of the camp will furnish employment for months for every carpenter, bricklayer and other workmen, both skilled and unskilled."[32] And the economic possibilities also prompted construction of a cantonment city as a private enterprise right next to the post. The new community, developed by the Belmont Development Company, planned to build a hotel, theaters, stores, houses, and an athletic field, utilizing 320 acres on lease from the St. Joseph Orphanage.[33] The small community of Belmont was bustling, but its viability only lasted through a short time. The army decided that it would provide that $3.5 million to build the Little Rock training facility.[34] By mid-June 1917, most of the cantonment sites were selected throughout the United States[35] and the survey of the Little Rock post had begun.[36] Major John Fordyce, who was connected with Arkansas, was selected to lead the construction of the central Arkansas post as the construction quartermaster. He arrived in Little Rock on June 17 from Washington DC to "take charge" as the *Gazette* reported.[37]

Major Fordyce was born in Huntsville, Alabama, on November 7, 1869, but moved to Hot Springs when he was very young; his father, who suffered from malaria he had contracted during the Civil War, hoped to regain his health in the springs. John's father, Samuel Wesley Fordyce, was an accomplished man in business and development. He had been the president of the Cotton Belt Railroad and was a major contributor to the development of Hot Springs. Samuel constructed the Eastman Hotel as well as the famous Arlington Hotel in the city and was involved in building bathhouses, including the Fordyce.[38] Regardless of the proverbial silver spoon, it appears that John's father expected him to find his own way in the world, which he did.

It is clear that John and his father had a good relationship, evidenced from the letters between them. But Samuel was not above a little gentle criticism when he believed it was warranted. While Major Fordyce served as quartermaster of the Little Rock cantonment, the two exchanged a series of letters regarding a longtime employee of the family at the Fordyce Bathhouse. His father believed that the employee was attempting to cheat them, while John believed the employee's motives were pure and aboveboard. Samuel wrote to John concerning the matter, stating, "I am afraid that by butting in to the Bath House situation, you have obligated yourself to [the employee] to pay the outrages [*sic*] sum he demands. I hope not. You are a splendid mechanic but I think very weak when it comes to general business matters."[39] Nonetheless, in other correspondence between father and son, there is a genuine respect and admiration between the two.

By the time Major John Fordyce was called to duty to build the

Major John Fordyce, who had roots in Hot Springs, was selected to oversee construction of Camp Pike. *Courtesy of the Arkansas National Guard Museum.*

Little Rock post, he had a distinguished career. After graduating from Washington University in St. Louis in 1892, Fordyce studied math and electricity at the Harvard Graduate School.[40] For three years, ending in 1900, he was the manager of a mill in Pine Bluff, Arkansas, and then spent two years as the chief engineer and vice president of the Little Rock Gin and Machine Company. Afterward, he worked at the foundry machine shop and woodshop for the Thomas-Fordyce Manufacturing Company in Little Rock, where he served as chief engineer and vice president. After a short time working out of state, Fordyce returned to the Thomas-Fordyce Company as the president and engineer, where he remained until June 1912. He then worked as an engineer in several locations, including Decatur, Alabama, and Galveston, Houston, and Texas City, Texas, until May 1917. Fordyce wrote that he planned on taking a position as an engineer in Mobile, Alabama, but, he said, "This was not carried out because of my call into active army service," which was to build the Little Rock cantonment.[41] During the 1890s, Fordyce went to the Arctic as part of an expedition headed by Frederick Cook. He possessed an innovative mind, developing several improvements in the cotton industry.[42]

As the survey continued at the cantonment location in late June, it was reported that a remount station was to be located on the post that would train between 8,000 and 12,000 horses for the military.[43] The use of the Little Rock cantonment was coming into focus. By June 25, construction began.[44] A few days later, General Leonard Wood finally made his long-awaited visit to the site, along with visiting Fort Roots. In a speech, he most assuredly pleased the local business and political leaders when he said "the cantonments of the Twelfth Army at Little Rock will be permanent," while also expressing the belief that the post "will remain at Little Rock, and it will prove even more valuable after war than now."[45] As the layout of the post developed, the streets were named on July 11, and a fire chief was named as well. The Argenta chief, Tom Exum, was named to the same position at the Little Rock post.[46] Finally, on July 16, the Little Rock cantonment was named Camp Zebulon Pike. A committee, headed by Brigadier General Joseph Kuhn, who was the chief of the War College Division, selected names for the posts that were connected to the area. Zebulon Pike, a military explorer who was killed during the War of 1812, trekked through the area that became Arkansas more than a century before.[47]

On June 22, the railroad spur line construction began[48] and reached the cantonment on July 11, without any major issues.[49] A few days later, building materials arrived on those tracks.[50] A railroad to the Camp Pike location was imperative for the construction of the post to proceed at a breakneck pace. Major Fordyce understood this, as he explained to the president and other leaders of the Missouri Pacific Railroad: "I told them the great need to rush the work, of the great difficulty of climbing up 250 feet on account of the abrupt face of the cliff which bordered the southern slope of the tableland on which the site is located."[51] The railroad complied.

By July 12, the telegraph on the post was "satisfactory," but telephone service was more of an issue because of "inexperienced help."[52] But that was a minor problem compared to routing water to the post. Before there was an attempt to drill the Argenta wells, not only was a permanent supply of water an issue but so was a temporary reservoir to

Argenta Fire Chief Tom Exum was named chief of Camp Pike's fire department as construction of the site developed. *Courtesy of the North Little Rock History Commission.*

Camp Pike.[53] In mid-July, the only water making its way to the post was hauled in from the wells at the St. Joseph Orphanage, located adjacent to the camp, and it was not adequate.[54] There was an attempt to get water to Camp Pike from the Little Rock side of the Arkansas River, provided by the Arkansas Water Company. However, the Iron Mountain Railroad had issues with building a pipe on their bridge. In order to construct the pipe on the Iron Mountain Bridge from Little Rock to the north side of the river, the company wanted "an agreement with the War Department absolving them from responsibility in connection with the operation of the draw on account of the location of the pipe line thereon."[55] E. B. Black, a consulting engineer on the project, wrote on July 13, "The Iron Mountain Railway has refused permission to cross their Upper Bridge with our pipe line on account of operating difficulties, but have granted permission to cross the lower bridge." However, the lower bridge caused problems because it was a drawbridge and river traffic could not be slowed. "The situation has been outlined in a telegram to Colonel [I.W.] Littell," wrote Black, "[and if it can't be settled, I'm] asking that we be authorized to proceed at once with the development of a well supply in Argenta."[56]

Fordyce had projected that two million gallons of water would be carried to the post through sixteen-inch redwood pipes, "six miles long from Little Rock, Ark. to five wood-stave tanks located near the center of the Cantonment; total capacity five tanks, 1,000,000 gal."[57] But getting to the water source proved to be the issue. To add insult to injury, some of the temporary wells at St. Joseph were found to have "colon contamination," and were declared unusable for drinking water.[58] But even two weeks before this early August contamination issue, drinking cups were provided at cost at the Post Exchange to help with sanitation problems.[59] Major Fordyce claimed that he never thought placing the pipe on a draw bridge was practical, and he was able to get approval for the water pipeline to be built across the "Free Bridge," which was not a drawbridge. This was accomplished at cost to the federal government, as the city made an agreement with the Secretary of War that Little Rock would not pay for the construction of the water supply system. However, Fordyce was concerned about possible sabotage of the pipeline across the bridge. "The pipe is in a very exposed position," he explained, "and could be easily broken by exploding a stick of dynamite under it." Therefore, guards were stationed at each end to protect the pipeline. Still, Fordyce believed that the pipe would continue to be exposed to danger. Although Fordyce acknowledged in his completion report that the city had drilled in Argenta and found a water supply, he never indicated if actual wells were drilled. It is possible that the Argenta wells were never drilled, as Fordyce wrote that "it was thought in Washington because of the broken condition of the rock strata that surface water would get in and that there always would be danger of contamination even in the deepest wells."[60]

The Arkansas National Guard was involved in the construction phase of Camp Pike through police duty. The Third Battalion of the First Arkansas Infantry Regiment was sent to the cantonment on July 18, for police duty, with Captain Walton Brooks of Blytheville as the commander.[61] In early August, the Machine Gun Company of the First Arkansas also arrived at Camp Pike for the same reason.[62] Although there do not appear to have been many issues with workers, there was one particularly interesting incident on August 1, 1917. Robert Parkinson was removed from Camp Pike and told to never return because of disloyal remarks he made to fellow workers. Apparently, Parkinson "cussed out" President Wilson and the U.S. government. He was given a severe lecture before being kicked off the post. Parkinson, who hailed from New Jersey, was relieved, as the *Gazette* reported, that the punishment was not more severe.[63]

During construction, Major Fordyce had to juggle numerous facets of the job and other business, such as people asking for jobs as favors, including a few requests from his own father. Fordyce even had a little back-and-forth with his brother, Sam. He wrote to his brother on August 11, explaining that he wished Sam would join him at Camp Pike, "and not wast[e] your time around Washington attending poker parties with the Senators."[64] At some point, Sam Fordyce made it to Camp Pike as indicated by some photos of him working at the post. Major Fordyce was also bucking for a promotion because the pay for his rank was not adequate. Fordyce wanted to be a colonel because, as he said, "I feel that my experience, especially in engineering, will easily enable me to hold my own among most officers of that grade who are now in the service."[65] But Fordyce never received that promotion at Camp Pike.

Major Fordyce wrote that he did not have an abundance of labor problems, but there were a few. It is clear that Fordyce was in no mood for labor upheaval during a time of war when the post needed to be finished and ready for soldiers by September. In August, the Carpenters' Union called for a closed shop throughout the country if construction was to continue at the cantonments.[66] But a closed shop at Camp Pike did not fly with Major Fordyce. The major wrote that there "was to be an 'open shop' when union and non-union men were to work together."[67] A demonstration of this cooperation came when it was reported that the plumbers would work on Labor Day. The plumbers, as with all workers, were encouraged to be patriotic and work when needed. A clause forbade plumber workers in their union to work on Labor Day, but that clause was suspended.[68] Fordyce wrote to his father, explaining that "I persuaded [laborers] to work on Labor Day, in violation of direct orders from their National Labor Union President. . . . I consider [this] one of the accomplishments of the summer."[69]

In a demonstration of his toughness on labor, Major Fordyce wrote that "any foreman found compelling a workman to join a union or discharging him because he was not a member was promptly placed in the guard house. He was worked from there three to five days at hard police duty under guard without pay, and then put off the reservation with orders not to return."[70] If workers were "idlers" Fordyce had them arrested and thrown into the guard house. When their time of confinement was complete, they were placed back into the post workforce or escorted off

Construction work at Camp Pike attracted so many workers that other industries complained of the competition. *Courtesy of the National Archives and Records Administration.*

the cantonment. "In this way," he wrote, "between persuasion and actual violence, I have been able to keep them working."[71]

Fordyce issued a flyer to his workers about working and patriotism that was packed full of rhetoric:

> TO CAMP PIKE WORKMEN
> Our country is at war.
> You are soldiers.
> This is your battlefield.
> Be an American.
> Be patriotic.
> Every blow you strike with ax, pick or hammer is a blow for liberty.
> Delay here in this Camp means death and destruction in France.
> Do all you can to rush the work and see that it is built without waste and on time.
> Show the enemies of our country that free Americans are not driven to duty, but, exalted and inspired, will work till death for the sacred cause of freedom.[72]

Once the railroad reached the post, construction became hurried. Major Fordyce understood that this was imperative if the post was to be ready for troop arrival in early September, although not finished. State lumber mills greatly benefited when they received contracts to supply the post with 15 million board feet of pine lumber.[73] Of course, problems arose, such as heavy rains, delay in receiving materials, and lack of manpower, but the work continued. Because there were not enough local men to bring the workforce to maximum capacity, workers were brought in from other states, and from as far away as Puerto Rico.[74] So many Arkansas men were hired to build Camp Pike that Fordyce received complaints because he was "stealing" workers from industries and farms. He wrote to his brother Sam that he "told the planters that it is their patriotic duty to work a little themselves and let the negroes come up and work for the government." By the middle of August, there were around 8,000 men working construction on the post, and there were many African Americans employed.[75]

Major Fordyce wrote on August 21 that 65% of the work was completed and that "work is progressing splendidly here."[76] Indeed it was. By the time the first troops arrived in early September, although not finished, Camp Pike was ready. Construction continued throughout the fall even after troops were training on post. By December, most of the construction work at Camp Pike was completed, although there was some small work to be done.[77] By this time, Major Fordyce's time at Camp Pike was winding down. Work at Camp Pike went so fast that at one point one million board feet of lumber arrived daily.[78] By December, more than 1,100 buildings were constructed, including several YMCA buildings and one for the Knights of Columbus.[79] Sesser wrote that "the structures at Camp Pike were functional but not grandiose."[80] And Sesser is correct. There was not time to build grand training facilities, and Camp Pike followed the basic model applied throughout the country.

During the summer, the army changed its numbering system for its divisions and Camp Pike became the training site for the Eighty-Seventh Division, which consisted of the same states as before. At the end of August, before the first troops arrived, the new commander of the Eighty-Seventh, General Samuel D. Sturgis Jr. was on post. Major Fordyce wrote to his father that "I am very impressed with him as a broadminded man as well as an efficient military officer."[81] Sturgis, who was born in St. Louis, Missouri, in 1861, was promoted to Major General when he took command of the Eighty-Seventh Division at Camp Pike.

Draftees arrive to begin their military training at Camp Pike. *Courtesy of the Arkansas National Guard Museum.*

On September 2, General Sturgis inspected the new post and said he was impressed with the progress of construction. At that time, it was disclosed that Camp Pike could accommodate 30,000 men.[82]

Sixteen Little Rock men were selected to be the first of the Eighty-Seventh Division to arrive for training at Camp Pike.[83] On September 5, 1917, troops arrived on post to begin training as part of the Eighty-Seventh Division.[84] By the end of the month, 23,000 men were on post.[85] When Private James Harris Atkinson, with whom we started our story, arrived at Camp Robinson in 1918, he was "issued two good pairs of shoes, two shirts (woolen), two pr. trousers, 3 pr. socks, belt, hat, two suits, underwear, comb, brush, two woolen blankets, 2 towels, toothbrush, soap, 1 pr. leggings, mess kit, knife fork spoon, cup, bed sack."[86] And this was typical of all soldiers. In addition, the training doughboys (as the soldiers were called) were encouraged to live chaste lives. Speaking at several of the YMCA buildings on post in January 1918, Dr. Clement G. Clark, who was touring several military training cantonments throughout the country, told the men, in his then "famous address" called "Sex-Life and Patriotism," to live clean lives as "a duty they owed to their God, their country, the women they may marry and themselves."[87]

A number of men were discharged from the Eighty-Seventh Division throughout 1917 and 1918 for physical problems.[88] By the end of January, 7.6% of the men from Arkansas, Alabama, Louisiana, and Mississippi had been discharged.[89] To help the men stay healthy, General Sturgis wanted each company at Camp Pike to participate in athletics. The general approved plans for competitions for regiments and the entire division. "Every man in athletics" was the slogan.[90] In November, athletic equipment arrived on post to be placed in all the barracks, although the men were temporarily quarantined because of a measles outbreak. Sporting events were difficult to conduct because of the constant coming and going of men. But the events were still managed.[91] In February, the first baseball game was played at Camp Pike between soldiers. Some of the men had even played professional baseball.[92] It is possible this game was played at the newly constructed Belmont Field, which was built by the owner of the local minor league team, the Little Rock Travelers.

Sports were good for morale and fitness, but military training was also required. Trenches were dug on post to emulate the conditions the men would experience when they fought in France.[93] In May 1918, a machine gun school was opened at Camp Pike.[94] Some unusual training was also provided at Camp Pike. For example, the Signal Corps experimented and trained in several methods to send messages, including homing pigeons. Pigeon training took place in the northwestern area of the cantonment, with signs that said "keep out." Eighteen soldiers trained at the Field Battalion Headquarters, of the 312th Signal Corps. Most of the birds came from the Boston, Massachusetts, area.[95] The *Trench and Camp*, the post newspaper, revealed that anyone caught shooting a homing pigeon would be fined $100 and sentenced to six months in prison.[96]

General Sturgis was ordered to a new post and transferred from Camp Pike around December 1, 1917. Brigadier General R. C. Van Vliet was named acting commander of the Eighty-Seventh Division and it was assumed that he would be appointed as the new commander.[97] However, Van Vliet was never named as the new permanent commander of the division. In mid-March 1918, more than 20,000 men of the Eighty-Seventh Division participated in a review. General Sturgis, who had just returned from an inspection assignment in France to again take command of the Eighty-Seventh, led the review. He was gone for more than three months, but once he returned, General Sturgis remained with the Eighty-Seventh and deployed with the division as its commander later in the year. The review was in honor of Sturgis's return from France. It

Athletics Great Training for Soldiers

THE RUNNER -

THE BALL PLAYER -

THE BOXER -

GOES OVER THE TOP QUICKLY AND ISN'T WINDED WHEN HE REACHES THE ENEMY.

MAKES GOOD AS A GRENADE THROWER.

MAKES AN EXPERT BAYONET FIGHTER ..

THE FOOTBALL PLAYER

WILL BE A GOOD MAN IN A MIXUP ....

R. Edgren.

By Robert Edgren

showed in many all-day battles with Persian invaders, where the Greeks sometimes killed ten of the enemy for every Greek in the fighting line. The Persians were war-like enough, but less skilled in athletic sports than the Greeks.

The sports that will be encouraged in the American training camps will all be useful in preparing men for battle. Boxing will be the chief sport. Every man will be taught to box, because a good boxer is sure to be a handy man with the bayonet. Bayonet fighting is practically boxing with a weapon. A lot of boxing tricks, including several that are barred in the Queensberry rules but considered quite the proper thing in a lumber camp fight, have been applied to bayonet fighting. In war there are no foul blows. In fact the blow that would be foul in boxing is most easily delivered with the bayonet.

Some of the new bayonet work is done with a shorthand gun, the muzzle grasped in one or in both hands. It was suggested by a boxer's infighting. And reports from the front say that the Canadians, who originated it, find it very effective.

"Snappy Blow" the Thing with Bayonet

The *Trench and Camp* newspaper at Camp Pike reflected General Sturgis' focus on athletics for the new recruits. Courtesy of the Arkansas National Guard Museum.

A review was held at Camp Pike to welcome General Samuel D. Sturgis as he took command of the Eighty-Seventh Infantry Division. *Courtesy of the National Archives and Records Administration Still Picture Branch.*

was the largest military ceremony ever held in Arkansas up to that point, and General Sturgis was accompanied by General J. B. McDonald from the Inspector General Department in Washington DC. The *Trench and Camp* proclaimed the review "a beautiful spectacle." In addition to the soldiers, about 4,000 people from the area came in automobiles to witness the review.[98]

African Americans also trained at Camp Pike in segregated units, such as the Field Remount Depot No. 351 of the Auxiliary Remount Depot No. 317.[99] The first African American troops arrived at Camp Pike in October 1917, with a total of just over 1,400 during the month. A year later, the number of African American men on post reached a high of 11,267.[100] In the summer of 1918, twenty-seven African American second lieutenants from Camp Pike were sent to a new Department of Central Officers' Training School to be educated in leadership. The goal for these men, taken from several units, was to have them lead black troops by replacing white officers.[101]

One of the most significant incidents at Camp Pike during World

War I involved African American soldiers. Captain E. C. Rowan, a white officer from Mississippi, was court-martialed for refusing to follow a direct order from a superior. Rowan refused to line up his white company during the morning parade because black companies were also there in formation. At his court-martial, Rowan's defense was that "he would have had to violate a strict military ruling—would have injured the self-respect of his men—had he carried out the order . . . . Captain Rowan pleaded that the order in itself was illegal in that it violated the 'custom regulation of the army.'"[102] Rowan was found guilty in his court-martial and dismissed. This was the first time in American history that a white officer was court-martialed in an issue involving race.[103]

Native Americans also trained at Camp Pike, although not in segregated units. One such doughboy was Choctaw Joe Green, who provided information about a typical training week to the superintendent of the Indian School he had attended. He wrote, "I have been in the army almost two months, drilling eight hours a day five days a week. Saturday and Sunday we have as holidays." But the first day of the weekend was not just for personal time. Green explained that "Saturday morning we stand rifle inspection. So far I have passed this test. Some of the boys fail and get extra duty." Green also saw other Native Americans while training at Camp Pike. "I saw some of the Chilocco [Indian School] boys here three weeks ago. I was certainly glad to meet them. They were: John Johnson [Seminole], Albert Barcelo, Martin Jackaway and Nelson Cooper. I had begun to think I was the only one here from Chilocco and was glad to see these old schoolmates."[104]

A noteworthy case involved Peter Defoe, a Chippewa from the White Earth Reservation in Minnesota. Defoe believed that he was not legally drafted into the army because Major General Enoch Crowder, who was in charge of the Selective Service, made the decision that Native Americans who kept their tribal affiliations active were not to be included in the military draft. Defoe attempted to be released from military service even before his transfer to Camp Pike from Camp Dodge in Iowa. However, as indicated in an article published in *The Tomahawk*, the White Earth Reservation newspaper, General Crowder's mandate did not apply to Defoe. Because of the Nelson Act of 1889, the White Earth Chippewa accepted allotments from the federal government, which also constituted citizenship. In addition, according to *The Tomahawk*, an amendment made it perfectly clear that Indians of "mixed blood" were undoubtedly citizens of the United States. The paper indicated that because Defoe was of mixed heritage, he was a subject to conscription. The paper also offered these words: "Our advice to Mr. Defoe is to stand by his enlistment and serve his country loyally as a good citizen, for citizen he is."[105] Indeed, Peter Defoe did continue to serve in the army and was killed in action on October 1, 1918, in France and is buried in the Meuse-Argonne American Cemetery in that country.[106]

When men arrived for training, they were quarantined for ten days to help prevent the spread of disease. The men were also vaccinated for a number of diseases such as smallpox. However, precautions such as quarantines and vaccinations did not prevent all diseases from spreading. By early 1918, Camp Pike had a high rate of venereal disease, so much so that the post led all army posts in this category. And levels of other diseases at the Arkansas cantonment were close to being the highest in the country. Measles socked the post particularly hard.[107] But even a month before troops arrived at Camp Pike, a construction worker was discovered to have smallpox and was quickly sent to quarantine.[108] Of course, the close proximity of men, especially because they arrived on post from a multitude of places, hastened the spread of diseases. Unsanitary conditions could be a health hazard as well, but at the end of August 1917, an army health inspector indicated after visiting the camp that sanitary conditions were very good.[109]

By December 1917, however, the death rate at Camp Pike from diseases was extremely high. Even by mid-November, there were 571 cases of measles on post.[110] Even malaria was reported.[111] However, in December, Major General W. C. Gorgas of the Medical Corps visited Camp Pike and erroneously said that the death rates at cantonments should not inspire fear.[112] Then in February 1918, to compound the problem, Camp Pike experienced a pneumonia outbreak.[113] Men were quarantined until they were no longer considered contagious. However, the worst was yet to come. On September 23, 1918, influenza was discovered on post. This was the beginning of the great Spanish flu epidemic that spread throughout the world in 1918 and 1919, killing millions. The number of influenza cases at Camp Pike quickly rose, even while officials attempted to downplay the epidemic, despite the realization that by the end of September, the post hospital had already treated more than 7,600 patients.[114] Finally, on October 3, the post was placed under quarantine, and officers were included a few days later. If fact, the hospital was so crowded with cases of influenza that infected men were placed in barracks with those not sick, exacerbating the problem.[115]

The first half of September saw seventeen new influenza cases a day check into the post hospital, but that soon tripled. By the last part of the month, around a thousand new flu cases reported to the hospital, which had 2,000 beds. About 1,400 influenza patients arrived from Eberts Training Field, located in nearby Lonoke County. To make matters worse, sixty-two of the 240 medical personnel at the Camp Pike hospital contracted the disease. By the time the epidemic ran its course, 466 had lost their lives from Camp Pike and Eberts Field. Camp Pike was one of the worst-hit military reservations in the country.[116]

In May 1918, Congress passed a new law that allowed men who were not citizens to become naturalized if they were soldiers, suspending the previous requirement of five years of residency. Soldiers at Camp Pike took advantage of the new law, as did most of the other military training cantonments across the country. For example, between May and December 1918, more than 3,000 naturalization petitions were processed. Only two were denied by the judge, because the men were from China. During those years, Asians born on foreign soil could not become American citizens. Of the men naturalized at Camp Pike, more than 22% were from the Scandinavian countries, and another 22% were from Eastern Europe. Close behind were men from Italy at 18%. Most of these men were not living in Arkansas when they joined the army.[117]

In August 1918, the men of the Eighty-Seventh Division were sent overseas. Most of these men came from Arkansas, Alabama, Louisiana and Mississippi. However, in 1918, men from Tennessee and Iowa were also sent to Camp Pike to train as part of the Eighty-Seventh Division. General Sturgis led the Eighty-Seventh in France. During two consecutive months during the late summer and early fall of 1918, more than 54,000 troops were on post at one time.[118] Most doughboys received six months of training in the United States, and then usually had around two months' more training overseas. As a rule, once soldiers were committed to the battlefield, or trenches, as it were, they were sent to a sector that was not so intense for a month before being moved to the real battle zone.[119] And this was most than likely the case for the men of the Eighty-Seventh.

After the War

Thousands of men trained at Camp Pike during the Great War. After the Eighty-Seventh deployed, the cantonment was used for

DIVISIONAL INSIGNIA

87TH DIVISION
KNOWN AS THE ACORN
DIVISION 141

TRAINED AT CAMP PIKE
TROOPS FROM ARKANSAS,
LOUISIANA AND MIS-
SISSIPPI

Soldiers from Arkansas, Alabama, Louisiana and Mississippi, Iowa and Tennessee trained at Camp Pike to serve with the Eighty-Seventh Infantry Division. *Courtesy of the Arkansas National Guard Museum.*

replacement training and, after the war, Camp Pike was utilized as a demobilization post for the Third Infantry Division. Around 105,000 soldiers demobilized at Camp Pike. Beginning in 1919, the Third Division, in partnership with the Knights of Columbus, established Camp Pike College on post to help returning soldiers with their transition into civilian life. Courses covered such areas as motor mechanics, sheet metal work, carpentry, and plumbing. In addition, there were courses offered in bookkeeping and dramatics, as well as a class in Americanization. It is important to remember that 1919 was the year of the first Red Scare in America, and understanding what it was to be an American was deemed important, even to those born in the country.[120]

In 1922, the U.S. government decided that Camp Pike was no longer

Camp Pike College was established in 1919 to help doughboys' transition to civilian life by teaching such skills as sheet metal work. *Courtesy of the National Archives and Records Administration Still Picture Branch.*

needed and deeded the post over to the State of Arkansas. At that time, Camp Pike College closed. The state had to utilize the post for military purposes, so the Arkansas National Guard took over the site. In addition, it was stipulated that if the army ever needed to use the camp again it would be federalized. During construction, Arkansas senator Joseph T. Robinson visited the post.[121] Little could he have known that, twenty years later, the camp would bear his name.

The legacy of Camp Pike is immense, especially to Arkansas. Thousands of doughboys trained on the post during the First World War, which also greatly enhanced the local economy. The soldiers were trained with the best methods of the day, and were treated to numerous programs and events that broadened their scope of the world, such as speeches on camp from former secretary of state and presidential candidate William Jennings Bryan and former president and later chief justice of the Supreme Court William Howard Taft. But the legacy of the post goes well beyond the World War I years. Indeed, the post survived the 1920s, and continues strong today.

The Arkansas National Guard has utilized Camp Pike/Robinson for more than ninety years, interrupted only during World War II. Only about two years after the post changed its name to Camp Robinson, after Senator Robinson's death, the U.S. Army took over the post in the fall of 1940, more than a year before the attack on Pearl Harbor but with the anticipation of America's entry into the Second World War.

Used mostly for infantry and medical replacement training during World War II, Camp Robinson saw more than 850,000 soldiers come through. The Sixty-Sixth and Ninety-Second Infantry Divisions trained at Camp Robinson. In addition, there was a German POW camp placed on post.[122] Camp Robinson was rebuilt in 1941, and from its World War I beginnings of 3,000 acres with 10,000 acres leased for training, the post was increased to 44,000 acres during the Second World War.

During the World War II years, some think that Camp Robinson might have been utilized for Indian code talker training, possibly as early as 1941. Major E. W. Horner, who was a soldier in the First World War, used Choctaw doughboys to send and receive messages in France through the telegraph for two days in October 1918, because the Germans had intercepted American communications sent in English. Horner wrote that the system "worked quite successfully." He was not if anything similar was being tried in 1942. But he said, "I did read in some Army Publication last summer [1941] that Sioux Indians were being trained at Camp Robinson, Arkansas along this line, and the article mentioned that I was the first to use the system during the World War."[123]

After WWII, Camp Robinson went back to state control and to the Arkansas National Guard. Today, now named Robinson Maneuver Training Center but still called Camp Robinson by most people, it is an important training facility for the Arkansas National Guard and continues to be an asset for the local economy, especially north of the Arkansas River. Most of the roughly 32,000 acres currently in the camp are for training, but the cantonment area is vibrant and always on the move, housing several training centers and armories, plus the Office of the Adjutant General. And, since the 1970s, Camp Robinson houses the ever growing National Guard Bureau's Professional Education Center, where thousands of National Guard soldiers from around the country have received advanced training. In addition, one corner of the post, using the original name of Camp Pike, is the site of the Army, Navy, and Marines Reserve Center.

Thousands of men (some who were even teenagers) worked to build

Camp Pike, earning money to help their families. One such young man was Clyde F. Gay, who was a junior in high school when he worked at Pike. Reminiscing in 1980 about his time at Camp Pike some six decades previous, Gay's memory was sharp. His principal provided him a ten-day pass to earn money at the cantonment site. "Each morning" Gay said, "I joined a truck at City Hall from which four short term colored prisoners were released to my custody for a day." He explained that "we were to walk [chain measures] every road and path in the area marked by Mr. [A. M.] Lund," who was Gay's Sunday School teacher, and an engineer who got Gay his job. All this work was before Little Rock won the honor to build the post. Gay said, "After the preliminary site was sent to Washington—General Leonard Wood came to Little Rock, toured it and decided to condemn and take for the U.S. at once." Whether Gay's account of how the cantonment was awarded to Little Rock is exactly accurate is not important because his work, along with others, provided the army with a blueprint of the layout.[124]

In addition to the Eighty-Seventh, other divisions who spent time at Camp Pike during the Great War and during the demobilization period of 1919 were the Third Division, the Fifteenth and Thirty-Fifth Divisions, along with the Ninetieth Division and the Thirty-Ninth Division, of which the Arkansas National Guard was a part. The 153rd and the Thirty-Ninth Infantry of the Arkansas National Guard mobilized for overseas service at Camp Pike, and the 142nd Field Artillery of the Thirty-Ninth Arkansas Guard regiment demobilized at the post. There were also a number of non-divisional units at Camp Pike during World War I.[125]

When the Board of Commerce of Little Rock petitioned for a training post, the members could not have known that the camp would continue, uninterrupted, 101 years later, with no signs of closing. Sure, the business and political leaders of Little Rock wanted the post to help central Arkansas economically, and hoped that the cantonment would last a few years, but it is doubtful they looked one hundred years into the future. For more than a century, Camp Pike/Robinson has provided training for soldiers, to Arkansans and those from outside the state's borders. It has also provided employment for local civilians and has been a positive addition for local businesses. That legacy continues to grow.

6 | Soldiers and Veterans at the Elaine Race Massacre

BRIAN K. MITCHELL

The role of active-duty U.S. soldiers in the Elaine Race Massacre has been well documented by scholars studying the event. Through the scholarship of Richard C. Cortner, Grif Stockley, and Robert Whitaker, we know the names of many of the commanding officers and that of the sole active-duty fatality of the campaign, Corporal Luther D. Earles.[1] From a wealth of primary sources, we can glean bits of information about what these soldiers did during the campaign and what they saw. Questions in regard to the accuracy and details within the reports and documents produced by the military officers, military intelligence, and federal authorities have perplexed researchers and scholars since these documents were first released to the public. While the role of the active-duty soldier is the subject of much debate in the narrative surrounding the event, there are two other groups of soldiers who were also active and visible components of the engagement: the black veterans and the white veterans. Although all three—the active-duty soldier, the white veteran, and the black veteran—fought for the same nation, their service would be viewed differently. For the white active-duty soldier and veteran, military service brought with it a sense of pride and respect. Their service was applauded, and their acts of valor were lauded and commemorated. However, the service of the black veteran went generally unappreciated and unacknowledged, or, worse still, it was feared by neighboring whites.

| DOI: https://doi.org/10.34053/christ2019.twah.6

The story of the Elaine Massacre is one of unfulfilled promises and expectations on the part of black soldiers who believed that their service had transformed them into full-fledged citizens of the United States. To understand their plight and the perilous perch that their protest placed them upon, one must first have an understanding of white supremacy and the unrelenting grip that this institution had on the lives of blacks, particularly those who were unfortunate enough to reside in agrarian portions of former Confederate states. The black veterans of World War I were the sons and grandsons of slaves, who, like their forefathers, committed themselves to war with the expectation that they too would be in return made true citizens of the United States. Unfortunately, the black veterans of the "War to End All Wars" returned from the war to an unchanged South. Their deeds, however noble or heroic, could not erase the stain of race, and their dreams, like those of their ancestors, remained dreams deferred. The soldiers' expectations that their government and neighbors would deal with them more equitably after serving in the Great War were unfulfilled.[2] With that in mind, this chapter examines the role that the three types of soldiers (the white active-duty soldier, the white veteran, and the black veteran) played in the Elaine Massacre.

The Spark and the Powder Keg

On September 30, 1919, under the cover of night, scores of black sharecroppers met secretly at a small church at Hoop Spur, about three miles from Elaine, Arkansas. Tired of being exploited by the South's brutal system of agricultural debt peonage, the farmers joined the Progressive Farmers and Household Union of America (PFHUA). The PFHUA was established in 1918 in Winchester, a community in Drew County, Arkansas, by a local resident Robert Lee Hill. Hill, a native of Chicot County and veteran of World War I, focused the union's work on fair wages and treatment within the sharecropping system.[3] To achieve that goal, Hill urged farmers to combine their efforts and resources to hire legal counsel in hopes of receiving fair compensation for their crops and a fair recording of debt at their landlords' plantation stores. Plantation owners and landlords perceived the economic exploitation of their sharecroppers as a right and sought to sustain the entitlement by intimidating tenant farmers who joined the union. To find out where the union's meetings were held and to identify farmers who were members, the landlords relied on "a few friendly negroes" to report "what was going on" within the union.

As the union members met at Hoop Spur and armed men stood guard outside, a firefight erupted outside of the church with a group of law enforcement officers who claimed to have stumbled upon the gathering after puncturing a tire and looking for help. The officers alleged that they had been in pursuit of a bootlegger before their car problems and had merely stopped at the church seeking assistance. Authorities maintained that armed black sentries posted outside of the church fired upon the unsuspecting officers first, killing W. A. Adkins, a special agent of the Missouri Pacific Railroad Co., and wounding Charles W. Pratt, a Phillips County deputy sheriff. "Kidd" Collins, a black trusty at the Phillips County Jail who had accompanied the officers, escaped the firefight unscathed and reported the incident to local authorities. The sharecroppers maintained that the law enforcement officers' claims of having stumbled accidentally upon their meeting and their allegations of having been fired upon first were untrue. The tenant farmers contended that the officers had surrounded the church and commenced to firing into the structure to intimidate and terrify them into abandoning their pursuit for fair treatment.[4]

Responding to Collins's report, a sheriff's posse made its way to the scene of the shooting. However, once there, the deputies discovered that they were outnumbered and returned to Helena for reinforcements. By the morning of October 1, the story of the gunfight and the number of black farmers had been exaggerated repeatedly. Rumors circulated that "between 1,000 and 1,500 negroes had assembled in the vicinity of Elaine and were armed with high-powered rifles." When the message of the shooting reached the city's telephone operator, she embellished the tale further by adding that the "fight was in progress in the streets [of Elaine]" and requesting that reinforcements, guns, and ammunition be sent.

Sparing little time, the returning deputies recruited members of Helena's American Legion Hall. Chief Deputy A. F. James of Phillips County provided details of the veterans' participation in the massacre during an interview for the *New Orleans States Item*, noting that after "realizing that they were outnumbered, the deputies returned and swore in a bunch of Legion men." James maintained that about seventy-five of the post's members were deputized and after being provisioned with rifles and ammunition from the sheriff's armory, returned to the site where the PFHUA's farmers had collected, outside of union leader Ed Ware's cabin. The chief deputy recounted that a "fierce gunfight ensued" and even though he maintained that the "negro gang," presumably the members of the union, was broken up after ten minutes, he contended that several skirmishes still sprang up during the course of the day. While noting that only five whites were killed, James estimated the death toll at between fifty and 100 blacks, most of whom were killed after the arrest of those sharecroppers who had attended the Hoop Spur meeting.[5]

When panicked messages of an ongoing race war reached his office, Governor Charles H. Brough responded by reaching out to Major General S. D. Sturgis, the commanding officer of the nearby army encampment, Camp Pike. Sturgis, having no authority to commit his soldiers to intervene, suggested that Brough contact the secretary of war. By October 2, with the intervention of both of Arkansas's U.S. senators, Brough secured orders for 583 soldiers from the Third Division and the Fifty-Seventh Infantry to accompany him to Phillips County. The provisions of Special Order 264 maintained: "By direction of the President, a detachment of troops consisting of four rifle companies of the Third Division, two rifle companies of the 57th Infantry, under command of Colonel Isaac Jenks, Infantry, 3rd Division, will proceed from Camp Pike, Ark., to Elaine, Arkansas, for the purpose of quelling disorders and protecting lives and property."[6]

An advance order dated October 1, 1919, divided the troops into four provisional companies and noted that soldiers assigned to the engagement would show up with "full field equipment ready to move out in short notice." (Appendix II)[7]

The Army Arrives

The contingent of soldiers requested by Brough traveled by train from Camp Pike to Elaine, arriving in the town at 8:15 a.m. on October 2, 1919. Among the soldiers was Father Edward J. Sliney, chaplain and first lieutenant from the Third Division. Sliney, a native of Boston, Massachusetts, and acting unit historian, brought along a camera in order to create a "photographic record or interest to supplement his report."[8] The chaplain's photographs complement the narratives in the officers' reports and provide images of what the troops saw during their deployment to Elaine.[9] Jenks reported that upon his arrival he found the town in "a great state of excitement" with "hundreds of white men, all carrying fire-arms" on the streets, "near the station and in groups, all over town." (See Figure 1)

Following up on reports of an ongoing engagement, the colonel dispatched one of his provisional companies under the command of

FIGURE 1 (ABOVE):
A mob gathers during
the Elaine massacre,
October 2, 1919.
*Charles Hillman
Brough Collection,
Arkansas State
Archives, Little Rock.*

FIGURE 2 (LEFT):
A dead woman's
body lies outside a
sharecropper's cabin.
*Charles Hillman
Brough Collection,
Arkansas State
Archives, Little Rock.*

Major N. E. Callen.[10] The company had advanced about a mile and a half when it found "a negro woman lying in front of her doorstep and barely alive, shot through the neck several hours before" (see Figure 2).[11] While Jenks's report failed to provide the name of the victim, Ida B. Wells's *The Arkansas Race Riot* described the details of the murder of Frances Hall, a mentally ill housekeeper and relative of two PFHUA members, Frank and Paul Hall, which was eerily similar to the scene depicted in Sliney's photograph. Wells noted that the mob that killed Hall "tied her clothes over her head, threw her body in the public road where it lay thus exposed till the soldiers came Thursday evening and took it up."[12]

After finding the body, Jenks reported that the battalion reconnoitered approximately two miles of the surrounding terrain. The report described the search for the alleged black rebels, noting only that they had "captured several prisoners" and "all the rest of the colored outlaws had disappeared." (Figures 3 and 4) The commanding officer noted that his unit suffered two casualties during the search; both soldiers were in First Provisional Company and had served in the Fourth Infantry before being assigned to Elaine. According to the report, Corporal Luther Earles and Sergeant Pearl B. Gay were both shot in a glade as they approached dense thickets. The sniper, who hid in the "impregnable" forest, shot both Earles and Gay. Earles was shot in the face and died the following day, while Gay was only slightly wounded and had returned to his duties before their colonel had completed his report of the incident. Jenks described the soldiers' assailant as a "negro outlaw" and made no consideration that the shots that came from the "jungle" may have come from a member of one of the white lynch mobs. Despite the fact that no one could identify a marksman in the bush, a local sharecropper, Sam Wilson, was charged with Earles's murder. Wilson pled guilty to second-degree murder on November 7, 1919, and was sentenced to twenty-one years in prison.[13]

Federal troops took hundreds of black citizens residing in the neighboring countryside into custody. Holding them in a school that had been commandeered to serve as a makeshift stockade, the troops interrogated the captured. Those black sharecroppers identified as members of the PFHUA were charged and confined, and those who were not union members were released and given passes so that they could return to work in the fields.[14] While searching the area for blacks who were believed to be hiding in the woods, the troops discovered a small farmhouse with a meager contingent of white men protecting it. Inside the home, soldiers discovered sixty-five white women and children hiding. When

FIGURES
3 AND 4:
United States
army troops
march pris-
oners seized
near Elaine
toward a stock-
ade. *Charles
Hillman Brough
Collection,
Arkansas State
Archives, Little
Rock.*

questioned, the white sharecroppers contended that they had crowded together, believing that it was safer that way. Describing the whites in the Elaine area as "panic-stricken," Jenks established a network of outposts throughout the area to protect and reassure the white citizenry. A detachment of twenty-five soldiers was sent to the town of Millwood after Jenks reported seeing "ten or more" white men patrolling the town's streets. Another group of troops was sent to the small farm where the white sharecroppers had gathered, and a third patrol was assigned to the Lambrook Plantation.[15]

Lambrook was owned by Gerald B. Lambert, the proprietor of Lambert Pharmaceuticals and manufacturer of the popular antiseptic Listerine. Ida B. Wells noted in her investigation of the massacre that several PFHUA members were sharecroppers on the Lambrook Plantation. Jenks, keenly aware of Lambrook's importance to the PFHUA membership, wrote that he had assigned troops "where there were several malcontents and ringleaders among the large number of negroes employed." Lambert documented the violence that occurred on his plantation, providing vivid testimony of what had been omitted from government and military reports.[16]

Lambert recalled that while traveling to his plantation on October 4, he saw white men in the woods of the surrounding area firing upon any suspicious person that they encountered. He further maintained that he saw whites shielded in a steel rail gondola pick off blacks hiding in the neighboring thickets. At his farm, Lambert maintained that Jenks's soldiers apprehended a PFHUA leader and tied him to one of his plantation store's wooden columns. Once he was secured to the column, the men poured kerosene over the union leader and began questioning him. When he refused to answer, he was set aflame. "The colored man went up like a torch," recalled Lambert, "and in a moment of supreme agony, burst his bounds. Before he could get a few feet he was riddled with bullets."[17]

Noted *Arkansas Gazette* journalist Louis Sharpe Dunaway described the Elaine Massacre as "the blackest day ever written by blood or bayonet in the history of Arkansas." His account of military involvement in the massacre also contradicted the sparse details provided by Colonel Jenks in his report. According to Dunaway, the troops sent to Elaine to quell the riot caused "a crusade of death that claimed the lives of nearly one thousand innocent victims." Calling the battalion's reconnaissance mission and subsequent hunt for union members a "March of Death," he maintained that troops participated in widespread carnage, killing an estimated 856 blacks before returning to Camp Pike. While Dunaway's account of the massacre affirms the violence described by Lambert, he dismissed the violence of mobs, sheriffs, and the American Legion members, instead placing the blame for the bulk of the deaths on the soldiers.[18] Dunaway made little effort to substantiate the number of dead, and there were no lists of missing or dead, nor city enumerations or explanation to show to how his calculation had been ascertained.

Jenks made no mention of his troops' alleged atrocities. His report maintained that his battalion's objectives were primarily those of a peacekeeping force. Outlining his priorities during the campaign, the colonel maintained that the operation of the federal troops consisted of five priorities: "(1.) Guarding inhabitants of outlying localities where danger seemed imminent; (2.) Sending out strong searching parties—patrols to apprehend ringleaders— and get their records and all other obtainable evidence; (3.) Prevent any disorders—lynching or shooting affairs throughout the district; (4.) Relieve the mental distress of the people, by furnishing security for them to return to work without fear; (5.) To protect the colored people from any kind of violence and enable them to resume their work under the protection of U.S. Troops."[19]

On October 7, 1919, Captain Edward P. Passailaigue of the Third Division's Ammunition Train wrote an assessment of the unit's campaign in Phillips County. The contradictions between Passailaigue's report and that of his commanding officer, Colonel Jenks, are striking. While Jenks maintained that the town was filled with hundreds of white men brandishing guns, Captain Passailaigue contended that there were only "small groups of white people armed with shot-guns, pistols, and rifles." In Passailaigue's account of the engagement, there were no white mobs or posses searching out black targets; instead, the captain described a region held hostage by "negroes holding the woods around the town" that "prevented them [the white populace] from getting out." Reversing the roles of blacks and whites found in the accounts of Lambert and Dunaway, Passailaigue contended that "negroes of the surrounding country had assembled and were killing the whites wherever they ventured out of their farms." While ripe with contradictions, Passailaigue's account contains an important acknowledgement. On the bottom of the report's second page, the captain confessed "that to the best of my knowledge about twenty negroes were killed by soldiers for refusing to halt when so ordered or for resisting arrest." Justifying the violence, he added, "had the troops not been sent to quell the disorder, the negroes would have succeeded in carrying out their murderous plans [of massacring the white populace]."[20]

Passailaigue's confirmation that the soldiers had in fact fired upon and killed blacks hiding in the woods appears nowhere in Jenks's report. Instead of a census of the captured blacks, or a casualty or fatality count, what appeared in the colonel's report was a cryptic sentence that makes little sense without the information provided by Captain Passailaigue. At the top of the fourth page of Jenks's report, he wrote, "The arrival of troops on the morning of October 2nd, put an end to the hopes of the negroes many of whom had been informed that the War Department was to send colored troops to protect them." Jenks made no clarification in regard to the sentence, and he offered no explanation as to why alleged rebellious black outlaws would have hoped that the War Department would rescue them. This is not the only perplexing statement in the commanding officer's report.[21]

On the third page of his report, the colonel discussed the investigation of the PFHUA, explaining that the "object[s] of this union were supposed to be better education and living conditions for the negroes and the absolute equality of the races." While benign and benevolent by modern standards, the goals of the union undermined the established agrarian social order and threatened to destabilize the fragile system of white supremacy that justified the economic exploitation of the black populace despite their numerical advantage in the county. Fear, intimidation, violence, and subjugation were as much tools of debt peonage as were the plow and the mule. Simply stated, the goal of the white landowner was to maintain his sharecroppers in a perpetual state of fear and indebtedness—too hungry not to work, too broke to leave the plantation, and too afraid to demand better wages and treatment.

For the plantation owner, the returning black veterans were especially dangerous men, empowered by their belief that they were owed respect and better treatment. Jenks identified the black veteran as a significant feature of the alleged "uprising," explaining that "among the plotters were several ex colored soldiers." While the white veteran, in the form of the American Legion member, could be called upon when the community was in peril, the black veteran was a threat and someone to be feared.[22]

The Black Veteran and Consequences of the Massacre

Men like Frank Moore and Ed Ware joined the PFHUA after leaving the military. They envisioned better lives for themselves and their families, and were convinced that if paid fair wages, they could purchase land and determine their own destinies. The black veterans were blamed for the violence and, in the instance of Moore, were accused of training the non-veterans in the union, preparing them for an impending revolution.[23]

On October 8 and 9, 1919, American Legion delegates from around the state gathered at the Marion Hotel in Little Rock for the organization's first annual convention. Governor Brough gave the opening address before granting the podium to the event's master of ceremonies, Chaplin John W. Inzer, Southern Field Representative for the American Legion of Mobile, Alabama. In his speech, Inzer "espoused three core ideals: the evils of Bolshevism, the threat of radicalism in America, and the maintenance of one-hundred-percent Americanism." On the following day, J. G. Lyford of Helena's Post 41 engaged in a heated debate on the floor of the convention. Undoubtedly influenced by the events of Elaine, Lyford led a campaign protesting "the formation of separate negro [American Legion] posts, citing Phillips County with two-thirds of the veteran population comprising negro veterans." Later that afternoon, the convention showed that a majority of its membership shared Lyford's fear of black veterans when it adopted a resolution "limiting posts to white veterans." Lyford and the members of American Legion Post 41 were honored as heroes, and the violence committed by whites during the massacre was excused. What remained radical in the minds of many white Arkansans were the views of equality and pleas for fair treatment embraced by the PFHUA, as well as notions that somehow black citizenship could be equated to that of white Americans.[24]

The members of the PFHUA paid a high price for their aspirations. With a mob crying for their blood rallying outside of the courthouse, the leaders of the PFHUA (Ed Coleman, Frank Moore, Ed Ware, Joseph Fox, Joseph Knox, Albert Giles, Alfred Banks Jr., John Martin, Paul Hall, William Wordlaw, and Frank and Ed Hicks) were sentenced to death in the state's electric chair. The fear of a potential insurrection at the hands of black soldiers lingered in the minds of white veterans who had violently put down the PFHUA. In the wake of the massacre, not a single white man was called to answer for the atrocities that occurred. There were no known attempts on the part of local, state, or federal governments to identify those killed, and by January 1920, the members of American Legion Post 41 were volunteering their services as a posse to put down another alleged "race riot" sixty miles from Elaine in Dumas, Arkansas.[25]

The black sharecroppers of Phillips County responded to the events of the Elaine Massacre in two ways: those who believed that the violence was too much to bear gathered their belongings and left, abandoning their claims to cotton to spare their lives; those who stayed remained quiet and returned to their work in the cotton fields and the cycle of exploitation inherent to sharecropping. The *Topeka Plaindealer* wrote of the former, saying, "There were in the neighborhood of 200 colored people who arrived in the city [Topeka, Kansas] from the immediate vicinity of Elaine, Winchester, and other farming communities in Arkansas."[26] Likely betting that they would fare better in Kansas—the state that had provided sanctuary to Robert L. Hill, founder of the PFHUA—some sharecroppers and their families gambled that Topeka would be more welcoming than anywhere in Arkansas.[27]

In the wake of the massacre, the leading businessmen of the neighboring agrarian community of Dermott stated their case in support of mob violence, writing, "Mob rule will never be checked by such acts as that of Governor [Henry J.] Allen [of Kansas] in the Hill Case. By his act, he has kindled a smoldering fire in the breasts of many southern men, that is liable to burst forth in one awful conflagration one of these days. In his refusal to grant this requisition [an extradition order requesting the return of Hill to Arkansas to stand trial], he has done not only Law and Order an irreparable injustice, but also the negroes of the South. The mothers, fathers, wives and children who have been made to suffer because of the atrocious crimes perpetrated by Hill, may forget Hill, but the memory of this act of Governor Allen is imprinted indelibly upon the minds of the southern people."[28] Dermott's business leaders acknowledged that innocents were "made to suffer" during the massacre, but they placed the blame for their suffering entirely on Hill. The PFHUA leader was not present at Hoop Spur shooting, yet he was accused of having committed "atrocious" unmentioned crimes. While keenly aware that Hill had broken some unspoken law, the wealthy businessmen gave no mention of the suffering meted out by the soldiers and white veterans in the mobs and posses.

There are few questions in regard to the identities of the white men killed as a result of the incident at Hoop Spur or the days of violence that followed. However, the identities of blacks slain during the massacre were not recorded by local newspapers, law enforcement, the military, or federal authorities investigating the altercation. While Dunaway provided a total of 856 blacks killed, he made no effort to list the deceased by name or to provide any identifiable details in regard to those individuals. Dunaway's total of the dead far exceeds all other estimates of the massacre. Chief Sheriff's Deputy A. F. James of Phillips County was a member of the posse that pursued PFHUA members following the shooting at Hoop Spur. James estimated the number of sharecroppers killed during the massacre at between fifty and one hundred, while Robert Whitaker, author of *On the Laps of Gods*, maintained that as many as 237 were blacks were killed.[29]

Despite these body counts, not a single grave site's location is known nor has a body been recovered that belongs to a black victim. The recovery of bodies or the discovery of a mass grave have the potential of resolving the debate as to who killed more sharecroppers, the mobs or the military. The discovery of remains could also indicate the weapons used by the assailants and the level of brutality that the victims were subjected to before their deaths. A mass burial site would indicate a high level of coordination and organization on the part of local officials or federal troops in Phillips County. A vast amount of manpower would have been required to collect hundreds of bodies scattered throughout the county, dig the grave(s), and fill and cover the site(s). Another lingering question in regards to the potential of a mass grave site is the lack of documents discussing the disposal of remains. How could officials have kept the collection of bodies and the location of grave sites a secret? Could such an undertaking have been completed without a single written reference?

While existing sources offer few answers and little consensus as to the participation of soldiers and veterans in the Elaine Massacre, historian Grif Stockley proposed a new direction to which future research should be directed to resolve perplexing problems dealing with the event. Noting that all of the existing sources cited in texts had come from members of the white community, Stockley put forth for consideration the idea that new sources should be collected from members of the black community whose family members survived the massacre. While these sources would likely be oral narratives given by the children or grandchildren of survivors, they provide a starting place for new archival research and give voice to a community that by virtue of their exploitation were kept silent.[30]

On November 16, 2018, in a small ceremony held in Helena, a group of local and state officials, members of the community, and distant relatives of Pvt. Leroy Johnston gathered for the posthumous awarding of service medals earned by the soldier during his service in World War I. Private Johnston, a member of the famed Harlem Hellfighters and the only known black veteran killed at the massacre, was one of four brothers abducted by a posse and brutally murdered; their bodies were left on the side of a road for their mother to find. The commemoration of Johnston followed the directive given by Stockley that future research of the massacre not follow the lives of well-known white men of Phillips County but instead should be directed toward the lives of the victims.[31] In closing, this author hopes that others will give voice to the voiceless and remember once again the forgotten.

APPENDIX I

Richard L. Kitchens American Legion Post 41— List of Members Who Served in World War I

Adkins, Dave
Aitken, Geo. L.
Bacharach, E. M.
Barnes, A. T.
Bealer, Harry L.
Beall, Allein, Jr.
Benthall, O. L.
Bernard, A. R.
Bickerstaff, Herman
Blair, Dave
Bowers, Chas. R.
Bradshaw, Joe
Brooks, R. L.
Broom, K. C.
Brown, Murphy
Burks, E. L.
Butts, J. B.
Byerley, E. F.
Campau, Harry
Carville, E. B.
Cavein, Milton
Chavey, W. C.
Clancy, Frank D.
Cohn, Millard
Connolly, Tom
Coolidge, W. A.
Cox, Aris W.
Crisp, Jesse
Dalzell, Frank
Danzinger, H. J.

Davidson, Abe
De Camp, E. C.
Dipola, Raymond
Dunavin, Roy
Dunnington, H. C.
Dwyer, J. H.
Edwards, Virgil
Erwin, Curtis O.
Etoch, Mike
Faulkner, A. D.
Faulkner, T. H.
Fielder, C. S.
Foreman, C. W.
Forte, C. S.
Gerlach, J. K.
Gist, Bogan
Gist, Warfield
Goldsmith, Abe
Goldsmith, M. W.
Goodwin, Jas.
Greenfield, Jack
Greer, C. F.
Gwin. W. T.
Hale, Roy
Hargraves, D. T.
Harris, John
Harthcock, A. G.
Hendricks, O. D.
Henley, H. H.
Hodge, Geo. L.

Hogue, J. H.
Hyde, V. N.
Hyman, John I.
Jacks, Eugene
Jacks, T. H.
Jackson, Jas. J.
Jeffett, W. F.
Jones, L. H.
Kahn, Mosler
Keeshan, Pat
Kelly, Thad R.
Kesl, Oldrich
Keys, W. H.
Krickel, Harris
Lambert, J. B.
Linson, Chas.
Lucy, B. H.
Lucy, W. H.
Lyford, C. C.
Mabie, L. E.
Madonia, Angelo
Mallory, Ned
Mangum, M. K.
Mayer, C. E.
McDaniel, Finis
McDonald, Jack
McKelvey, R. E.
Messina, John
Meyers, David
Miles, E. G.

Miller, K. T.	Porter, T. P.	Stratton D.D.
Moody, L. W.	Pounds, Roy	Strotherm, F. M.
Moody, W. C.	Purvis, Chas.	Syler, F. L.
Moore, John I.	Raff, Alfred	Tanner, W. B.
Nance, Roy L.	Ralston, J. Y.	Tappan, Moore
Naylor, A. B.	Rawes, R. C.	Thomason, Victor
Newkirk, J.R.	Rawlings, H. P.	Thornton, James C.
Newkirk, R. L.	Ray, Jas. R.	Tillman, Clyde
Nick, Tom	Ruane, Ellis	Toney, Edgar
Notto, L.	Sanders, A. C.	Vineyear, Geo.
Otis, Henry	Sheffield, John	Vondermau, Malcolm
Otis, R. M.	Snyder, Albert	Wahl, J. F.
Papa, Joe	Solomon, Alvin	Wall, J. C.
Papa, Sam	Solomon, Philip	Ward, C. H.
Parker, Verne	Solomon, Victor	Weirman, Geo.
Phillips, W. T.	Spratt, B. B.	Wooten, T. E.
Plumlee, Sam	Stingley, F. J.	

Source: List was compiled by the Post Historian, David Solomon of Richard L. Kitchens American Legion Post 41 on March 10, 2017.

APPENDIX II

Composition of Provisional Companies of "Elaine Massacre" Army Troops

PROVISIONAL COMPANY NUMBER	HOME UNIT	TROOP COMPOSITION
Company No. 1	4th Infantry	1 Captain, 3 Lieut., 75 enlisted
	3rd Ammunition Train	1 Lieut., 25 enlisted
Company No. 2	7th Infantry	1 Captain, 1 Lieut., 50 enlisted
	8th Machine Gun Battalion	1 Lieut., 10 enlisted
	9th Machine Gun Battalion	1 Lieut., 20 enlisted
	10th Field Artillery	1 Lieut., 20 enlisted
Company No. 3	30th Infantry	2 Lieut., 50 enlisted
	38th Infantry	2 Lieut., 50 enlisted
Company No. 4	18th Field Artillery	1 Captain, 2 Lieut., 70 enlisted
	78th Field Artillery	2 Lieut., 30 enlisted
Medical Detachment		5 Medical Officer, 15 enlisted

SOURCE: Advance Order from 1st Lieut. T.A. Breen, Headquarters Third Division, Camp Pike, dated October 1, 1919, File 370.6, Elaine, RG407, NARA

Vehicles Deployed with Troops:

Six Liberty Trucks • Two Motor Ambulances • Two Motorcycles with Sidecars

SOURCE: Report of Capt. Edward P. Passailaigue, Infantry, 3rd Ammunition Train to the Asst. Chief of Staff, 3rd Division, dated October 7, 1919, Military Intelligence Division—Negro Subversion, RG 165, NARA M1440.

7 Epidemic!

The Great Influenza Epidemic of 1918
and Its Legacy for Arkansas

THOMAS A. DEBLACK

In late January and early February 1918, a doctor in remote Haskell County, Kansas, began to see patients complaining of fever, body aches, headaches, and coughing. He had seen the symptoms before, and he correctly diagnosed the patients with influenza. But there was something different about this flu. It was "violent, rapid in its progress through the body, and sometimes lethal." Unlike most flus, this one did not conform to the traditional "U" curve, infecting the oldest and youngest most severely. Instead, it followed a "W" curve, attacking not only the extremes but those in the middle—healthy people of young and middle age.[1]

Soon the doctor was overwhelmed, and some of his patients began to die. Alarmed, he began to send reports to national public health officials about the outbreak. Schools in the county closed. Then in March, the disease disappeared as quickly as it had emerged. The schools reopened, and life returned to normal. The doctor remained concerned, but few outside the county paid any attention. Influenza was not then considered a "reportable" disease (one that the law required physicians to report).[2]

But in fact, what the Kansas doctor had diagnosed was the first strand of what would become a worldwide pandemic dubbed the "Spanish flu." The flu was not Spanish at all. In May 1918, the Spanish king, the prime

| DOI: https://doi.org/10.34053/christ2019.twah.7

minister, and the prime minister's entire cabinet all came down with the disease, and the country's newspapers—not hindered by the censorship that hampered the press in the warring nations of Europe—freely reported on it.[3] Thus the name "Spanish flu" was born. It quickly became apparent that there was no inoculation (no "flu shot"), no remedy, no medicine, and no cure. One historian of the disease noted, "Your best chance of survival was to be utterly selfish. Assuming that you had a place that you could call home, the optimal strategy was to stay there . . . not answer the door (especially to doctors), jealously guard your hoard of food and water, and ignore all pleas for help."[4]

Historians still argue over just where and how this flu originated. Both historian Alfred Crosby in his 2003 book *America's Forgotten Pandemic: The Influenza of 1918* and John Barry in his 2004 book *The Great Influenza: The Epic Story of the Deadliest Plague in History* accept the hypothesis that the disease originated in rural Kansas, where rural people worked and lived close to animals and consumed the meat. The virus most likely originated in swine or poultry and spread to humans.[5]

And, yet, the outbreak might have ended right there, as well. As John Barry points out, "As sparsely populated and isolated as Haskell [County] was, the virus infecting the county might well have died there, might have failed to spread to the outside world. That would be so, except for one thing: this was wartime."[6] Some 300 miles to the east of Haskell County was Camp Funston, an army training camp located on the grounds of Fort Riley just southwest of Manhattan, Kansas. In 1918, it was the second-largest army base in the country, holding on average about 56,000 trainees. Soldiers inducted from Haskell County trained there.[7]

On March 4, 1918, a camp cook reported to sick call with influenza-like symptoms. Within three weeks, more than 1,100 soldiers were admitted to the hospital with similar symptoms, and thousands more were treated at makeshift infirmaries around the base. Thirty-eight men died of influenza or accompanying pneumonia at the camp, a number that, Barry notes, was higher than normal, but not sufficiently so to draw attention. Some soldiers went home on leave and returned. Others continued to transfer in and out of the camp. Many traveled to other bases on crowded trains. Others sailed for France in crowded ships.[8]

Some of them undoubtedly ended up at another large base in Arkansas—Camp Pike. Located just north of Little Rock, Camp Pike, like Camp Funston, had been hastily constructed in 1917. At its peak, it held just over 52,000 men, making it easily the second-largest city

African American recruits line up for sick call at Camp Pike. *Courtesy of the Butler Center for Arkansas Studies, Central Arkansas Library System, Little Rock.*

in Arkansas, trailing only Little Rock's population of 58,000. The first recorded incidence of a soldier reporting to the base hospital with the flu took place on September 23, 1918. The hospital administrator was highly concerned. By this time, the War Department had reported 20,000 cases of the flu at bases throughout the country. Just five days later, 754 men at Camp Pike were sick with the disease. Before the month of September was out, some 7,600 cases of the flu were reported at the camp.[9]

On October 3, the camp commander issued an order for a partial quarantine and quickly expanded it to a complete quarantine, with no one allowed to enter or leave the base. It was too late. By that time, a thousand soldiers a day were falling ill with the flu. The base infirmary was quickly filled to overflowing, and some of the sick were quartered in barracks, often with soldiers who were still healthy. As historian Kim Scott noted, "A more effective method of insuring the spread of the disease could hardly be imagined."[10] And, of course, new recruits continued to arrive daily, further negating the effects of the quarantine.

Notices of deaths at the camp began to fill the Little Rock papers, spreading fear throughout the city. On October 13, Col. Charles Miller, the camp commandant, told Owens and Company undertakers in North Little Rock to stop releasing such information to the newspapers.[11] Scott noted, "The mortician was in no position to refuse the order: his firm held the contract for the post and had been assigned nine government embalmers just to keep up with the rush."[12]

Some twenty miles to the southeast of Camp Pike, near the small town of Lonoke, Eberts Field, an aviation training field, was also hard hit. Like Camp Pike, Eberts had been hastily built, with construction of seventy-two structures beginning in December 1917 and finishing in the spring of 1918. At its height, Eberts was home to approximately 2,500 men. When the flu outbreak struck the camp, the base hospital was quickly overrun. Hangars meant for aircraft were converted to hospitals and convalescent wards.[13]

Both the federal and state governments and the U.S. military responded slowly. Dr. Michael Osterholm, director of the Center for Infectious Disease Research and Policy at the University of Minnesota, wrote, "The U.S. government didn't want our own vulnerability to be known around the world."[14] But those on the ground knew the real story. "You ought to see this hospital tonight," wrote Francis Blake, one of the four members of the army's pneumonia commission at Camp Pike. "Every corridor and there are miles of them with a double row of cots and every ward nearly with an extra row down the middle with influenza patients and lots of barracks about the camp turned into emergency infirmaries and the Camp closed. . . . There is only death and destruction."[15]

Historians disagree on the exact number of persons contracting and/ or succumbing to the flu at Camp Pike and Eberts Field. Citing the Office of the Surgeon General's report, *The Medical Department of the United States Army in the World War* and the *Medical and Casualty Statistics*, as well as the November 1, 1918, edition of the *Arkansas Gazette*, Kim Scott wrote that a total of 7,642 soldiers contracted the flu at Camp Pike in September, and 105 of those died. In October, another 6,364 soldiers contracted the disease, and seventy-nine died, bringing the total for two months to 14,006 contracting the disease with 184 fatalities.[16] However, a researcher for the Arkansas National Guard Museum at Camp Robinson discovered a 1919 study, titled *Pneumonia Following Influenza (at Camp Pike, Ark.)*, which concluded that 13,892 men at Camp Pike fell victim to the flu or pneumonia resulting in 468 deaths at that camp alone.[17]

John Barry believes that Camp Pike played a huge role in the spread of the disease to Europe. Noting that nearly 40% of the two million American troops who arrived in France disembarked at Brest, France, Barry wrote, "The first outbreak of [the flu] with high mortality [in Brest] occurred in July, in a replacement detachment of American troops from Camp Pike, Arkansas."[18]

In retrospect, the early reaction to the disease seems puzzling. The Arkansas State Board of Health, created in 1913, not long before the outbreak, initially did little or nothing to respond to the outbreak. Scott noted, "Influenza was not among the twenty maladies listed by the board as being subject to reporting and quarantine by Arkansas doctors." By the time that problem was corrected, the epidemic was rapidly spreading through the state.[19]

On September 20 the *Arkansas Gazette* carried a story in which Dr. Jacob C. Geiger, the United States Public Health Service officer for Arkansas, said that the new influenza was "simple, plain old-fashioned la grippe." The pronouncement was strange given that the disease had claimed 265 lives in Boston in the two weeks since it first appeared in the city on September 7. As late as October 4, Geiger assured the *Arkansas Gazette*, "Situation still well in hand."[20]

By the time he made that statement, however, the cities of Little Rock and North Little Rock were reporting 506 cases of the flu. Located less than ten miles away from Camp Pike, those two cities received the full brunt of the epidemic. On October 5, the *Gazette* reported an additional 296 cases, but that same day Geiger told the paper, "The disease has reached its highest point here and the number of cases will begin to decline from now on." He concurred with the conclusion of the State Board of Health that a mandatory quarantine was not needed. "A general quarantine is both unwise and unnecessary," he told the *Gazette* on October 6. "Were such drastic measures necessary, the [United States] Public Health Service, which has the interests of the people always in mind, would have declared a quarantine before now." Two days later, with 1,800 cases being reported around the state, the Arkansas Board of Health did just that.[21]

The quarantine consisted of five points:

1) All children younger than eighteen were to be kept off the streets. Parents would be held accountable.
2) The "congregation" of people anywhere was forbidden. (This order closed schools, churches, and all public gatherings of people.)
3) It was strongly suggested that all people finish their business transactions and return to their homes immediately. Farmers were told to go home and not enter town for the immediate future.
4) Only immediate family, preacher, and necessary pallbearers should attend funerals.

5) All doctors were to report cases of Spanish flu daily to the county health office.[22]

Though accurate figures are impossible to determine, it is clear that by October the disease had struck Little Rock in epidemic proportions. Citing the records of the United States Surgeon General, Scott wrote, "Out of a population of approximately 58,000, Little Rock reported 9,813 cases of influenza during the month of October alone; 351 of the sufferers died." Scott puts the situation in central Arkansas in some perspective by pointing out that "one out of every four people reported sick during September and October . . . ; every man, woman, and child must have either had influenza themselves or at least knew someone who did."[23]

By the end of the month, the epidemic began to taper off in the capital city, and the quarantine rules began to be gradually lifted. On October 25, the State Board of Health announced that local boards would be permitted to authorize the resumption of church services, and colleges were granted permission to resume classes as conditions indicated. Public schools were to remain closed, and children under eighteen were restricted to their homes. The following day, it was announced that stores in the capital city were allowed again to remain open on Saturday evenings, and pool halls were permitted to reopen, albeit "for players only." On November 4, the quarantine for Pulaski County was fully ended.[24]

However, the end of the quarantine in Pulaski County did not signal the end of the epidemic in the state. In Fort Smith, the state's second-largest city with a 1918 population of more than 25,000, the epidemic was not declining in late October. A report from the city dated October 23 stated, "Eighty-four new cases of Spanish influenza were reported here today, a *marked increase* over the past several days, and 23 more than reported yesterday (emphasis added). From indications, the epidemic is not abating. There were two deaths today."[25]

The state's institutions of higher learning were also impacted by the outbreak. Classes at the University of Arkansas in Fayetteville, which generally started in mid-September, were delayed for about a month, beginning in late October. Many students were already on campus, including future Arkansas congressman Brooks Hays, who was returning to campus for his junior year. He found the campus, in Scott's words, "transformed into a military enclave." Scott continued:

Surrounding the YMCA hut just west of the Arkansas Avenue-Dickson Street intersection in the southeast corner of the campus, a small city of frame barracks had sprung up to house the newly formed Student Army Training Corps (SATC). Uniformed guards positioned at the campus main gate barred anyone from entering unless they had a pass signed by Major George Martin, the university commandant who shared administrative power with [university] president John C. Futrall.[26]

The quarantine did not sit well with Hays's girlfriend (and future wife) Marion Prather, who was making plans to come to Fayetteville by train to visit him. "If you're in quarantine, can't you meet the train?," she wrote in a letter date October 3, 1918. "I don't want you to be in quarantine."[27]

Hays would soon get out of quarantine, but not in the way that he or his girlfriend had hoped. Within days, he and a significant number of his 600 fellow students were in the school infirmary with severe cases of the flu. Soon the infirmary was filled, and sick soldiers were forced to remain in the barracks. Eventually about half of the contingent of 600 soldiers at the university came down with the disease. An urgent appeal went out to the local community for pillows and bedsheets and later for fifty women "with or without medical training" to help nurse the sick. Hays made a speedy recovery, but six of his comrades died.[28]

Other colleges were also impacted. In early October, the Second District Agricultural School in Russellville (today's Arkansas Tech University) as well as the town's public schools were suspended indefinitely by order of the State Board of Health. The Russellville *Courier* reported on October 10, "The epidemic of Spanish flu which has been sweeping the country the past few weeks has reached Russellville. . . . There are hundreds of cases in Russellville, and there were 62 absentees from high school alone Monday."[29]

In Magnolia, the Third District Agricultural School (today's Southern Arkansas University) was also impacted. School president Elbert Austin canceled classes and some students went home, leaving only about forty-five on campus. Still, almost everyone remaining on campus—students, faculty, administrators, and staff—were stricken. With the adults ill, the few students who managed to avoid the illness were left to fend for themselves. Amazingly, given the widespread nature of the epidemic, there were no fatalities on campus.[30]

Galloway Women's College in Searcy shut down for two weeks in early October. It resumed classes on October 23, but the school remained under quarantine and local students were not allowed to attend. Approximately 100 students contracted the disease, but none were reported to be seriously ill. The *Gazette* reported, "Owing to the shortage of nurses, President J. M. Williams and Mrs. Williams, with members of the faculty, worked day and night." The paper reported, "While there has been a large number of cases in Searcy, the majority were in a very light form, and there have been only two deaths in town from the malady."[31]

In Arkadelphia, six deaths had been reported by the middle of October, but the *Arkansas Democrat* reported on October 21, "Work at Ouachita and Henderson-Brown colleges has not been retarded a single day by the flu although a large per cent of the students have had their case, most of which were light. One serious case has been reported at each college but these are on the road to recovery." Still, the colleges were under quarantine, with dormitory students restricted to campus. The Student Army Training Center (SATC) corps at both schools were also under quarantine, and those who became ill were taken to a special hospital.[32]

The experiences at Conway, another multi-college town, demonstrated the capricious nature of the epidemic. The establishment of an SATC unit on campus forced Hendrix College to postpone its opening until October 3. A record 415 students enrolled for classes, but the semester had barely gotten underway when the flu hit both the town and the Hendrix campus hard. On October 8 Conway was put under quarantine, closing all public schools and the town's three colleges. By that time, there were more than 200 cases of the flu at Hendrix. As the outbreak appeared to subside, Hendrix's president Dr. John Hugh Reynolds announced that the school would reopen on October 15. But on October 14, SATC member Tabor Bevins of Booneville died of complications of the flu. The following day, another SATC soldier, James L. Craddock of England, died. The deaths caused Reynolds to postpone the reopening to October 29.[33]

While the outbreak ravaged Hendrix, the campus of the Arkansas State Normal School (today's University of Central Arkansas) and Central College (today's Central Baptist College) remained largely free from the disease, though both closed their campuses during the quarantine that was in effect from October 8 to November 4. On October 19 both the State Normal School and Central College reported that they had no cases of the flu. By December a few cases had appeared at the Normal School, and

Men on the "Service" Roll, who Lost
Their Lives

James A. Dowdy   Robert W. Young   William Arthur McGuire

Tabor Bevins   J. Watson Reynolds   James L. Craddock

Men on the Hendrix College Service Roll who lost their lives in
World War I. Tabor Bevins (bottom left) and James L. Craddock
(bottom right) were both victims of the Spanish flu outbreak on
the Hendrix campus in 1918. *From* The Troubadour, *Hendrix
College, 1918, used with permission of the Hendrix College Archives.*

officials there gave permission to all students to withdraw until after the
Christmas holiday. However, only about forty students took the school up
on its offer, and classes continued without interruption.[34]

Fayetteville also had good news to report. The October 23 edition of
the *Fayetteville Daily Democrat* ran a headline that read, "Flu Epidemic
at U of A Nearly Eradicated." The accompanying article noted, "Of
the three hundred and some odd men who have been ill at university
barracks, base hospital, and infirmary, all have been discharged except 45,

and all but five of those are now on solid food and considered convalescent. None of the five is in a dangerous condition."[35]

While the state's larger cities and college towns provide interesting case studies, they were not typical of Arkansas as a whole. In 1918 the state remained almost 80 percent rural, defined not only as people living on a farm but also in small towns. At Nashville in southwestern Arkansas (population approximately 2,500), the public schools opened as normal in late September. A large Liberty Loan rally was planned for Saturday, October 12. On October 9, a headline in the *Nashville News* read, "Big Crowd Will Hear Sousa Band. City's Largest Crowd Expected Saturday." It urged people from all parts of Howard County to attend the concert, with proceeds to go to the war effort. But the concert never took place. A special from Nashville to the *Gazette* dated October 14, read, "On account of the statewide quarantine against the assembling of crowds, the Liberty Loan rally, which was to have been held here Saturday, was called off." It went on to note, "Up to date no cases of Spanish influenza have been reported here." A second article noted, "No quarantine has been made on the schools, churches and theaters here to date, as no cases of Spanish influenza have been reported in this community."[36]

That changed quickly. A headline in the October 16 issue of the *Nashville News* read, "Quarantine Placed on County." The accompanying article noted, "Dr. D.A. Hutchinson, the Howard County Health Officer, announces that all of Howard County is being placed under official quarantine to halt the spread of the Spanish flu." A subsequent edition on October 23 restated the quarantine rules and announced that Lt. R. B. Magee, scientific assistant of the United States Public Health Service, had arrived to aid Dr. Hutchinson in enforcing the quarantine. Magee warned all violators, including doctors, that failures to report cases of the flu were subject to punishment by federal authorities. The article concluded by noting that the disease was spreading rapidly and new cases were developing daily.[37]

The report from October 14 that there were no cases of Spanish flu in the county and the subsequent report from October 16 that the disease was spreading rapidly are hard to reconcile. Was the local paper or the state government suppressing news about the flu, or did it just break out incredibly suddenly? It is impossible to say with any certainty.

Anecdotal evidence makes it clear that the flu was present in Howard County and that it was deadly. Leo Puryear was just shy of his sixth birthday in October 1918 when his entire family—mother, father, five brothers and a sister—were stricken by the disease. Young Leo remembered that a neighboring family would bring food to his family, place it outside the house near the family mailbox, and then holler to alert the family that food was there; they wanted to make sure that the Puryears did not come out until they had left. All the Puryears survived, but Leo's son, Frank Puryear, remembered that, later in his life, his father would point out a nearby house and relate the story of five children in one family who died of the disease.[38]

Forty miles to the south of Nashville, the city of Texarkana, with a population of about 8,000, was also hard hit, and the fatalities there indicated clearly that factors such as wealth, status, youth, or spiritual leadership were no protection against the disease. In its October 24 edition, the *Gazette* reported, "Several deaths from pneumonia, developing out of the Spanish influenza, have occurred in Texarkana within the last 24 hours. Among this number are J.D. Williams, former treasurer of Miller county, who died last night, aged forty. He was one of the well-known cotton planters of the county, owning a large Red River plantation near Index, 10 miles north of here. The Rev. E.D. Meredith, aged 66, a pioneer Baptist minister of this section, died yesterday afternoon at his home on Rose Hill." Three other victims listed in the article were in their twenties.[39]

A dispatch to the *Gazette* from Fordyce in south-central Arkansas dated October 14 read, "The schools are closed, no church services will be held, and no public gathering will be allowed until the influenza epidemic is checked. Dr. H.H. Atkinson has been sick for several days and the other doctors have all the work they can attend to. Thus far only one death has been reported." A dispatch from Crossett noted, "A total of 125 cases of influenza have been reported here. Some of the cases are very serious."[40]

A correspondent from Hardy in the northern part of the state wrote to the *Gazette* on October 24, "On account of the influenza the meeting of the Tri-County Teachers' Association, consisting of the teachers of Sharp, Lawrence, and Randolph Counties, which was scheduled to meet at Williford October 25 and 26, has been postponed."[41]

Reports from around the state indicated that much of Arkansas was suffering from the epidemic:

> Coal Hill—The influenza situation here is improving, only 500 cases remaining. The physicians are badly overtaxed. The school and theater have been closed.

Calico Rock—Because of the influenza situation the Calico Rock fair has been postponed.

Piggott—On account of the influenza, Judge Dudly has notified the jurors not to appear Monday, the day for convening the civil division of the court.

Guion—The Spanish "flu" has a grip on this place, there being approximately 50 cases in the town.[42]

Some reports from around the country suggested that African Americans were less affected by the flu than whites. "As far as the 'Flu' is concerned the whites have the whole big show to themselves," J. Franklin Johnson wrote to the *Baltimore Afro-American*.[43] However, reports from around the state suggest that this may not have been the case in Arkansas. A dispatch from England, Arkansas, noted, "Up to Tuesday deaths from Spanish 'flu' have been 48, 13 white and 35 negroes. Local physicians say the epidemic among negroes is increasing."[44] A correspondent from McCaskill reported, "The flu is getting better around this place, but there have been several deaths among negroes." A white resident of Ozan wrote to the *Washington Telegraph*, "Our folks have not taken the 'flu' yet, although our colored man, Robert Muldrow, and all his folks have it."[45]

In much of the state, particularly the more populated areas, the epidemic had largely subsided by mid-November. But in the southern counties and in the more remote areas it was still raging. In Pine Bluff, November proved to be a particularly devastating month. In the week between November 20 and November 27, a "second wave" of the disease hit the city, with 440 new cases reported in a population of slightly less than 20,000, although these cases tended to be milder in nature than earlier incarnations.[46] On December 15, the *Pine Bluff Graphic* announced, "The usual [Elks] Christmas tree for poorer children of the city will not be had this year on account of the 'flu' situation." It also reported, "There will be no church services today, according to an announcement by Dr. F. C. Rowell. The 'flu' situation is decidedly improved, but the ban will not be lifted for several days."[47] Camden did not lift its quarantine until Christmas Day.[48]

By late November, the situation was so bad in parts of the state that Dr. Charles Willis Garrison, head of the Arkansas State Board of Health, warned that another statewide quarantine might be in the offing. Some have speculated that this November flare-up may have been a somewhat milder second (or maybe third) strain. A few unfortunate persons managed to be stricken twice, providing further evidence that the November

Dr. Charles Willis Garrison, head
of the Arkansas Department of
Health, contemplated a statewide
quarantine as the Spanish flu
spread in November 1918. *Courtesy
of the Historical Research Center,
University of Arkansas for Medical
Sciences.*

outbreak may have been a mutation of the initial virus. As Scott noted,
"Just when this second wave of the epidemic ended depended on where
in Arkansas you lived." A soldier returning home to Gentry in far northwestern Arkansas on December 20 found that the epidemic had passed,
while a few miles away in Gravette, the situation was so bad that a new
quarantine was ordered.[49]

By the beginning of 1919, the epidemic had largely run its course
in the state. Officially, it had claimed over 7,000 lives, though that figure
is almost certainly low, perhaps dramatically so. Like many disasters,
the epidemic brought out the best in many people. All across the state,
doctors and nurses worked themselves to exhaustion, and in so doing
made themselves even more susceptible to the disease. Dr. Christopher
Columbus Gray of Independence County had so many patients that
his two eldest sons were made to be his chauffeurs. While making his
lengthy rounds from house to house, the overworked physician caught
what sleep he could in the back seat of his Maxwell while the boys piloted
the vehicle. Five doctors died in Fayetteville and Fort Smith alone.[50]

Exhaustion may have contributed to the absence of bedside manner in a doctor from Center, Arkansas, who told a flu sufferer he was treating, "This is my 25th case and I've lost the first 24!" In an ironic twist, even Dr. Geiger, who had consistently downplayed the severity of the epidemic, contracted the disease on October 14. Eight days later his wife died of it. She was thirty-two years old.[51]

Heroism and sacrifice were not limited to members of the medical community. Scores of others with little or no medical training also stepped forward to help, often at great personal risk. In his centennial history of Southern Arkansas University, James Willis noted, "When the [campus] cook became sick, a student, Carl McCollum, who had been the 'stove wood boy,' assumed responsibility for preparing meals. There was then no campus nurse. A sophomore, Bess Lowe, worked day and night caring for those with the flu. Miraculously, she never became sick."[52]

All around Arkansas, people from various walks of life tended to those stricken with the disease. When the epidemic hit Everton, a small community of fewer than 200 located just south of Harrison in Boone County, a local doctor asked thirty-eight-year-old Nina Byrom Stephenson to look after a family that had contracted the flu and had no one to take care of them. Despite being warned to "be selfish" and not risk exposure to the disease, this mother of six children ranging in age from six to eighteen agreed. Due in no small part to her unselfish efforts, all members of the family recovered. But Nina Stephenson contracted the disease and was confined to bed at her home.[53]

Stephenson's granddaughter, Nan Snow, remembered, "As Christmas drew near, she became steadily worse. Realizing the dire nature of her situation, she called her two youngest daughters—Faye, age 8, and Rua, age 6—to her bedside on Christmas Eve, 1918. She gave each of them a gold locket and gold chain, told them she loved them, hoped they would always be good girls, and to mind their Daddy." Nina Stephenson died on December 30. She was buried at Crossroads Cemetery near Harrison. Snow recalled, "Her family would forever remember watching in disbelief as a black buggy bearing her body made its way to the cemetery carrying yet another casualty of this deadly epidemic in Arkansas."[54]

While people like Nina Stephenson represented the best in human nature, the epidemic brought out less-than-noble motives as well. As in any disaster, there were those who hoped to profit from the disease. An ad in the October 1 issue of the *Arkansas Gazette* informed readers that by using Dr. Jones Catarrhal Oil, they could prevent "Spanish Influenza

Nina Byrom Stephenson volunteered to care for a flu-stricken family. The family survived, but she died of the flu on December 30, 1918. *Courtesy of Nan Snow.*

and Other Dangerous Colds, Catarrh, Etc." It contained "campher [*sic*], menthol, eucalyptus, etc." and came in twenty-five-cent and fifty-cent bottles. On December 3, the *Pine Bluff Graphic* printed the testimonial of Mrs. Mary Kisby, 533 Princeton Avenue, Spokane, Washington, who wrote: "Our little boy found relief in wonderful Foley's Honey and Tar. It surely cured me. I am 75 years old; had very bad cough from la grippe." The wonderful curative was for sale at Mann's Pharmacy.[55]

A dispatch to the *Arkansas Democrat* from October 22, headlined "New Cure for Flu," read, "Dr. George S. Kimball, who discovered the lignite fields underlying 50 square miles of Ouachita County many years ago, and who has spent the last 30 years experimenting with the coal and its products, declares that vapor from lignite oil is a cure for influenza. Dr. Kimball has treated a number of cases with splendid results. The oil is vaporized by heating over a lamp or on a stove, and boils easily at ordinary heat."[56]

Another large ad in the *Pine Bluff Graphic* promoted the benefits of

Goodbye Old "Flu"

We've Started to Taking
Brunson's Famous Prescription
"The Great Restorative"

Down in Louisiana where the "Flu" has been raging for several weeks, the people were in a terrible plight. Scores of people were dying and hundreds of others were in a dangerous condition. And then—

Someone discovered that a few people who were taking Brunson's Famous Prescription for general run-down condition had not caught the disease. That started others to taking it. It was soon learned that Brunson's Famous Prescription was an ideal preventive against infection from influenza.

Telegrams galore began pouring in to REINBERGER & COLLIER, of Pine Bluff, manufacturers of the medicine. They were swamped with orders. People who already had it recovered in many instances. Those who didn't kept well.

IT HAS BEEN THE SAME WAY IN PINE BLUFF, though on a smaller scale because the disease was not so prevalent here. Brunson's Famous Prescription has therefore achieved another triumph. Whether you have the "Flu" or not, if your health isn't what it should be, you need a bottle. Price $1.00 at all leading drug stores.

NEWT BYRD, well known local resident, took two bottles of Brunson's Famous Prescription and gained 10 pounds. He also escaped the "Flu." Didn't he get his money's worth?

HOW IS YOUR LIVER THESE DAYS? Inactive, sluggish livers make you easily susceptible to colds, malaria, chills and fever and loss of weight. For your livers sake try the remedy.

BRUNSON'S LIVER PILLS

A new product of the Reinberger & Collier laboratories. 25c a box. Leading druggists have them.

An ad for Brunson's Famous Prescription, sold as a preventative/curative for the Spanish flu. Pine Bluff Daily Graphic, *November 12, 1918.*

an Arkansas-based product that had performed wonders in the state's southern neighbor.

> Down in Louisiana where the "Flu" has been raging for several weeks, the people were in a terrible plight. Scores of people were dying and scores of others were in a dangerous condition. And

then—Someone discovered that a few people who were taking Brunson's Famous Prescription for general run-down condition had not caught the disease. That started others to taking it. It was soon learned that Brunson's Famous Prescription was an ideal preventive [*sic*] against infection from influenza.

The ad noted that telegrams had begun pouring in to Reinberger and Collier of Pine Bluff, manufacturers of the medicine. "People who already had it [the flu] recovered in many instances. Those who didn't kept well." It closed with the results obtained by "well-known local resident" Newt Byrd, who took two bottles of the miracle elixir and gained ten pounds while also escaping the flu. The ad asked, "Didn't he get his money's worth?" At $1 a bottle, it certainly must have seemed so.[57]

Not all the flu-related ads were for preventatives or curatives. One from E. B. and F. R. Bloom, "Hazard Experts," plaintively asked, "Has the 'flu' added increased burdens to your living expenses?" If so, the ad urged readers to "prepare for another emergency by letting us write you a Health and Accident Policy. The cost is low—the benefits great."[58]

Even real doctors were not immune to bad science. Dr. Albert J. Croft of Chicago wrote a paper read before the Chicago Medical Society, "Poison Gas in Air Cause of Flu Epidemic." In it, he "advanced the theory that the condition termed influenza is in reality a non-bacterial, non-contagious disease caused by inhalation of small amounts of depressing, highly irritating, high density gas present in the atmosphere, especially at night and when the air is surcharged with moisture, more particularly near the surface of the earth."[59] Those gases had been let loose during four years of war and could largely be attributed to the Germans, who were the first to make use of poison gas in the conflict."[60] While the theory fed into a widespread grievance against Germany as the major perpetrator of the war, an article in the *Dallas Morning News* dated December 8, 1918, concluded that Dr. Croft "does not seem to have affirmed the correctness of his theory" and noted that his explanation "will get a more tolerant reception from the nonscientific than the scientific mind."[61]

After the War

The wild inaccuracy of causal explanations and the almost total ineffectiveness of patent medicines notwithstanding, by 1919 the pandemic was largely over. Cases continued to be reported throughout that year and in some rural areas even until 1920 but at nowhere near the death rates of the fall of 1918.

Few events in human history have had such a dramatic worldwide impact as the Spanish flu pandemic of 1918. In her 2017 book titled *Pale Rider: The Spanish Flu of 1918 and How It Changed the World*, Laura Spinney wrote, "The flu resculpted human populations more radically than anything since the Black Death. It influenced the course of the First World War and, arguably, contributed to the second. It pushed India closer to independence, South Africa closer to apartheid, and Switzerland to the brink of civil war. It ushered in universal healthcare and alternative medicine, our love of fresh air and our passion for sport, and it was probably responsible, at least in part, for the obsession of twentieth-century artists with all the myriad ways in which the human body can fail."[62]

In a review of Spinney's book, Scottish physician Gavin Francis noted, "It is estimated that five hundred million people contracted the Spanish flu—a third of the global population in 1918—and that between fifty and a hundred million of them died. Asians were thirty times more likely to die than Europeans. The pandemic had some influence on the lives of everyone alive today. Donald Trump's grandfather Friedrich died from it in New York City. He was 49. His early death meant that his fortune passed to his son Fred, who used it to start a New York property empire."[63] Around the world, most people who survived the flu returned to their normal lives, albeit with an increased fear that another new disease or even an old disease might appear without warning at any moment.

The impact in Arkansas went far beyond the lives cut short by the disease. In her essay in Michael Polston and Guy Lancaster's book *To Can the Kaiser: Arkansas and the Great War*, Nancy Hendricks cited a 2007 study by Thomas Garrett, an economist for the Federal Reserve Bank of St. Louis, that gave evidence of the tremendous economic toll the flu inflicted. Quoting from an article in the October 19, 1918, issue of the *Arkansas Gazette*, the study noted:

> Merchants in Little Rock say their business has declined by 40 percent. Others estimate the decrease at 70 percent. The retail grocery business has been reduced by one-third. One department store, which has a business of $15,000 daily, is not doing more than half that. . . . Little Rock businesses are losing $10,000 a day on average. . . . The fact that males aged 18 to 40 were the

hardest hit by the influenza had serious economic consequences for the families that had lost their primary breadwinner.[64]

Hendricks also speculated that the flu may have impacted the election of November 1918 because "many voters were too sick or too afraid to vote." The resulting low voter turnout may have doomed to defeat the proposed new state constitution that included provisions for women's suffrage and prohibition. Other effects would take years to become apparent. Garrett's study found that babies born or in utero during the 1918 pandemic had "reduced educational attainment, higher rates of physical disability, and lower income" throughout the rest of their lives. Children of infected mothers were 15% less likely to graduate from high school.[65]

Arkansans would have to wait less than a decade for the next big disaster, the Great Flood of 1927, and then only two years more for the onset of the Great Depression. And, of course, new strains of the flu would reappear periodically. In 1957 it was the Asian flu, in 1968–1969 the Hong Kong flu, and in 2009 the swine flu. But none of those events and none of those flus would match the human toll wrought by the great epidemic of 1918.

The author wishes to thank the following people for their help in preparing this chapter: Frank Puryear of Nashville; Nan Snow of Little Rock; Jimmy Bryant of the University of Central Arkansas Archives at Torreyson Library, University of Central Arkansas, Conway; and Marcia Crossman of the Winfred D. Polk Archives for the Arkansas Conference of the United Methodist Church at the Olin C. Bailey Library, Hendrix College, Conway.

8 | World War I and Woman's Suffrage in Arkansas

BY JEANNIE M. WHAYNE

The decades-long struggle of suffragists, together with the sacrifices women made during the Great War, resulted in the weakening of opposition to suffrage, so much so that at least thirty-one belligerent countries in Europe—as well as the United States—enfranchised women either during the war or shortly thereafter.[1] Women throughout the war fronts in Europe made tremendous sacrifices and bore the brunt of horrific death tolls among a generation of young men. Although women in the United States did not experience the war's effects directly and endured a much smaller cost in terms of the loss of its young men, they contributed in many ways in the homefront effort to support the troops.

Once President Woodrow Wilson abandoned his earlier position of neutrality and called for a declaration of war on April 6, 1917, most of the American women who had adopted his earlier calls to remain neutral in thought as well as in deed flocked to the cause of saving the world for democracy. Although woman's suffrage associations nationwide continued to function, many suffragists in Arkansas and elsewhere began to divide their time between homefront activities and agitation for suffrage. Most were mindful, however, that in doing so they were establishing their credentials as full-fledged participants in the civic and political life of the country. Even when Alice Paul and other members

| DOI: https://doi.org/10.34053/christ2019.twah.8

of the National Woman's Party (NWP) continued to agitate for suffrage in very public ways and endured arrest and shocking treatment at the hands of authorities, it merely raised the profile of the women's suffrage campaign. President Wilson eventually pardoned the NWP women, and a congressional committee was established to consider the proposition of votes for women.[2]

Although the NWP founded an affiliate organization in Arkansas in 1916, most Arkansas women allied with Carrie Chapman Catt's National American Woman Suffrage Association (NAWSA). In fact, when the NWP picketed the White House during the Great War, some Arkansas suffragists "adopted a resolution condemning 'the actions of the Woman's Party leaders in their misguided picketing of the White House and in their determined efforts to harass the president at this, the most critical time in the history of the republic.'"[3] Catt and the NAWSA advocated securing the ballot on the state level, while Paul and the NWP agitated for a remedy at the federal level: an amendment to the United States Constitution. Arkansas suffragists, like those in other southern states, were traditionally adherents to local and state solutions, and only gradually came around to the federal approach. When they did, however, the state followed and became the twelfth state and the first southern state to ratify the Susan B. Anthony (Nineteenth) Amendment to the Constitution in July 1919. By that time, Arkansas suffragists had already accomplished a partial victory in their long struggle to secure the ballot. In February 1917, two months before the United States entered World War I, the state legislature voted to allow women to vote in the Arkansas primary elections. Governor Charles Brough, whose wife Anne was a suffragist, happily signed the measure and, in fact, traveled the state calling on women to register to vote. According to Freda Hogan, a socialist and labor activist in Sebastian County, the governor's remarks led sixty-seven women to register in that location alone.[4] Indeed, more than 40,000 women voted in the Arkansas primary election in May 1918.[5]

The outbreak of the Great War led women in Arkansas and other suffragists in the United States to step back from pursuing their suffrage agenda and turn their attention to supporting the war effort. This was not the first time that suffragists in the United States had put aside their own interests for a larger cause. American suffragists in the North during the antebellum period had struggled mightily to secure equal rights but had allowed their cause to be relegated to the larger struggle against slavery both before and during the Civil War. They were dis-

Dr. Anna Howard Shaw (left) and Carrie Chapman Catt were leaders in the national effort to afford women the right to vote. *Courtesy of the Library of Congress.*

appointed when they were not rewarded immediately after the war for their sacrifice. As Reconstruction politicians debated the issue of votes for black men, women's rights advocates struggled in vain to have women's rights written into the Fourteenth and Fifteenth Amendments. In fact, for the first time, enfranchisement was specifically designated as a "male" prerogative in the Constitution and this caused the woman suffrage advocates to two split into two camps. In one camp, Elizabeth Cady Stanton and Susan B. Anthony campaigned against ratification of both the Fourteenth and Fifteenth Amendments, while Lucy Stone, Julia Ward Howe, and Elizabeth Blackwell supported them. In 1869, the division became organizationally codified with the founding of Stanton/Anthony's National Woman Suffrage Association (NWSA) and Stone/Howe's American Woman Suffrage Association (AWSA).

This struggle between suffragists hardly registered in the South, however. Because the suffrage cause was so closely associated with abolitionism in the North, it was far from popular in the antebellum South. According to historian Stephanie McCurry, in fact, as the antislavery movement arose in the North, the southern defense of slavery in the 1830s became linked to the subordination of women and other dependents (such as slaves) within the household. Not until after the

Civil War did suffrage begin to surface in southern states like Arkansas. Suffrage first emerged in the contest over congressional Reconstruction in Arkansas in 1868, when Miles Ledford Langley, a Republican delegate to the constitutional convention that year, proposed the enfranchisement of women in the new Arkansas constitution, arguing that "men and women were created equal" and that a woman did not "differ from man in any particular that disqualified her from exercising the same political rights." He spoke specifically to the qualifications of his own wife, who was "as well qualified as himself to vote" and "in every way worthy of the confidence" that he wished to place in her. According to historian A. Elizabeth Taylor, his proposal was met with "hostility and ridicule." Echoing the sentiments of other opponents, one argued that the woman's sphere was in the home, and vesting voting privileges in women would lead to "revolutions in families." The measure was tabled.[6]

The unwillingness of delegates to the 1868 constitutional convention to give serious consideration to the woman suffrage cause in Arkansas reflected the point of view that national Republicans held on the issue and also showed the deep conservatism within the state even among the so-called radicals. Indeed, as the suffrage struggle gained momentum elsewhere in the country in the post–Civil War United States, it developed slowly in the South. However, in the last three decades of the nineteenth century, women in Arkansas and other southern states began to venture from the sphere assigned to them by joining the Woman's Christian Temperance Union (WCTU), arguing that since drunkenness had a detrimental effect upon the family, women were merely extending their sphere in an acceptable manner. By the 1880s, many of these women began to speak out about the issue of woman suffrage. In Eureka Springs, Eliza A. Dorman Fyler, a WCTU member, founded the Arkansas Woman's Suffrage Association in 1881.[7] Fyler had moved to Eureka Springs from Missouri and studied law. She began to practice in 1884, but she was not allowed to plead cases in court because of her gender. In that same year, she attended a woman suffrage association meeting in Washington DC, but she died in 1885 and her small organization died with her.[8]

The void Fyler's death left was filled in 1888 by Clara McDiarmid, a dedicated member of the WCTU, who founded the Arkansas Equal Suffrage Association in Little Rock and started publishing the *Woman's Chronicle*. McDiarmid was a native of Indiana who moved to Arkansas in 1866 to marry a Union officer who had commanded a black regiment during the Civil War. Both McDiarmid and her husband were unapologetic Republicans who brought a particular northern sensibility with them to Arkansas. Clara's outspokenness rankled many, but she found a receptive audience with certain women who, like her, gave talks at social meetings and introduced measures to allow women to vote in school, mayoral, and other such non-partisan elections. It appears they were having some influence and, with the Republican Party increasingly marginalized within the state, their appeal crossed party lines. In February 1889, the *Woman's Chronicle* lauded Susan B. Anthony's speaking engagements in Helena, Fort Smith, and Little Rock, and, significantly, reported that Governor James Eagle, a Democrat, introduced Anthony to a large and enthusiastic audience, manifesting "every evidence of approval although she advocated woman suffrage."[9] The suffrage struggle in Arkansas revealed in 1891 that it had departed far from its 1868 origins. During a session when poll tax and new election rules were proposed in order to disfranchise African Americans and poor whites, a woman suffrage measure was introduced in the Arkansas Senate by E. P. Hill "to confer the right of suffrage upon white women." In explicitly excluding black women, it was almost certainly unconstitutional. It secured a second reading but was then tabled. The abandonment of African American voting rights very nearly coincided with the unification of the two national suffrage associations, Stanton/Anthony's NWSA and Stone/Howe's AWSA, into the National American Woman Suffrage Association (NAWSA).[10]

McDiarmid continued to promote the woman suffrage cause until her death in 1899.[11] Her organization did not survive her, and advocacy for woman suffrage lost its public face as women activists devoted most of their attention to other causes, fighting for temperance in the state, establishing literary clubs, and promoting certain Progressive Era reforms such as education and public health. However, suffragist speakers visited Little Rock in the first decade of the twentieth century and events were held in conjunction with their appearances.[12] The suffrage cause was not forgotten.

The organizational hiatus ended in 1911, when Arkansas suffragists founded the Political Equality League in Little Rock, but they faced a formidable opponent: liquor interests. By this time, Arkansas suffragists had long been associated with the WCTU, and in 1910 the organization joined the Anti-Saloon League in promoting a statewide ban on alcohol. The ban failed to secure sufficient votes, but the liquor interests were not entirely satisfied with their victory and identified women—whether they were associated with the WCTU or not—as dangerous opponents of alcohol. Their potency as an enemy of woman suffrage manifested itself in 1911, when a woman suffrage constitutional amendment was introduced in the Arkansas legislature. It passed in the Senate but was defeated in the House, largely because of the concerted opposition of liquor interests. The origins of the woman suffrage bill are sketchy. According to historian Bernadette Cahill, some women representing themselves as members of an equal-suffrage society tried to meet (and maybe did meet) with Arkansas senator James P. Clarke in Washington that year. Cahill further suggests that the bill may have had its origins in the publicity accorded to the national struggle for woman suffrage. Women suffrage activists had engaged in speaking tours across the country and were attracting wide attention in the first decade of the twentieth century. Arkansas women, according to Cahill, were hardly likely to have been unaware of these activities and found a sympathetic reception among at least some progressives in the legislature. Nevertheless, the liquor interests defeated them in 1911. The Political Equality League, however, with Mary Fletcher of Little Rock at the helm, began a more concerted campaign to achieve its ends. These kinds of organizations spread to other towns in the state.[13]

While elite and middle-class women in Little Rock were pressing for the vote, Freda Hogan, the socialist editor of the *Huntington News* in Sebastian County, joined a suffrage association—possibly a local branch of the Political Equality League—and was serving as its secretary by 1912. While most Arkansas women advocated suffrage as an individual right and characterized their voting as an opportunity to influence government in ways that supported home and family, Hogan promoted it as a means to challenge American capitalism itself. The daughter of a Socialist Party leader with a national profile, she lived in southern Sebastian County and witnessed a level of class exploitation and poverty that radicalized her. She believed that working women "were more ruthlessly exploited than men by their employers" and that woman's suffrage would provide them with some means of addressing this inequality. As historian Michael Pierce suggests, she also believed that "women—whose maternal instincts make them the natural enemy of economic exploitation—would use the franchise to challenge the economic system from which all forms of exploitation sprang." In other words, "For Freda Hogan, the fight for women's suffrage became the main front in the larger battle for a more just economic system." In addition to joining the local suffrage

Sebastian County newspaper editor Freda Hogan (right, pictured with Ida Callery) saw women's suffrage as a means of combating capitalism. *Picture Collection No. 3710, Special Collections, University of Arkansas Libraries.*

association, Hogan also joined the Socialist Party of America's Women's National Committee (WNC) in 1914. When she joined that committee, it had been preoccupied with educational services and produced literature of that nature. Along with three other women, however, Freda advocated for an expansion of their activities "in anticipation of the extension of the vote" to women. They were successful in turning the attention of the committee in that direction and "the WNC called for special organizers and the publication of a newspaper dedicated to women's issues. If the party failed to act, the committee warned, the two major parties would organize women and use their votes to strengthen its grip over the nation's political system." The WNC's new agenda was too much for the Socialist Party's leadership to accept. According to Pierce, "For them, discrimination against women arose out of class exploitation, and the campaign for women's suffrage and the mobilization of women were so integral to the party's existence that they should not be segregated as women's work." Whether Hogan and her cohort knew it, this willingness to submerge the interests of women to the larger cause echoed that of Republican proponents of the Fourteenth and Fifteenth Amendments decades earlier. Ultimately, the Socialist Party refused to launch the educational campaign that Freda and her friends sought.[14]

In voicing an anti-capitalist rationale, Freda Hogan was a minority voice among woman suffrage advocates in Arkansas, and it is understand-able that the focus of most scholars on the topic in the state has remained on the middle-class and elite white women. Even as Hogan became embroiled in the controversy within the WNC, in 1914 the Political Equality League held a convention and, along with other smaller suffrage organizations, reorganized as the Arkansas Woman Suffrage Association (AWSA)[15] with an explicit goal of securing a state constitutional amend-ment. They continued to position themselves as representing the women's voice on issues of the family and did not articulate anything like a critique of capitalism. They remained dedicated to a state rather than a federal solution, affiliated with NAWSA, and pursued their conservative strat-egy of securing individual state constitutional amendments in favor of suffrage.[16] In conjunction with a suffrage march in Little Rock, members of the AWSA, according to Cahill "persuaded business owners on Main Street to decorate their stores in honor of the event and a procession went from the rally at the Old State House to the celebratory luncheon at the Capital Hotel."[17]

In May 1915, the Arkansas Federation of Women's Clubs, which heretofore had refrained from association with suffrage, endorsed the cause without a dissenting voice at its annual meeting in Fayetteville.[18] In a speech that connected women's activism in Arkansas to World War I, Mrs. Max Lane, president of the resolutions committee, declared that just as the Germans had a custom of toasting "Der Tag" (This Day) "when they would annihilate their enemies" so too the federation was assem-bling in Fayetteville to have "their day" on a range of issues, including woman suffrage. Addressing the men in the audience, who included the president of the University of Arkansas, "in whimsical vein," Mrs. Lane said, "Please, kind sirs, give us a try at this voting business." According to Lessie Stringfellow Read, a member of the federation and writer for the local newspaper, one of the men present was heard to say, "By Jove, you couldn't refuse a magnificent woman like that anything, could you!"[19] In adopting a "whimsical" tone and addressing herself to "kind sirs," Lane had couched her appeal in a deferential manner and had successfully made her pitch to the male members of the audience.

As the momentum for suffrage grew, the suffrage amendment was again presented to the Arkansas legislature. Minnie Rutherford, a mem-ber of the AWSA, spoke to the House hearing committee, and Florence Brown Cotnam, a former president of the Political Equality League and secretary-treasurer of the new organization, spoke to the House

Florence Brown Cotnam was a leader in Arkansas's efforts to give women the right to vote. *Picture Collection, Number 3607, Special Collections, University of Arkansas Libraries, Fayetteville.*

itself. Although the substance of these addresses is unknown, it can be assumed that it conformed to the deferential tone Lane had adopted, and that Rutherford and Cotnam attempted to assure legislators that they were respectable ladies who would merely seek to represent the interests of women and families. As Arkansas was in the midst of a period of progressive reform that included aid to education and public health, the suffragists appealed to legislators who could be counted upon to be sympathetic to at least some of the goals of AWSA. In the end, the amendment passed but was undone by unfortunate circumstances: Three other unrelated amendments also passed, and according to Arkansas law, only three amendments to the state constitution could be presented to voters in one year. The people of Arkansas had no opportunity in 1915, therefore, to vote on the woman suffrage amendment.[20]

In 1916, the leaders of both national woman suffrage organizations came to Arkansas, but while one found a ready audience, the other did not. Carrie Chapman Catt of the NAWSA received a warm welcome. She was met at the railroad station by enthusiastic suffrage supporters, and "eighteen automobiles decorated with suffrage emblems paraded the streets for a half hour" after her arrival. Alice Paul of the National Woman's Party received a less-than-enthusiastic welcome but was listened to "politely" when she spoke at the Marion Hotel. It was clear that her advocacy of a federal amendment did not appeal to southern women generally. Despite the differing treatment of Catt and Paul, the distance between the two national organizations had narrowed. Carrie Chapman Catt had come to believe by 1916 that the state-by-state approach had gone about as far as it could go. Meanwhile, the Arkansas chapter—and those of other southern states—remained wedded to the state solution. Catt was careful to allow maneuvering room for herself and the organization by pursuing a two-pronged approach: She redirected the national organization to pursue a federal amendment while at the same time sanctioning continued work toward state-based efforts. This kept the Arkansas AWSA loyal to Catt and the NAWSA.[21]

Although most Arkansas women did not support the goals or the tactics of the NWP, there is some evidence that among those who supported them was a prominent Little Rock matron, Adolphine Fletcher Terry, a sister to suffragist advocate Mary Fletcher. Terry was a member of the AWSA but, according to Bernadette Cahill, Terry "presided over a meeting of the Congressional Union (CU)," the mother organization of the NWP, in Little Rock in 1916. The meeting coincided with Alice Paul's visit to the state, and it may have been the same one that received the tepid welcome mentioned above. Again, members of Arkansas AWSA attended and were polite but restrained in their response to her remarks. While her Little Rock cohort was cool to the NWP, Adolphine Fletcher Terry served on the "National Advisory Board of the [Congressional] Union and [as] an ex-officio member of the Executive committee for Arkansas." Her photograph appears in the NWP's archives, and in her memoirs, written many years later, she recollected fondly about how "we acted like complete hellions to get the vote. We of the 'lady' class had always been on a pedestal . . . beauteous womanhood, all that kind of junk." Speaking almost certainly to the NWP's silent sentinels who began activities in January 1917, Terry declared, "We changed that attitude when we tied ourselves to telephone poles and did unseemly and unladylike things to attract attention to our cause." Terry was probably using the royal "we" here, indicating sympathy with the NWP rather than participation with them in their efforts. As she indicates in her memoir, Terry found it necessary to refrain from public activities during the Great War because of anti-German sentiment (she was of German descent). In

Arkansas suffragist Adolphine Fletcher Terry curtailed her activities during World War I because of anti-German sentiment in the state. *Courtesy of the Butler Center for Arkansas Studies, Central Arkansas Library System, Little Rock.*

any case, acting like "hellions" was hardly the kind of behavior condoned by the women of Arkansas's AWSA, and Terry was a prominent and respected member of the Little Rock community who also maintained her membership in the AWSA.[22]

Regardless of their affiliations with national organizations, the sentiment for woman suffrage was growing in the state. Indeed, by 1917, on the eve of America's entry into the Great War, the momentum for women's suffrage had reached a critical point. Having failed to secure a state constitutional amendment, Arkansas suffragists took a new course of action. They sought passage of a bill—not an amendment to the state's constitution this time—allowing them to vote in the state's primary elections. Two months before the United States entered World War I, state Representative John A. Riggs of Hot Springs introduced the woman's suffrage primary bill on February 7. Although the outcome was initially in doubt, it easily passed in the House (54–27) as anticipated. It passed in the Senate by the narrowest of margins but only because two of its most dedicated opponents had been arrested for "boodling"—bribe taking—(17–15) and were absent when the vote was taken. Once the governor signed it, Arkansas became the first southern state and the first non-suffrage state in the Union to allow women the right to vote in the primary elections.[23] While generally lauded and certainly appreciated by suffragists, it was not universally popular. The *Arkansas Gazette* published a letter from a disgruntled man in March 1919 who complained, "When woman knocks at the door of the political arena, it reflects upon my chivalry," and suggested that the legislature ought to "expunge this silly and effeminate law from the statutes of the great state of Arkansas."[24]

Although far from the state amendment to the constitution that Arkansas suffragists desired, it marked an important milestone. However, it did not enfranchise black women, who were unable to vote in the all-white Democratic Party primary. Considered by scholars as the last of three disfranchising measures in Arkansas, the white primary was intended to exclude those African Americans who managed to overcome two other disfranchising measures passed in the state legislature in 1891: a poll tax amendment and state election laws that gave local registrars the ability to turn away illiterate voters. According to historian J. Morgan Kousser, the poll tax alone eliminated 21% of black voters and 7% of white voters. Given that 56% of black voters were illiterate, the state election law further impacted black voters, but the black middle class continued to vote.[25] The white primary, aimed specifically at the state's black middle class, began to be employed informally in the late 1890s by county primary committees but became formalized in January 1906 when the State Democratic committee ordered its use throughout the state. After implementation of the white primary rule, blacks had only two options: voting in the fall elections for a slate of Democratic Party candidates chosen by whites only or voting for Republican candidates who had no expectations of winning election. Court challenges failed to secure satisfaction for black voters until the Supreme Court overturned the white primary in *Smith v. Allwright* in 1944.[26]

As southern historians like Marjorie Spruill Wheeler have argued, white women in the South eschewed association with black women's organizations generally and failed to welcome black women as compatriots in the woman suffrage struggle.[27] Black women organized separate book clubs, WCTU chapters, and suffrage societies. Little has been writ-

Mame Stewart Josenberger of Fort Smith was likely a supporter of women's suffrage by virtue of her involvement in the National Association of Colored Women. *From the* National Cyclopedia of the Colored Race, Volume One, *1919.*

ten about Arkansas black women on woman suffrage in the state and, like Freda Hogan, they are not part of the traditional narrative on the subject. Historian Cherisse Jones-Branch suggests that Mame Stewart Josenberger, a successful Fort Smith businesswoman, was likely a pro-suffrage advocate by virtue of her ties to the National Association of Colored Women (NACW) and her affiliation with the Arkansas branch of the organization. As Jones-Branch put it, "Suffrage for women and African Americans was a primary objective for black clubwomen in the early years of the 20th century and was among the many departments established by the NACW immediately after its founding." The Arkansas branch of the organization embraced the woman suffrage struggle as their own, believing that only through the ballot could they begin to overcome the marginalization of blacks in American society. Likely disappointed when white suffragists resorted to securing the ballot through their inclusion in Arkansas primary elections, black women persisted in their dedication to securing the right to vote. For example, in July 1919, an article appeared in the *Arkansas Gazette* concerning the meeting in Pine Bluff of more than 500 black women from Arkansas and other states who expressed enthusiasm over the recently passed Nineteenth Amendment. They were "attending the Royal Grand Court, Order of the Eastern Star," at the Masonic Temple. After the passage of the federal suffrage amendment in 1920, "*The Arkansas Gazette* noted with concern that 122 black women members of the Little Rock Women's Political League had paid poll taxes at the Pulaski County Collector's office in response to an appeal from the National Women's [*sic*] Suffrage Association." According to Jones-Branch, "It is likely that these women were AACW members who, like Josenberger, positioned voting rights as an integral part of their activist agenda."[28]

In other southern states, some suffragists argued that extension of the vote to white women would counter the black male vote in the places where black men had managed to get through the obstacles to voting. Whatever they might have been saying to legislators behind closed doors in their lobbying efforts, white women in Arkansas were apparently silent publicly on the issue of black voters. Opponents to woman suffrage in Arkansas were not so reticent, however. Although some considered the possibility of enfranchising women as a way to offset the black vote, few found this appealing. Instead, as historian Barney R. McLaughlin argues, they articulated a racial argument in opposing woman's suffrage. For example, in 1915, "Senator I. C. Burgess of West-Central Arkansas argued that granting women the vote would 'turn the Negro women loose to vote and more of them will vote than white women.'" Given the demographics of the Arkansas Delta, this was of special concern to white politicians in Delta counties, and Senator J. Monroe Smith spoke to that issue during that legislative session, suggesting, "The gravest question came from the 'black belts,' where black women's votes would mean that white men would have to 'take the law into their own hands.'" The specter of black women voters surfaced again during the debate on woman suffrage in 1917. One White County representative "opposed woman suffrage because it would force white women to serve on the same juries as 'negro wenches.'"[29]

Once the primary bill passed in February 1917, the Arkansas Woman Suffrage Association reorganized as the Equal Suffrage Central Committee in order to prepare women to begin exercising the ballot. Their attention was diverted, however, by America's entry into World War I in April 1917. Like the NAWSA, Arkansas suffragists under the banner of the AWSA embraced the war effort and, perhaps at least in part, motivated by the opportunity to demonstrate their eligibility for full citizenship, worked in Red Cross workrooms, sold liberty bonds, and promoted the war savings stamps program.[30]

While the NAWSA and the AWSA "avowed full support for the war," the National Woman's Party remained focused on the cause of woman's suffrage. Membership in the Woman's Peace Party, an organization found in 1915 when President Wilson was still advocating peace, declined sharply nationwide.[31] Indeed, support for the war became a kind of litmus test. Even before the United States entered the conflict raging in Europe, President Wilson created an organization, the National Defense Council, intended at first as much for maintaining peace as preparing for war. Established in August 1916, the council included the cabinet offices of war, agriculture, commerce, and the interior but also a civilian advisory board. In January 1917, a Women's Committee was created and the honorary head of the NAWSA, Dr. Anna Howard Shaw of Massachusetts, was appointed to head the new organization. English born and a practicing physician in Boston, Shaw set about the task of creating state Women's Committees. The wife of Governor Charles Brough, Anne, became the honorary head of the Arkansas Women's Committee, and four other suffragists within the state were among those who held one of the nine leadership positions. Minnie Rutherford Fuller, who played a crucial role in the suffrage struggle in 1915, served as secretary of the Arkansas Women's Committee.

While Anne Brough was honorary chairman, Ida Frauenthal, a prominent Conway woman, was named the official chairman. As Elizabeth Hill explained, "Chairmen were responsible for the departments of legislation, child welfare, registration, food administration, home economics, health and recreation, publicity, training for service, education, women in industry and home and foreign relief, as well as maintenance of existing social service agencies, the speaker's bureau, Liberty Loans, War Savings Stamps, and Americanization."[32] Frauenthal carried a heavy portfolio of responsibilities but she shared these with nine officers and department heads, most of whom were from Little Rock.[33]

The committee reached into communities throughout Arkansas through two major initiatives: a food conservation campaign and a registration-for-service campaign. To address the first campaign, it organized a food conservation pledge drive that promoted conservation of food, particularly, as Hill stated, "control of food in storage, better methods of transportation, and elimination of speculation in foodstuffs."[34]

In January 1918, in response to the need to encourage more women to participate, the committee organized the registration-for-service campaign to encourage women to pledge their willingness to be of service. Registration cards were distributed through county committees, and the governor designated February 17–26, 1918, as Registration Week. The program was promoted as an effort "to indicate the chief usefulness of the women of Arkansas in this crisis, to give strength to the government and mobilize the spiritual resources that did much to help prosecute this righteous war." [35]

To reach women in rural areas, the food conservation program worked through the Cooperative Extension Service and the accompanying Home Demonstration programs that were enacted as part of the 1914 Smith-Lever Act. County Home Demonstration agents introduced rural women to a variety of food preservation techniques, home gardening, and other programs that were consistent with the goals of the Home Demonstration program. According to historian J. Blake Perkins, "About fifty percent of Arkansas's farm women had participated in a program . . . to teach women how to make their own soap in lieu of buying it."[36] One presumes they were not asked to sign anything in connection to this endeavor, as Frauenthal reported to the chairman of the State Council of Defense a disappointing overall response to the food conservation campaign. She lamented that most women exhibited "a decided objection to 'signing anything'" because "their husbands have cautioned them against putting their names to any sort of paper." Some feared they would be required to give up their canned goods and even "that families would be forced to eat cornbread."[37] Similar problems occurred during the Registration-for-Service campaign. As Hill wrote, some refused to sign because they believed they might be conscripted, others because of the "[f]ear they would be forced to vote," and at least one "prominent war worker . . . said she would not register because it was the work of the suffragists, and was not authorized by the president."[38]

Although Frauenthal reported a disappointing 10% participation rate in the registration campaign, the women of Arkansas earned a reputation for making a significant contribution to the war effort. In addition to serving on Red Cross committees, they sewed clothing for sailors and soldiers, entertained troops at Camp Pike, and sold war bonds.[39] According to Perkins, "Many women borrowed organizational skills pioneered by women activists for progressive causes in the late nineteenth and early twentieth centuries and adapted them to wartime mobilization

drives." He argued that they "helped the war effort in various ways, ranging from the administration of Red Cross and Liberty Loan drives to
helping with draft registrations in their communities."[40] As Hill wrote,
young women from Arkansas were provided "training in military, hospital,
and Red Cross. Classes were held in home nursing, surgical dressing,
fever nursing, dietetics, bacteriology, anatomy, first aid, life-saving, battalion drill, setting-up drill, and target practice." These were entirely new
experiences for most women, but hardly more so than the "almost 1,000
Arkansas women [who] worked in box factories, planing mills, sawmills,
and certain lines of office and railroad work." Hill reported that problems sometimes arose, however: "At the Missouri Pacific Railroad's Fort
Smith Crossing, fifteen yard clerks quit their jobs because nine women
had been hired to labor alongside them. According to the general manager, the men said they were afraid the women might hear objectionable
language."[41] Although some women endured the opposition of working
men and may have had to defy husbands who did not want them to
"sign anything," many women apparently shied away from participation
entirely. Nevertheless, the women of Arkansas and across the country
earned a reputation as having provided a valuable service during the
war, and, significantly, the participation of prominent suffragists in the
leadership positions gave them a profile they could carry into the postwar
period to promote a women's suffrage amendment to the constitution. As
Perkins stated, "Governor Brough bragged on the Woman's Committee
and, more generally, the patriotic women of Arkansas: 'With a meagre
fund, . . . this organization has thoroughly mobilized the woman power
of our state, until it is now a vital dynamic force in our midst, battling to
make the world safe for democracy.'"[42]

While women affiliated with NAWSA in Arkansas and elsewhere
in the country reduced their activities associated with securing the ballot
for women during the war, the NWP continued to demand a national
suffrage amendment and captured headlines and notoriety by staging
non-violent protests in the form of vigils. The NWP's founder, Alice
Paul, was a descendant of William Penn and a lifelong Quaker who had
learned the strategies of protest from British suffragists when she lived
for a time in England. Beginning in January 1917, Paul and other activists began protesting in front of the White House and became known
as "silent sentinels." The authorities responded harshly. Paul and approximately 200 other suffragists were arrested on charges of obstructing
traffic, and many of them were subsequently sentenced to terms in the

Alice Paul, a leader of the national effort for women's suffrage, was jailed for her activities. *Courtesy of the Library of Congress.*

Occoquan Workhouse. When Paul and some of the others began a hunger strike in protest of abysmal conditions in the workhouse, they were force-fed raw eggs mixed with milk. The image of respectable women arrested for peacefully protesting and then being subjected to such conditions troubled many Americans and created a public relations problem for the president.

Meanwhile, southern suffragists like those in Arkansas sought to distance themselves from the tactics employed by the NWP. Nevertheless, the NWP forged ahead in its campaign for the vote, recollecting "how women were betrayed by denial of the vote after the Civil War, even though they had given up their own suffrage campaign and worked for the war and the abolition of slavery." Paul and others had not forgotten the failure of Congress to include the protection of women in the Fourteenth and Fifteenth amendments.[43] Although there was an affiliate of the NWP in Arkansas, most of the state's women took the conservative position. In November 1917, for example, the Little Rock chapter went so far as to publish in the *Arkansas Gazette* an objection to a visit by Mabel Vernon, one of the silent sentinels of the NWP, writing, "Arkansas women need no White House picket nor Woman's Party to protect their rights. Assisted by men who know and understand that every Arkansas suffragist repudiates any connection with the militant organization, which has so long annoyed the president, Arkansas women will be able to take care of themselves. The Arkansas Woman Suffrage League will certainly make Miss Vernon realize, when she arrives in Little Rock, that the only welcome which awaits here is a Jack Frost welcome."[44]

However, there were women in Arkansas, like Adolphine Fletcher Terry, who supported the NWP's determination to continue agitating for suffrage during the war. In November 1917, according to Cahill, "Vernon met with 45 people in Little Rock who 'adopted a resolution to be sent to the president and members of Congress from Arkansas urging the passing of a national suffrage amendment at the next session of Congress.'"[45]

Paul's nonviolent protests were also having an influence on the national level. President Wilson, who had shown no interest in woman suffrage, began to change his mind precisely because of the horrific treatment of the incarcerated "silent sentinels." Not only did he pardon the women, by September 1918, he stood before a joint session of Congress urging members to "guarantee women the right to vote." The House had already passed a measure for a federal amendment to the constitution extending suffrage to women, but it was struggling in the Senate. Despite the president's plea, the amendment failed in the Senate by two votes. While this was playing out on the national stage, suffrage was making progress within Arkansas on another front but was doomed to a similar end. It was during 1918 that Arkansas citizens and politicians became preoccupied with rewriting the Arkansas constitution, and suffrage for women was included in the document submitted to voters in November 1918. However, the new constitution failed to secure sufficient votes to become the law, in part because of low voter turnout attributed to the Spanish flu epidemic.[46]

Despite these disappointments, another and ultimately successful effort to secure passage of a federal suffrage amendment was submitted to Congress on May 21, 1919, and passed in the House of Representatives by a vote of 304 to 89—42 votes above the required two-thirds majority. All seven members of the House from Arkansas voted in favor. It went to the Senate, where the vote would be much closer. Senator Joseph T. Robinson of Arkansas, a strong supporter, was enthusiastic enough to write a pamphlet that was distributed by the NWP in an ultimately unsuccessful attempt to sway the votes of senators in Mississippi and Louisiana. He failed to persuade them, but on June 4, 1919, the measure passed by a vote of 56 to 25, the necessary two-thirds, and went to the states for ratification.[47] It was quickly ratified in Wisconsin, Illinois, Michigan, Kansas, New York, and Ohio. Arkansas was the first southern state to approve the amendment (coming in as the twelfth state to approve) and by August 1920, the amendment needed only one more state to secure ratification. With the exception of Arkansas, it had failed uniformly across the South. Voting against it were Alabama, Georgia, Louisiana, Maryland, Mississippi, South Carolina, and Virginia. The crucial moment came, however, with another southern state and Arkansas's neighbor to the east: Tennessee. On August 18, 1920, Tennessee became the thirty-sixth state to ratify when it secured passage there by one vote. That one vote was cast by a twenty-four-year-old Republican legislator, Harry Burn, who intended to vote "nay" but was persuaded by a now famous missive from his mother, urging him to vote for suffrage: "Don't forget to be a good boy and help Mrs. Catt with her 'Rats.' Is she the one who put rat in ratification, Ha! No more from mama this time." With Tennessee's vote, the Susan B. Anthony amendment had secured the required number of states to make it officially the law of the land.

After the Great War

By the time the Nineteenth Amendment was passed and ratified, the Great War was over, but the battle had just begun as far as women were concerned. Even before the ratification of the amendment, Carrie Chapman Catt, president of the NAWSA, oversaw the creation of a league of women who would, in exercising the ballot, influence legislation. At the NAWSA's annual meeting in Chicago on February 20, 1920, the League of Women Voters was formally organized. It was intended to educate women on the principles and practices of citizenship, and although the new organization was to be bipartisan in membership, Catt declared that the league was not meant "to lure women from partisanship but to combine them in an effort for legislation which will protect coming movements, which we cannot even foretell, from suffering the untoward conditions which have hindered for so long the coming of equal suffrage."[48] Florence Brown Cotnam of Arkansas's AWSA organized the Arkansas League of Women Voters, joined the National Woman's Party, and was an early supporter of an Equal Rights Amendment, a measure proposed in 1923.[49]

From the moment that women became eligible to vote, politicians and political parties attempted to appeal to them. According to historian Lorraine Gates Schuyler, Congressman Thaddeus Caraway, who was running for the U.S. Senate, crafted an advertisement from passages in letters he had received from prominent suffragists, trumpeting: "When Suffrage Needed a Friend Congressman Caraway Responded Loyally." According to one of the suffragists he quoted, however, he had misrepresented the strength of his support, and she pledged to vote for his opponent.[50] This rebuke was not entirely warranted. As historian Sarah Wilkerson Freeman noted, Caraway "stood apart from most southern Democrats as a stalwart advocate of white women's suffrage and an original supporter of the Equal Rights Amendment proposed by feminists in the National Woman's Party."[51] While many Democratic politicians did their best to curry favor with female voters, the Republican Party also actively appealed to women and enjoyed some success. According to Schuyler, "A former democrat who described herself as a 'new republican' recruited support for the Republican ticket in Arkansas."[52] Some white Republicans in the state in 1920, signaling their association with a resurgent "lily-white faction," attempted to recruit white women for state legislative races.[53]

Seeking elective office in order to influence legislation favorable to women was one of the major objectives of both suffragists generally and the League of Women Voters in particular. Two women were elected to the Arkansas General Assembly in 1922, and the town of Winslow elected an all-female government in 1925.[54] Arkansas political leaders saw an opportunity, however, to use the enfranchisement of women to their own advantage. They were quick to recognize the opportunity to hold congressional seats left vacant by the untimely deaths of congressmen William A. Oldfield, who died in 1928, and Otis T. Wingo who died in 1930 by appointing their widows as placekeepers. Accordingly, Effiegene Wingo filled out her husband's term and then obligingly retired to allow a white man to run for the position. Likewise, Pearl Oldfield subsequently followed suit, establishing a precedent that, unfortunately for the state's Democratic political establishment, was not followed by Hattie Caraway in 1932.

When Senator Thaddeus Caraway died in late 1931, his widow, Hattie, was appointed by Governor Harvey Parnell to finish his term and was confirmed in a special election in January, making her the first woman elected to the U.S. Senate. Regarded as a "harmless innocuous compromise" designed to allow future white male candidates equal footing to compete for the important position in the coming Democratic primary, Hattie stunned them all when she announced her candidacy. Her campaign was enlivened by the presence of Senator Huey Long of Louisiana, who hoped to enlarge his profile regionally and to annoy his rival in the Senate from Arkansas, Joe T. Robinson. She won the election and spent the next thirteen years in the Senate, defeating in 1938 Representative John McClellan, who declared during the campaign that "we need another man in the Senate." She was defeated in 1944 by J. William Fulbright.[55]

Although electing women to office was of importance to the League of Women Voters, the organization devoted considerable attention to its primary purpose: educating women on the political process, preparing them for the practical aspects of exercising the ballot, and using the power of the ballot in influencing legislation aimed at bettering the circumstances of women and children in Arkansas. The Washington County League of Women Voters, organized on April 1, 1920, stands as an example of what the fledgling organization was attempting to do on the ground level during its first two years of existence. The league sponsored programs that included a presentation by the superintendent of the Fayetteville schools on the school situation on May 6; a lecture by University of Arkansas professor David Y. Thomas on "candidates and issues" on June 10, and Citizenship School in early August. The next year, they heard "five-minute talks" by three candidates for the office of local mayor; "released an informal study" on paying the poll tax; and supported a woman seeking election to the school board. The minutes of their June 9, 1921, meeting revealed that they encountered discrimination "against women at the polls," and declared their intention to run "two candidates for membership on the school board next year."[56]

The attempts to secure the election of women were intimately connected to the goal of representing the interests of women and families in the state, and there were some early successes in that regard. As Schuyler pointed out, "The 1921 session of the General assembly granted women equal guardianship of their children and raised the age of consent." The most important legislative achievement came with the passage of the Promotion of the Welfare and Hygiene of Maternity and Infancy Act, better known as the Sheppard-Towner Act. Proposed by a Texan, Senator Morris Sheppard, and an Iowan, Representative Horace Mann Towner, the act was intended to do precisely what the title suggests: promote the medical welfare of mothers and infants. According to historian J. Stanley Lemons, the legislation had its origins in the "United States Children's Bureau developed from [a] White House conference in 1909, and the Bureau's first major investigations were into the causes of infant and maternal mortality."[57] Although the seeds of the act were planted before women voted and held office, it was the advocacy of women that secured its passage in 1921, and it was the determination of women within Arkansas that secured the necessary matching funds by the state legislature in 1923. In that year, according to Schuyler, "the Arkansas General Assembly appropriated matching funds for the Sheppard-Towner program, the first state monies ever made available for child-hygiene work in Arkansas."[58]

While the end of Progressive Era reforms stalled further achievements by the mid-1920s, the advent of the New Deal marked a new era in reforms that worked to the benefit of women and families. When President Franklin Roosevelt appointed Frances Perkins Secretary of Labor in 1933, the first woman to hold a cabinet-level position, he was selecting a woman with a long history of advocating for the welfare of working women and children. Many women were aided indirectly by other New Deal agencies, and some women found employment in a few New Deal agencies, such as Dorothea Lange, who worked for the Farm Security Administration's photography program. Several women found work in the Works Projects Administration (WPA) in Arkansas, contributing to one of two programs: (1) the WPA slave interviews; (2) a county history program that necessitated intensive interviews within virtually every county in the state.

After World War II

While changing political fortunes and World War II forced a reckoning with some Depression-era advances, many women found employment in industry during the war and, for a time, enjoyed a new economic independence. The post–World War II era signaled a return to the household for many, and the politics and social conservatism of the 1950s led to a resurgence of the idea of subordination of women within the household, despite the fact that a larger percentage of women were entering the workforce at low-paid, lower-level positions. The volatile 1960s marked another transition as many women became involved in civil rights and anti–Vietnam War activities. They found, however, that even in these "liberal" organizations, they were expected to assume subordinate positions, and their relative inability to break out of this stereotype played a role in the emergence of a new woman's movement in the 1970s.

One idea that was resurrected was the notion of an Equal Rights Amendment, an idea that was first introduced in 1923. The AWSA's Florence Brown Cotnam had supported the ERA in 1923 but to no avail, and in the 1970s the ERA had its day in Arkansas but came face-to-face with the conservatism of a large segment of the female population, one that echoed the opposition of some women to signing registration cards during the Great War.

Although the ERA was passed by Congress in 1972 and seemed assured of easy victory, a concerted opposition arose from deeply conservative roots, ones that held the position of women as subordinate to their male superiors as sacrosanct. Phyllis Schlafly was largely credited with pulling these forces together, but they reflected a long tradition of deeply conservative women—and men—who held to an ideology of female domesticity and male superiority that had hardly subsided since Mrs. Max Lane of the Arkansas Federation of Women's Clubs asked the men attending the federation's 1917 banquet, "Please, kind sirs, give us a try at this voting business." Lane's tone of address was what was expected of women in the early twentieth century, but such obsequiousness was anathema to the ERA advocates of the 1970s. Diane Kincaid Blair, a respected political science professor at the University of Arkansas, found it particularly galling when she asked a reluctant legislator for his opinion of an expert's testimony, hoping that he had been persuaded to the ERA cause. He responded in a manner meant to place her in the all-too-familiar subordinate position. "What I think, Diane," he replied, "is that you are absolutely gorgeous in green."[59]

In the final analysis, the contribution of suffragists and women generally to the Great War played an important role in setting up the circumstances that made possible the passage of the Susan B. Anthony amendment, and since then, gains have been made in terms of addressing issues of importance to women. However, on the eve of the celebration of the one-hundred-year anniversary of the Anthony amendment's passage, progressive and independent women are facing new challenges as the political discourse at the highest levels has shifted against them. Still, a record number of women secured election to Congress in 2018, and they may yet break the barriers that keep many of them in subordinate positions.[60]

9 | Paris to Pearl in Print

Arkansas's Experience of the March from the Armistice to the Second World War through the Newspaper Media

ROGER PAULY

In the earliest hours of November 11, 1918, the exhausted staff of the *Arkansas Gazette*, led by the editorial team of brothers John and Fred Heiskell, waited by their new Associated Press teletype machine for an anxiously anticipated message. Their Little Rock office had been answering phone call after phone call for hours throughout the previous evening and was still doing so now, well after midnight. One can imagine how these exchanges went. "Is the war ending yet?" another excited voice would ask. "Still no word," comes the tired reply. Finally, at exactly 2:15 a.m. the teletype machine springs into life with its famous "clackity-clack" sound. There is a confirmation "flash." The Great War will end in just nine hours.

The newspaper staff immediately passed word to a crowd of people waiting outside the office, and the news shot from mouth to mouth, corner to corner, neighborhood to neighborhood, and town to town. Spontaneous revelries broke out across Little Rock as the city experienced the "wildest celebrations of its history."[1] A few hours later, blaring factory whistles ushered in the break of dawn. They blew not to summon workers, but rather in festive acknowledgment of the imminent peace. The *Gazette* itself would later describe the event as a reign of pandemonium.

| DOI: https://doi.org/10.34053/christ2019.twah.9

There was no past experience to compare it with. It had all the joy of all the Christmases that have ever been, all the fire and patriotism of all the Fourths of July, the color and noise of 47,000 circus days and the confetti-covered camaraderie of a million street carnivals, the whole lot jumbled up into one tremendous occasion.[2]

The party went on all day and into the night. Despite a statewide prohibition on alcohol having come into effect a year earlier, a significant amount of booze managed to appear out of nowhere. At the time, few Arkansans could have imagined that in just a little over two decades, their sons and daughters would again be fighting in yet another, even more destructive cataclysm. After all, had not this first conflict also been nicknamed the "War to End All Wars"? How was it that the 2,183 Arkansans who died in World War I would be followed by another 3,519 who died in World War II?

For decades, historians, political scientists, and other scholars have tried to make sense of this question. In the simplest terms, it is clear that the seeds of the Second World War lay in the story of the First.[3] Beyond that broader equation, the exact nature of this causality becomes less and less clear the more we study the problem. Can we trace a direct timeline from November of 1918 to September of 1939 or December of 1941? Can we find a blueprint for World War II in the text of the 1919 Treaty of Versailles? The terms of this treaty ended the conflict but humiliated Germany by stripping it of overseas colonies, reducing its land area by 14%, and saddling it with $33 billion in reparations payments.[4] In enacting such severe terms, did the victorious Allies indirectly help put the ultra-nationalist German chancellor Adolf Hitler into office and thus set the world back on the path to war? While the simplest response to these questions is probably "yes," the full story remains more nuanced.

Let us tackle this challenging puzzle by first reviewing the manner in which a number of notable scholars have explored connections between the two wars. Next, we will need to paint a broad picture of how the end of World War I set in motion a series of key political and diplomatic events throughout the interwar period that helped drive the world back toward conflict. At the same time, we will try to glean some sense of how Arkansans received and understood these developments. To accomplish this last task, we will draw on perhaps the most readily available and comprehensive primary historical source of the era: the newspaper media.

Since historians have literally given the two World Wars *the same name*, it may come as no great surprise that they have seen connections between the events. Indeed, fighting had not even ceased in World War II when political writer Walter Lippmann claimed that President Woodrow Wilson, one of the key players in developing the peace terms of 1919, did not really understand the importance of stopping dictators nor the idea of a balance of power.[5] That same year, Stanford historian Thomas Bailey offered even harsher criticism of the president in a book with the rather unsubtle title of *Woodrow Wilson and the Lost Peace*.[6]

In truth, neither Lippmann nor Bailey were breaking much new ground, even at this early stage. Criticism of the Treaty of Versailles already had a rich history well before the Second World War actually broke out. The most famous early voice denouncing Versailles belonged to noted British economist John Maynard Keynes, who wrote two blistering attacks, *The Economic Consequences of the Peace* (1919) and *A Revision of the Treaty* (1922). In these works, Keynes suggested that the terms of the treaty were morally wrong and too severe. He felt the obligations of Versailles would cripple Germany's economy and, in doing so, drive the nation into aggressive and militant directions. In the first book, Keynes warned that when the economic situation in any nation becomes bad enough, "man shakes himself, and the bonds of custom are loosened. The power of ideas is sovereign, and he listens to whatever instruction of hope, illusion, or revenge is carried to him on the air."[7] In the second work, he more directly warned that the treaty "endangered the life of Europe."[8] Keynes predicted that a renewed Germany might eventually look eastward to pursue its ambitions, a plan echoed by Adolf Hitler a mere three years later in his notorious book *Mein Kampf* (1925).[9]

Not only economists and aspiring dictators made these criticisms. Harvard historian William Langer referred to the Treaty of Versailles as "unbelievably harsh" in 1936.[10] Although he did recognize Hitler's regime as a danger, Langer was so opposed to the treaty's terms that the following year he proposed giving back to Germany its overseas colonies.[11] Of course, none of this prevented Langer from later re-writing his own narratives and criticizing the policy of the appeasement (the policy of giving in to Hitler's demands in the vain hope of avoiding war) once World War II was safely over.[12]

The historiographical pattern of linking the Second World War to the First World War, noted above in the cases of Lippmann and Bailey, continued in later decades. This was a popular approach found from

Winston Churchill himself in 1945, to German historian Hans-Ulrich Wehler in 1995, to British historian Martin Francis in 2014 on the very centenary of the start of the war. Both Churchill and Wehler spoke of a "second Thirty Years War" to describe World Wars I and II as being, in essence, one global conflict.[13] For his part (in an essay that is otherwise a horrific example of academic gibberish), Francis re-confirmed the ideas of Churchill and Wehler by noting that "the relative chronological proximity of the two World Wars made it possible for both conflicts to be experienced in a single (auto-) biographical frame."[14]

Indeed, the idea that World Wars I and II were just episodes in the same longer tragedy may have played into arguably the most famous event in the historiography of World War I: the Fischer controversy.[15] Fritz Fischer was a German historian whose peers savaged his contention that the outbreak of World War I was primarily Germany's fault.[16] To be fair, there were some serious holes in Fischer's argument, but the ferocity of the debate over it was unprecedented amongst German historians.[17] The intense vehemence was probably due to the following equation: if the First World War created Hitler and his regime, and if Germany was not to blame for the that war, then at some level Germany was also not fully at fault for the Nazi tragedy. Fischer threatened this comfortable psychological arrangement.

While the Fischer controversy generated much attention and many arguments, by no means did it write the final word in this historical conversation. As the reference to Martin Francis's work above suggests, interest in World War I grew as the centennial of the event approached. Indeed this very essay, written as part of the Arkansas World War I Centennial Commemoration, is evidence of the trend. Among the slew of essays and books that have appeared in the last decade or so have been some that repeat the same arguments about causality between World Wars I and II. In 2014, German historian Klaus Schwabe reiterated a now-old theme, noting that "Hitler's rise to dictatorship is unthinkable without the humiliation and misery that resulted for the German people out of their defeat."[18]

Not all centenary voices focused on Germany or Hitler. Woodrow Wilson likewise again fell under the microscope in 2014, albeit in new ways. John Tierney Jr., an American International Relations expert, argued that the World War I experience as understood and defined by Wilson created an internationalist, democratic-crusading mentality that has molded American foreign policy to the very present.[19] The United

States was certainly not to blame for the onset of World War II, but our involvement greatly shaped the expansion and nature of the conflict.

In 2015, Australian historian John A. Moses offered an interesting essay analyzing war guilt and historiography. He likewise continued to support the old idea that World War I and the Treaty of Versailles helped lead to World War II, saying "The entire anti-Versailles movement was one of the most powerful factors in popularizing Adolf Hitler and assisting him to power."[20] Moses continued:

> Further, the German preoccupation with these issues during the nineteen twenties was of such dimensions that it effectively prevented the population from accepting with any degree of conviction the spirit of the democratic Weimar Constitution. . . . Instead of democracy and liberalism, a virulently pathological nationalism nourished itself in a passionate semi-hysterical anti-Western, anti-Versailles movement.[21]

Incidentally, the term "Weimar" that Moses uses comes from the German city of that name. It was in Weimar that liberal reformers successfully proclaimed a democratic constitution in 1919. While Berlin, and not Weimar, continued to serve as the nation's capital, the informal name "Weimar Republic" is often applied to the German state that preceded the Third Reich.

This brief survey of academic literature has shown that a significant number of professional scholars and writers have seen connections between World War I and World War II. However, back in 1984, historian Anthony Linter very correctly pointed out that what mattered the most about the Treaty of Versailles was not how historians saw it in much later decades, but how contemporaries viewed it.[22] Given that the essay you are now reading is part of a project for the Department of Arkansas Heritage, it seems logical that we should narrow the focus of Linter's question even more. How did contemporary *Arkansans* understand the Treaty of Versailles, the rise of Hitler, the appeasement of the Nazi regime, and other events that set the world on the path to a second global conflict?

This is a challenging question to answer, especially given the lack of public-opinion polls in Arkansas the 1920s and 1930s. Since the late nineteenth century, people had used polls to predict elections, but not to gauge the opinions of ordinary citizens on other news-making events. Indeed, it was not until 1937 that pollsters took the first non-election

American public-opinion poll. Coincidentally, in that poll, Gallup asked U.S. citizens if American entry into WWI back in 1917 had been a mistake. Seventy percent of those polled believed that it was![23] This statistic gives us a little bit of insight into Arkansans' thoughts as part of the wider American public in the late 1930s. In all likelihood, like other Americans, Arkansans were on the whole probably quite pacifistic and isolationist.

But what about Arkansan sentiments more specifically? How about their opinions in the 1920s? Or even at the exact time of the Paris Peace Conference itself in June 1919? One possible method to gauge popular sentiment in the "Wonder State," as Arkansans called it back then, is through the press—in particular, daily newspapers.

Looking at newspapers to get a sense of Arkansans' opinions in the 1920s and 1930s has two potential drawbacks, however. In the first case, it is entirely possible that a newspaper's editor held a certain opinion about, say, the Treaty of Versailles or Adolf Hitler, and his or her readership may not have shared this viewpoint. However, newspapers are a business, and then, just as now, they had to serve their customer base. Presumably, these editorials could not be too far off general public sentiment if the newspaper wanted to remain in print. Along those lines, local editorials are thus almost certainly a better source of Arkansas sentiment than articles reprinted from the Associated Press or the United Press. Those "outsourced" stories obviously would have reflected a broader national sentiment.

The second problem is that the majority of Arkansas newspaper editions printed in those key decades have not made a successful transition to microfilm or microfiche. Most microfilm collections from those decades have only particular newspaper editions from perhaps just a few days over the course of an entire given year. Thus, surviving copies of a small-town paper might include two single days in 1919, maybe none in 1920, three in 1921, and so forth.

Fortunately, the *Arkansas Gazette* is quite complete on microfilm and, as the flagship newspaper based in the state's capital city, it represents an excellent newsprint source. Nonetheless, it would be a shame if this was our only newspaper of record and if there were no smaller-town publications that we could use as a second source to compare to the *Gazette*. Once again, we are fortunate, in that the surviving collection of the *Fayetteville Democrat* is very nearly as complete as that of the *Gazette* and likewise offers plenty of commentary on international developments.

The *Arkansas Gazette* was the area's oldest and most respected newspaper, literally pre-dating the state itself. It was founded in 1819, the year Arkansas became a territory, a full century before the Paris Peace Conference that ended World War I. At the time of the Great War, the brothers John and Fred Heiskell (mentioned earlier) owned and edited the *Gazette*.[24] Incidentally, John had served as an acting U.S. senator for a few weeks back in 1913, which might in part explain the exceptionally strong opinions often expressed about the Senate in the paper's editorial pages. In addition, it is of note that one biographer seemed to believe that John Heiskell wrote almost all of the *Gazette*'s editorials during this era.[25] While it is likely that John wrote most of them, the possibility remains open that Fred and other staff members may have occasionally lent a hand.

Of further importance is the fact that the paper was far and beyond the most successful in the state. In 1922, it enjoyed a robust circulation of 50,000.[26] If nothing else, this statistic alone helps justify using the *Gazette*'s editorials as a window into the average Arkansan's response to international events.

While not quite as old as the *Gazette*, the *Democrat* was still rather venerable, having been founded back in 1860. By World War I, it was called the *Fayetteville Democrat* and entrepreneur Jay Fulbright owned it.[27] After his death in 1924, his widow Roberta took over running her late husband's numerous business ventures, including the newspaper.[28] In addition to overseeing the *Democrat*'s general affairs, she occasionally wrote an opinion column titled "As I See It." After her passing in 1952, one friend estimated that in composing her column and other editorials, Roberta Fulbright wrote over two million words in her lifetime.[29]

Roberta Fulbright also re-wrote the name of the paper more than once, turning it into the *Fayetteville Daily Democrat* and eventually the *Northwest Arkansas Times*. The U.S. Senate may have been on this particular editor's mind, too, since she is largely credited with eventually getting her son, J. William Fulbright (yes, *that* J. William Fulbright), elected as a senator in the midst of World War II. It is possible that some of the editorials in the *Democrat* were also her direct work while others likely came from her managing editor, Lessie Stringfellow Read, another notable figure in the history of Arkansas women working in the press. However, Fulbright's editorial writer, Charles Richardson, probably composed the lion's share of this work.[30]

What do these two papers actually suggest about Arkansas's perspectives on the march from the First to the Second World War? This is not a simple question to answer, as the connections between the two events are

Fred Heiskell may have written some of the editorials in the *Arkansas Gazette*, but most were likely written by his brother and coeditor John. *"Fred Heiskell," ASA_Photo_G5567_083, Arkansas State Archives, Little Rock.*

Lessie Stringfellow Read was the managing editor of the *Fayetteville Democrat*, but most of the editorials were likely written by Charles Richardson. *Courtesy Shiloh Museum of Ozark History / Washington County Historical Society Collection (P-1975).*

a little more complex than Versailles = World War II. As Schwabe argues, only World War I made Hitler possible, but the path was not "immediate."[31] To follow this long trail accurately requires a chronological review of certain specific, crucial international events from 1918 to 1941. In addition, it will be useful to make a corresponding analysis of how the *Gazette* and *Democrat* responded to them. While not perfect, this methodology should provide a solid sense of how Arkansans experienced, and tried to make sense of, the path from the first global catastrophe to the second.

To begin, how was the end of the War to End All Wars itself received? Due to an erroneous statement by U.S. admiral Henry Braid Wilson, the *Fayetteville Democrat* and dozens of other American newspapers actually jumped the gun and declared that the war ended on November 7, 1918.[32] However, once the world was sure that peace truly had broken out on the 11th, both the *Gazette* and *Democrat* welcomed the news. The former recounted the celebrations in Little Rock described at the beginning of this essay while the latter made certain its readership understood that *this time* the ceasefire was for real. The Fayetteville paper stated solemnly that the end of the war was "Officially Announced By The Authorities At Washington."[33] Incidentally, the Associated Press may have jinxed the establishment of a lasting peace by proclaiming that the Allies were going to guide Germany "to a place in the family of nations from which they can take a part in assuring that another such 1,300 days of blood and horror need never come again."[34] To be fair, World War II was 2,194 days of blood and horror, so perhaps the AP was right after all.

The extent to which these Arkansas papers heaped praise upon President Woodrow Wilson at this time may strike the modern reader as curious. Perhaps this is the result our having had a press corps in 2018 that was exceptionally hostile to the sitting president, and vice versa. However, the *Gazette* and the *Democrat* both seem strikingly sycophantic to Wilson. John Heiskell's biographer, John A. Thompson, noticed this tendency. When considering World War I, Thompson admitted, "The war years marked a low point in Heiskell's editorial career basically because he displayed relatively little independence of thought."[35] Thompson speculated that Heiskell's pattern of readily following the White House line "may have been as much to his Democratic loyalty and his interest in aiding the success of Wilson, the first Democrat to serve in the presidency since he had become editor."

The Fayetteville paper largely followed suit. As the war ended, the *Democrat* likewise lathered praise on Wilson, making such statements

John Heiskell's editorials in the *Arkansas Gazette* were largely sympathetic to the government line of the Wilson Administration. *"John Heiskell," ASA-Photo-G5567_083, Arkansas State Archives, Little Rock.*

as, "The lustre of his achievements are undimmed. He remains, unchallenged, the 'first citizen of the world.'"[36] Certainly, Arkansans were excited about the victory, but this passage seems like something *Pravda* might have written about V. I. Lenin. This pattern would repeat itself later on with both the *Democrat* and the *Gazette's* coverage of Franklin Roosevelt. To be fair, the editors of both papers occasionally singled out certain individual Republican politicians for praise.

On November 12, 1918, the *Democrat* more soberly praised the soldiers who actually fought in the war and then cautioned, "It remains for the people at home to do their part, and make sure and permanent the fruits of victory."[37] That permanence would fail, of course, in part because America did not do its part but retreated into isolationism. The same editorial also proclaimed, "Everyone knows what the war was fought for," which is interesting since today very few people seem to know what World War I was fought for.[38]

As noted above, many scholars see a key origin of World War II in the text of the Treaty of Versailles. As diplomats were signing the treaty on June 28, 1919, Arkansas editorials were supportive, particularly for American participation in the League of Nations. However, joining this international organization generated a lot of opposition amongst

Republicans in the U.S. Senate who feared membership in the league might weaken U.S. sovereignty. The *Arkansas Gazette* drastically overestimated national support for the league, stating:

> The Republicans—or at least those Republicans who are fighting the League of Nations—are suffering from a depression. The recent wave of feeling against the league which rang through the country has passed its crest and is subsiding rapidly—so rapidly, in fact, that there is great danger that those who so courageously climbed off the fence to combat the League of Nations will find themselves left high and dry.[39]

The *Democrat* was more realistic. Even as early as June 30, two days after the signing, the editorial page complained that the debate over the League of Nations had become so partisan that it was now difficult for any newspaper to comment upon it without being "suspected of undue influence of some sort."[40] The league was not without its problems, but America's refusal to join it left the organization short of a key world leader who might otherwise have been able to do more to promote international peace efforts.

By November, the battle to join the league had been lost in the Senate, and while the *Gazette* bemoaned the "stubborn fight," its criticism of the Republicans gradually dimmed. Perhaps the Heiskell brothers had discovered that support for the league in Arkansas was not much stronger than elsewhere in the country.[41] In fact, in May 1921, when the Allies announced the final amount of the reparations bill that Germany was required to pay (known as the London Schedule of Payments), the *Gazette* and *Fayetteville Democrat* did not even directly editorialize on whether or not they thought the $33 billion amount was excessive.

This ambivalence about reparations changed rather drastically in January 1923. The London Schedule allowed Germany to pay some of its debts by cash and some in raw commodities such as timber and coal. The Weimar Republic, however, had consistently failed to meet its coal obligations. Starting in December 1922, Germany also began defaulting on timber deliveries, and France lost its patience. On January 11, 1923, French and Belgian troops garrisoning a demilitarized zone in western Germany called "the Rhineland" moved farther into Germany and occupied the Ruhr Valley. France and Belgium conducted this invasion in order to extract the required reparations by force.

Initially, the *Gazette* put blame for this state of affairs squarely on

Germany: "It was Germany's use of might, including the use of might against virtually defenseless Belgium, that brought her present afflictions upon her. Might was Germany's religion. Who was it but the German Kaiser who glorified the 'mailed fist'"?[42] However, as the days and weeks went on and Germany's economic condition spiraled downward, the Little Rock paper began running a string of articles from other newspapers and the Associated Press that were increasingly sympathetic to the former enemy nation. On January 18, a *Gazette* editorial expressed concern over reports that the French intended to seize large amounts of timberland: "These forests are owned for the most part by communities and we are told that they are a source of livelihood for the majority of the people of the regions in which they are situated, while others depend upon them for fuel. We are also told that the newspapers of Germany are dependent upon them for their paper supply."[43] The later point was probably near and dear to the heart of a newspaper editor. A week later, the feisty yellow-dog Democratic *Gazette* also laid partial blame for the crisis on the anti-league Republicans in the Senate. "If the unspeakable catastrophe of another European War should come, to what acts could America point by way of showing that she had neglected to do nothing she might have done to keep peace in Europe?"[44]

Incidentally, it was during this crisis that Arkansans probably read the name Adolf Hitler for the first time. He was the central character in an Associated Press article about anti-French meetings of "German Fascisti" in Munich, Bavaria. Little Rock readers learned how "Herr Hitler went from one meeting to another and was loudly cheered when he declared that 'All German eyes today are turning to Munich where the thought of national unity is being vigorously promulgated.'"[45]

The *Fayetteville Democrat* was a little slower to editorialize about the Ruhr crisis, but in early February, it too weighed in. The paper complained about how France had seized four-fifths of Germany's coal resources and had left millions of German families in the cold: "Morally and legally Germany seems to have a poor case for complaint. But practically the situation must be judged by different standards. The principle of 'an eye for an eye' will never make France and Germany good neighbors and never will solve Europe's problems."[46] It would seem that feelings in Arkansas against the former enemy had eased considerably over the past four years.

The situation in Europe improved in August of the following year through the U.S.-backed Dawes Plan, named after banker Charles Dawes, who spearheaded the effort. The plan stabilized Germany's economy by means of a massive influx of U.S. cash loans to German banks. In exchange, Germany agreed to the resumption of more-regular reparations to France but at a reduced schedule of payments. The *Gazette* was supportive of the agreement and by this point clearly seemed more critical of France than Germany, and accused the former of dragging its heels.[47] The *Democrat* also praised the agreement, arguing, "There is no question of the attention given to German finance, industry and trade by this settlement. Though severe in some of its conditions, it is more definite and practical than previous reparation arrangement has been and gives the Germans something fairly definite to build on."[48]

Despite French reservations, the Dawes Plan did improve the situation in Europe to the point at which Germany, France, Belgium, Italy, and Britain were able to hammer out a series of secondary treaties collectively known as the "Locarno Pact" or "Locarno Treaties." These more or less reaffirmed major provisions of Versailles and even added more security protocols, but the key positive point of the treaties was that Germany agreed to them. The Weimar Republic was a partner in the negotiations, rather than simply having terms dictated to it. The *Gazette* astutely recognized this fact. An editorial cited British Foreign Secretary Austen (not Neville) Chamberlain, who observed that Locarno had the advantage of having Germany enter voluntarily into the agreement unlike "the treaty signed in the Hall of Mirrors" (a reference to the palace of Versailles) that was "imposed upon a defeated country."[49] Later, after diplomats formally signed the agreements on December 1, the *Fayetteville Democrat* only had praise for "the Locarno peace pact that guarantees to Europe there will be less of arms and none of war."[50]

This new era of goodwill culminated in August 1928 in the Kellogg-Briand Pact named after its key architects, U.S. secretary of state Frank Kellogg and French foreign minister Aristide Briand. Signatories to this protocol pledged to refrain from the use of war to solve international disputes. Following the lead of France and the United States, dozens of nations signed the pact, including future Axis powers Germany, Italy, and Japan. The *Arkansas Gazette* found some weaknesses in Kellogg-Briand but approved of its intent:

> Nevertheless, every action taken to mark war as an evil legacy inherited by the present from the past, a bad and destructive habit mankind has handed down from generation to generation, is a step taken toward the firmer establishment of peace, and the

substitution of conciliation and reasonable argument for international dealings.[51]

At this point, we can make a brief summary of Arkansas's perspective on the search for peace in the decade following World War I. Appearing in newspapers in a solidly Democratic state, the editorials greatly bemoaned the United States' refusal to enter Woodrow Wilson's League of Nations. Beyond that, the editorials seemed to follow a generally pacifist approach that was not unlike that of most American foreign policy makers, Democratic and Republican alike.

The picture became far more complex, though, as the world experienced a massive depression and witnessed the rise of aggressive totalitarian states in the following decade. The 1930s in Germany saw Adolf Hitler's highly militaristic National Socialist Party come to power. This "Nazi" regime was bent on revenge for what Hitler saw as the humiliation of Germany at the end of World War I and into the 1920s. Benito Mussolini's fascist Italian state gradually fell into Hitler's orbit and would become an active ally in World War II. Japan, which like Italy had fought against Germany in World War I, increasingly provoked its former allies by taking aggressive actions against China. Such policies would ultimately lead to confrontation and the attack on Pearl Harbor in December of 1941.

Reading through Arkansas editorials that comment upon these events in the 1930s is a depressing exercise. Editorial writers repeatedly and fruitlessly called for peace in a world marching toward war. Such sentiments in Arkansas were probably not much removed from similar feelings in Oregon, Arizona, Maine, or Florida.

In 1935, Benito Mussolini began threatening Ethiopia in anticipation of a full-fledged invasion. In late August, the despairing Ethiopian emperor, Haile Selassie, called for international support. He even offered generous oil leases to British and American petroleum interests in hopes that this might improve the chance of foreign intervention against the fascists. The *Arkansas Gazette* was critical of Mussolini but remained unimpressed by Selassie's actions. In an early September editorial, Little Rock's flagship paper flatly asserted, "The United States is not going to war in Africa for Standard Oil interests."[52] Incidentally, it is remarkable how much this particular editorial echoed the "No Blood for Oil" arguments that appeared prior to the Gulf War in 1991 and the war against Iraq in 2003.

On March 7, 1936, Hitler sent armed forces into the previously demilitarized "Rhineland" area of Germany near the border of France. This action was supposedly in response to a newly announced Franco-Soviet alliance but, in actuality, it was part of the Nazi leader's broader plan to right the supposed wrongs of World War I. The *Gazette* tried to downplay concern by suggesting the Rhine was such an intrinsic geographic part of Germany that the Fuhrer's actions might be understandable. The paper argued that "for the most part the Rhine flows through German Territory just as the Arkansas flows through Arkansas and not wholly on one side of the state as the Mississippi does."[53] The editorial also pointed out that the Treaty of Versailles only required Germany to keep the Rhineland demilitarized through 1935. Lastly, the editorial actually offered criticism of *France* by reminding Arkansas readers that the French government wanted to annex this German territory back in 1919 but Wilson and the British blocked the unjust attempt.[54] In a second editorial issued the same day, the *Gazette* spoke somewhat more negatively of Hitler's actions by admitting, "Germany goes on arming as she has never armed before."[55]

Almost as interesting as what the Arkansas newspapers chose to editorialize on are those international news stories they chose to ignore. In many cases, the papers reprinted Associated Press or other newspapers' stories that were critical of Germany or Japan but offered no opinions in their editorial pages. For example, the *Fayetteville Democrat* had little to say about the Rhineland remilitarization. The editorial staffs of both the *Democrat* and the *Gazette* were equally silent about the Japanese invasion of Manchuria in 1931, as well as the start of the Second Sino-Japanese War in 1937. Rather than commenting upon Japan's invasion of China, the *Gazette* angrily denounced plans to suspend the search for Amelia Earhart.[56] Likewise, neither paper seemed to have opinions on the several Neutrality Acts passed in the mid-to-late 1930s by the U.S. Congress and signed into law by President Franklin Roosevelt. While one might imagine that these events would warrant significant commentary in the *Gazette* or *Democrat*, such does not appear to be the case.[57]

One of the last great steps on the path from the First World War to the Second was the notorious Munich Conference of September 28–30, 1938. By this point, Hitler had grown used to defying the allies of France and Britain with impunity. Those nations had informally fallen into a policy or a pattern of appeasement. Appeasement was a product of World War I revisionist thinking, in that the theory of appeasement held that it was better to give in to Hitler's demands rather than risk war, especially if Hitler was justifiably reacting to terms that had been too harsh in the first place.

Some of Hitler's demands were territorial in nature, either seeking land stripped from Germany in 1919, or entirely new territory holding ethnic Germans. Prior to the Munich Conference, Hitler had been threatening war over the so-called "Sudetenland," a border region of Czechoslovakia that held some three to four million ethnic Germans. Hitler invited the leaders of France, Britain, and Italy to Germany to resolve the situation. At the conference, Édouard Daladier of France and Neville Chamberlain (Austen's brother) of Britain essentially agreed to giving Hitler the Sudetenland in exchange for a promise that the German leader would make no further territorial demands in the future. The British and French advised Czechoslovakia to hand over the disputed border regions or fight Germany alone. Faced with such odds, the Czechs capitulated. Over the next few months, German forces occupied *all* of Czechoslovakia, not just the border regions, and by the spring of 1939, Hitler was demanding Polish territory that held ethnic Germans.

On September 29, 1938, the *Gazette* had applauded the Munich Conference. Although Roosevelt was not even in attendance, an editorial praised him up and down and speculated that it may have been the American president who moved Hitler to call the peace summit.[58] The editorial also spoke of Roosevelt as the "head of one great nation" and Hitler as "the ruler of another great nation." By the following day, Team Heiskell had made a 180-degree turn and attacked Hitler, arguing that the Fuhrer still had dreams of conquest in Eastern Europe as part of the plan he had first laid out in *Mein Kampf*.[59] One wonders how the *Gazette* staff had gotten its wires quite so crossed between September 29 and the 30.[60]

The former *Fayetteville Democrat*, now re-branded as the *Northwest Arkansas Times*, was less optimistic. Even before the Munich meeting took place, the paper presciently argued that a great war was coming between communism and fascism and that the democracies of the world needed to prepare to defend themselves. The *Times* cautioned, "You can't reason with a mad dog. You can only shoot him down in all kindness and mercy if he invades your home or runs amuck in your community."[61] This mad-dog theme would prove to be a favorite of the *Times* editorial staff, who repeated it with regularity. Somewhat more in the tin-foil-hat camp was the paper's claim that Germany was building secret underground airfields with money lent to the country by the United States.

Owner-editor Roberta Fulbright also directly weighed in on the Munich Conference several times in her personal column, "As I See It." She too offered the obligatory praise of Roosevelt and denounced "Adolph" as a "megalo-maniac."[62] By this point, too, the *Times'* editorial page was regularly running political cartoons insulting Hitler. However, Fulbright also praised the allied leaders for ultimately managing to avoid bloodshed, an effective endorsement of appeasement, saying, "There should be nothing but praise for the Czechoslovakian, the French and British statesmen who swallowed their pride, possessed themselves in patience and practiced a great tolerance in a most trying situation."[63]

A little less than a year after the Munich Conference came the Molotov-Ribbentrop Pact. Scholars often see this alliance as a final stepping stone on the path from World War I to World War II. Named after Soviet foreign minister Vyacheslav Molotov and his German counterpart Joachim von Ribbentrop, the pact was a non-aggression and strategic trade agreement between the Nazi state and its communist rival. The agreement ensured that the Germans and Russians could carve up Poland quickly between them.

An attack on Poland, however, had the chance to trigger a general war with France and Britain against Germany. However, if Poland collapsed quickly enough, the Third Reich would be able to avoid a prolonged two-front conflict, something that was devastating to the German war effort in World War I. Incidentally, Hitler would later throw away this advantage on June 22, 1941, when he betrayed Joseph Stalin's trust and invaded the Soviet Union. However, when Molotov and Ribbentrop first announced their pact back on August 23, 1939, most of the world's diplomatic corps understood that a second general war was only a matter of weeks away. Unfortunately, it is less clear what the Arkansan press corps thought of the Nazi-Soviet agreement, as neither the *Gazette* nor the *Times* editorialized upon it.

Both papers did have plenty to say once armed conflict actually broke out on September 1, 1939, after Germany invaded Poland. Britain and France gave the Nazi regime forty-eight hours to recall its armed forces before reluctantly declaring war on Germany on the September 3. The *Gazette* took the opportunity to blast Democratic and Republican senators who earlier had blocked a plan by Roosevelt that would have allowed for arms sales to Britain and France.[64] However, the paper also calculated that "neither 'isolationists' nor 'Jingoes' represents the prevailing sentiment of the great masses of the American people. The average American

Newspaper publisher Roberta Fulbright attacked Adolph Hitler and Nazi Germany in her column in the *Northwest Arkansas Times*. *Picture Collection No. 3848A. Special Collections, University of Arkansas Libraries.*

hopes this country can escape involvement but fears that some turn of events might drag it in."[65] The *Gazette* must have regretted its September 29, 1938, editorial even more once general fighting in Europe had broken out. "In the light of today's situation, that Munich 'appeasement' looks sadder than ever." The editorial concluded, "Now that it is too late, it can be seen that if a choice had to be made between peace and war, Munich was the time and place for England and France to force the issue."[66]

While the *Gazette* was now more consistent than it had been in editorializing on the Munich Conference, this particular crisis was an opportunity for the *Northwest Arkansas Times* to spin in contradictory circles. As Germany marched into Poland on September 1, somehow Roberta Fulbright managed to imagine that the Japanese might team up with Britain against Germany.[67] Meanwhile, her editorial staff again stated that the only thing to do with a mad dog was to shoot it. One might logically take this as a call for France, Britain, and possibly even the United States to shoot the mad-dog Hitler, presumably by going to war against Germany.[68] By September 4, with the reality of a full-scale European war setting in, the *Times* seemingly changed its tune, calling for strict U.S. neutrality and reminding its readers that "we must bear in mind that war is Europe's problem, not ours."[69] The paper even argued that the United States should defend American soil but "never" send U.S. military forces to Europe or Asia. So now the idea was to allow mad dogs to live and let live? Fulbright's personal column echoed this pacifism, arguing that, "The United States must use its head and not its hate."[70] She did, however, agree with calls to sell weapons to the European democracies.

War had indeed broken out, but Arkansans—along with the rest of their countrymen—would not join in the fighting for another year and a half. In that time, German and Italian armies would defeat both Poland and France before sweeping into the Balkans, North Africa, and the Soviet Union. The United States attempted to help in March 1941 with the Lend-Lease Act, which supplied war materiel to Britain (and later Russia). Meanwhile, Japanese forces continued a brutal campaign in China that eventually provoked the Roosevelt administration into declaring an embargo of oil sales against Japan in August 1941. This action led to Japan's decision to go to war against the United States, starting with the bombing of Pearl Harbor that December. For reasons that are not entirely clear, Germany and Italy followed the Japanese move by declaring war against the United States a few days later on December 11.

How did Arkansans keep abreast of these final steps in the march from World War I to World War II? Paradoxically, the *Gazette* did not devote much attention to the Lend-Lease Act beyond praising Republican minority leader Joseph Martin for vocally supporting it.[71] The *Northwest Arkansas Times* apparently had even less interest. Likewise surprising is the fact that the oil embargo against Japan failed to generate any specific editorial commentary in either newspaper. To be fair, while the *Times* did not editorialize on the embargo itself, it continued to call for maintaining a strong standing army while an unnamed "menace" continued to exist.[72] The paper was not clear, though, on whether this threat came from Germany, Italy, Japan, or all three, now known collectively as the Axis Powers.

The *Gazette* did have more to say about international developments as relations between the United States and Japan deteriorated on the eve of the Pearl Harbor attack. One editorial on December 5, 1941, took Kansas senator Arthur Capper to task for arguing that the United States should avoid foreign entanglements:

> The fact of the matter is that whatever course the United States followed it would still be "entangled" along with the rest of the world in the world-wide war which afflicts this generation of mankind. We'll be entangled if we stand aloof; we'll be entangled if we throw the weight of our industrial and technological resources against the Axis. The only question is, which is preferable from the viewpoint of this free and peaceful nation, an Axis victory or an Axis defeat?[73]

In that same edition, another editorial squarely blamed Japan for its own economic suffering due to Tokyo's aggressive actions in China.[74]

The next edition of both papers following the actual air raid in Hawaii were, of course, filled with commentary from Mr. Heiskell, Ms. Fulbright, Mr. Richardson, and perhaps other members of the respective editorial teams. On December 8, the *Gazette* ran a particularly enraged editorial, stating, "The attack made on Hawaii by Japanese planes was one of the most insane acts in all the history of nations. It was enough to rouse the American people to righteous fury, but vengeance will be deliberate and ordered—and unsparing to the end and to the death."[75] The *Times* was not too far off this mark, stating, "Never in history has such a dastardly act been committed as the unprovoked, murderous, savage assault by prepared Japanese who knew they were actually at war with the United States while we were entertaining and listening to their peace envoys."[76] The Fayetteville paper also suspected that the Germans and Italians had something to do with the raid. Fulbright's team felt so rushed by the events that this editorial contains some grammatical errors, such as the claim that "Arkansts has always done its part."[77]

The *Gazette* and *Times* editorials were similarly enraged at Germany and Italy after these nations issued their declarations of war on the United States. The *Times* in particular continued to insist on some level of collusion between the European and Asian branches of the Axis powers. "Germany, Italy, and Japan—they're all in the same boat."[78] The *Times'* earlier insistence that America would "never" fight enemies overseas in Europe or Asia now seemed completely forgotten (and more than a little illogical). The *Gazette* bizarrely managed to claim that Germany did not want war with the United States at this time—even though *Germany had just declared war on the U.S. at that time*: "We may be sure that nothing could have suited Hitler better than to keep the United States on the side-lines as a non-belligerent until he had realized his hope of subduing Europe, cracking Russia as a military power, and sending Britain down in defeat."[79] The *Gazette* did admittedly leave us with a witty one-liner on the editorial page in that same issue: "Nobody enjoys isolation more today than an isolationist."[80] Since she so often got the last word in any given discussion, it seems somehow appropriate to give Roberta Fulbright the final say on this subject—as she saw it: "Defeat Japan and the Axis is written in glowing words everywhere. Isolationists are swallowed up; pacifists are lost in the shuffle."[81]

So what can we conclude? In many ways, the two newspapers reviewed here appear to reflect the general American impression of international events from late 1918 through 1941. There are some more "Arkansan elements" to the editorials, most notably the fact that Arkansas was adamantly Democratic and both papers stuck firmly to the party line. This tendency may not have been just a matter of politics, though. One gets the impression that both papers were legitimately convinced that the League of Nations truly was the key to peace in the world. Today, the league seems like a discredited, failed experiment, but that conclusion was by no means universal in the interwar period.

Also of interest is the sharp response to the French Ruhr invasion. While the *Gazette* and *Democrat* ignored other important events, one senses that the invasion of 1923 was truly a public-relations disaster of global proportion for France. The tone toward defeated Germany shifted drastically, even in a small, rural American state half a world away from Europe. This fact alone might help explain why so many international leaders of the 1930s came to decide that maybe Versailles had been too harsh and perhaps giving the Germans some slack was a good idea.

Unfortunately, that calculation of course led to appeasement. The Little Rock and Fayetteville papers both seemed bewildered at times by these later events. One editorial would seem to have the perspective of an activist Wilsonian internationalism. This might be followed a day or two later by a call for further retreat into isolationism. That second editorial in turn might give way to a jingoistic demand to shoot the mad dog, Hitler. Confusion reigned in Arkansas editorial rooms at least as much as it did in European foreign ministry offices.

Given the wild, unpredictable actions of Hitler's expansionist policies, perhaps this is not surprising. We have the hindsight of knowing that the Nazi story would end badly for the world. Neither John Heiskell, nor Roberta Fulbright, nor Charles Richardson, nor anyone in Arkansas had that luxury. It is easy to forget that between bouts of militant bluster, Hitler was clever at waving olive branches at just the right time to a weary world still recovering from the bloody experience of 1914–1918. Of course, we need to limit such conclusions to events in Europe. While the papers' editors paid surprisingly sharp attention to inter-war affairs in Germany, France, and Britain, East Asia was out of sight and out of mind in the Wonder State. It was not until the very eve of the air raid on Pearl Harbor that Arkansas editorials began to address Tokyo's aggression in a serious manner.

In the end, whether the *Gazette* or the *Times* had paid enough attention to one branch of the Axis powers perhaps did not matter very much. As anger over Pearl Harbor spread through the state, thousands of young Arkansans would come to join the ranks of kith and kin who, only twenty years earlier, had first trod that long, long, and deadly trail a-winding. Arkansans had watched events that they had almost no control over from a great distance for two decades. All that time, many of them had hoped and prayed for peace with apparently little effect. They could not have known that the first catastrophe had already sown seeds for the second almost before the smoke had cleared from the trenches.

NOTES

Chapter 1

1. President Wilson's Declaration of War Message to Congress, April 2, 1917; Records of the United States Senate; Record Group 46, National Archives. https://www.ourdocuments.gov/doc.php?doc=61 (accessed November 26, 2018).

2. "Thomas Gibson." The Arkansas Great War Letter Project. https://chs arkansasgreatwar.weebly.com/gibson-thomas-h.html (accessed November 26, 2018).

3. President Wilson's Declaration of War Message to Congress, April 2, 1917; Records of the United States Senate; Record Group 46, National Archives.

4. John Keegan, *First World War* (New York: A. Knopf, 1999), 1.

5. Winston Churchill, *The World Crisis, 1911–1918* (New York: Free Press, 2005), 291.

6. Washington Gladden, *Christianity and Socialism* (New York: Eaton & Mains, 1905), 58.

7. Keegan, *First World War*, 1.

8. Herbert Read, "Ode Written During the Battle of Dunkirk, May, 1940," as found in Paul Fussell, *Great War and Modern Memory* (Oxford: Oxford University Press, 2013), 72.

9. Keegan, *First World War*, 1.

10. Edward A. Gutièrrez , *Doughboys on the Great War: How American Soldiers Viewed Their Military Experience* (Lawrence: University Press of Kansas, 2014), 30; *The War with Germany: A Statistical Summary* (United States. War Dept., 1919), 25.

11. Gutièrrez , *Doughboys on the Great War*, 14.

12. "America's Wars," https://www.va.gov/opa/publications/factsheets/fs _americas_wars.pdf (accessed November 26, 2018); *The War with Germany: A Statistical Summary*, 25.

13. Richard Faulkner, *Pershing's Crusaders: The American Soldier in World War I* (Lawrence: University Press of Kansas), 4; *Summary of Casualties Among Members of the American Expeditionary Forces* (United States. War Dept., 1919).

14. *The War with Germany: A Statistical Summary*, 13; Faulkner, *Pershing's Crusaders*, 4; *Summary of Casualties Among Members of the American Expeditionary Forces*.

15. President Wilson's Declaration of War Message to Congress, April 2, 1917; Records of the United States Senate; Record Group 46, National Archives.

16. *Congressional Medal of Honor and Distinguished Service Cross* (United States. War Dept., 1919), 52.

17. *Congressional Medal of Honor and Distinguished Service Cross*, 52.

18. Awards and Decorations: World War I Statistics, https://history.army.mil/documents/wwi/23awd.htm (accessed November 26, 2018).

19. *The War with Germany: A Statistical Summary*, 23.

20. Kim Allen Scott, "Plague on the Homefront: Arkansas and the Great Influenza Epidemic of 1918," *Arkansas Historical Quarterly* 47 (1988): 342.

21. *Summary of Casualties among Members of the American Expeditionary Forces.*

22. Mark K. Christ and Cathryn H. Slater, *Sentinels of History: Reflections on Arkansas Properties on the National Register of Historic Places* (Fayetteville: University of Arkansas Press, 2000), 107.

23. David W. Blight, *Race and Reunion: The Civil War in American Memory* (Cambridge, MA: Harvard University Press, 2001), 386.

24. Jennifer M. Murray, *On a Great Battlefield: The Making, Management, and Memory of Gettysburg National Military Park, 1933–2013* (Knoxville: University of Tennessee Press, 2016), 166.

25. Murray, *On a Great Battlefield*, 16.

26. Blight, *Race and Reunion*, 272.

27. United Daughters of the Confederacy, Minutes of the Annual Convention, Vol. 24, 1918, 341.

28. John Milton Cooper, *Woodrow Wilson: A Biography* (New York: Vintage Books, 2011), 168.

29. Carl Moneyhon, *Arkansas and the New South, 1874–1929* (Fayetteville: Arkansas University Press, 1997), 96.

30. Laura Mattoon D'Amore and Jeffrey Meriwether, *We Are What We Remember: The American Past through Commemoration* (Cambridge Scholars Publishing, 2012), 372.

31. *Confederate Veteran* 26, no. 10 (Nashville, TN, October, 1918), 1.

32. Foy Lisenby, *Charles Hillman Brough: a Biography* (Fayetteville: University of Arkansas Press, 1996), 8.

33. Lisenby, *Charles Hillman Brough: a Biography*, 18.

34. "The Reunion in Brief," *Confederate Veteran* 26, no. 11 (Nashville, TN, November, 1918), 468.

35. *Confederate Veteran* 26, no. 1 (Nashville, TN, January, 1918), 7.

36. "The Reunion in Brief," *Confederate Veteran* 26, no. 11, 36.

37. *Minutes of the Annual Convention*, vol. 24 by United Daughters of the Confederacy, 342.

38. *Minutes of the Annual Convention*, 342.

39. *Minutes of the Annual Convention*, 342.

40. "The Reunion in Brief," *Confederate Veteran* 26, no. 1, 42.

41. "The Reunion in Brief," 42.

42. "The Reunion in Brief," 42.

43. Report of the Arkansas State Council of Defense, May 22, 1917 to July 1, 1919, 36.

44. Report of the Arkansas State Council of Defense, 6.

45. Report of the Arkansas State Council of Defense, 7.

46. Report of the Arkansas State Council of Defense, 13.

47. Committee on Public Information, Four-Minute Man Bulletin, No. 17 (October 8, 1917).

48. Michael D. Polston and Guy Lancaster, *To Can the Kaiser: Arkansas and*

the Great War (Little Rock: Butler Center Books, 2015), 13; Kenneth C. Barnes, *Anti-Catholicism in Arkansas: How Politicians, the Press, the Klan, and Religious Leaders Imagined an Enemy, 1910–1960* (Fayetteville: University of Arkansas Press, 2016), 83.

49. Report of the Arkansas State Council of Defense, May 22, 1917, to July 1, 1919, 36.

50. "Wireless Station a Wooden Derrick," *Arkansas Democrat*, April 5, 1917, 1.

51. "Collegeville Is Hostile at Sight of German Flag," *Arkansas Democrat*, April 8 1917, 3.

52. "Collegeville Is Hostile at Sight of German Flag," 3.

53. James L. Gilbert. "World War I and the Origins of U.S. Military Intelligence" http://www.firstworldwar.com/features/propaganda.htm (accessed November 29, 2018).

54. The Arkansas Great War Letter Project. http://chsarkansasgreatwar .weebly.com/ (accessed February 1, 2018).

55. "Heber McLaughlin Called By Death," *Arkansas Gazette*, May 29, 1931, 6.

56. Matthew J. Davenport, *First Over There: The Attack on Cantigny, America's First Battle of World War I* (New York: St. Thomas Press, 2015), 59.

57. The Arkansas Great War Letter Project. https://chsarkansasgreatwar .weebly.com/heber-mclaughlin.html (accessed November 29, 2018).

58. "Heber McLaughlin Called By Death," 6.

59. "Grady H. Forgy," The Arkansas Great War Letter Project. http://chs arkansasgreatwar.weebly.com/forgy-grady.html (accessed November 29, 2018).

60. "Homer Grissom," The Arkansas Great War Letter Project. https://chs arkansasgreatwar.weebly.com/grissom-homer-c.html (accessed November 29, 2018).

61. Jim McDaniel, "William Jayson (Bill) Waggoner," Central Arkansas Library System Encyclopedia of Arkansas, https://encyclopediaofarkansas.net/ entries/william-jayson-2991/ (accessed November 29, 2018).

62. "Bill Waggoner," The Arkansas Great War Letter Project. http://chs arkansasgreatwar.weebly.com/bill-waggoner.html (accessed November 29, 2018).

63. "Lane Herman," The Arkansas Great War Letter Project. http://chs arkansasgreatwar.weebly.com/lane-herman-o.html (accessed November 29, 2018).

64. "James Lankford," The Arkansas Great War Letter Project. https://chs arkansasgreatwar.weebly.com/lankford-james.html (accessed November 29, 2018).

65. "James Lankford," The Arkansas Great War Letter Project.

66. "Lane Herman," The Arkansas Great War Letter Project. http://chs arkansasgreatwar.weebly.com/lane.html (accessed November 29, 2018).

67. "Lane Herman." The Arkansas Great War Letter Project.

68. "Glenn Cole." The Arkansas Great War Letter Project. https://chs arkansasgreatwar.weebly.com/cole-glen.html (accessed November 29, 2018).

69. "Glenn Cole." The Arkansas Great War Letter Project.

70. "Glenn Cole." The Arkansas Great War Letter Project..

71. "Foreman Kelley." The Arkansas Great War Letter Project. http://chs arkansasgreatwar.weebly.com/foreman-kelley.html (accessed November 29, 2018).

72. "L. A. Girerd." The Arkansas Great War Letter Project. http://chs arkansasgreatwar.weebly.com/girerd-l-a.html (accessed November 29, 2018).

73. "L.A. Girerd." The Arkansas Great War Letter Project.

74. Randy Finley, "Black Arkansans and World War One," *Arkansas Historical Quarterly* 49, no. 3 (Autumn 1990): 260.

75. Gutièrrez, *Doughboys on the Great War*, 58.

76. Cameron McWhirter, *Red Summer: The Summer of 1919 and the Awakening of Black America* (New York: Henry and Holt, 2011), 219.

77. Finley, "Black Arkansans and World War One," 263.

78. Finley, "Black Arkansans and World War One," 260.

79. Finley, "Black Arkansans and World War One," 260.

80. Finley, "Black Arkansans and World War One," 260.

81. Finley, "Black Arkansans and World War One," 260.

82. Finley, "Black Arkansans and World War One," 260.

83. Kieran Taylor, "'We Have Just Begun': Black Organizing and White Response in the Arkansas Delta, 1919," *Arkansas Historical Quarterly* 58, no. 3 (Autumn 1999): 266.

84. Taylor, "'We Have Just Begun': Black Organizing and White Response in the Arkansas Delta, 1919," 271.

85. Taylor, "'We Have Just Begun': Black Organizing and White Response in the Arkansas Delta, 1919," 270.

86. Taylor, "'We Have Just Begun': Black Organizing and White Response in the Arkansas Delta, 1919," 271.

87. McWhirter, *Red Summer*, 219.

Chapter 2

1. For a discussion of Arkansas's club women, see Frances Mitchell Ross, "The New Woman as Club Woman and Social Activist in Turn of the Century Arkansas," *Arkansas Historical Quarterly* 50 (Winter 1991): 317–51.

2. For a discussion of industrialization and women's roles, see Carl N. Degler, *At Odds: Women and the Family in America from the Revolution to the Present* (New York: Oxford University Press, 1980), 155.

3. Cherisse Jones-Branch, "Segregation and Desegregation," Central Arkansas Library System Encyclopedia of Arkansas, https://encyclopediaof arkansas.net/entries/segregation-and-desegregation-3079/ (accessed November 30, 2018).

4. "Donate Site for School," *Arkansas Gazette*, January 31, 1917.

5. "Donate Site for School," *Arkansas Gazette*. In response to the women's request, Governor Brough promised the delegates that he would consider the matter.

6. "School and Demonstration," *Arkansas Gazette*, April 27, 1917.

7. Elizabeth Griffin Hill, *A Splendid Piece of Work 1912–2012: One Hundred Years of Arkansas's Home Demonstration and Extension Homemakers Clubs* (CreateSpace: 2012), 14.

8. Elizabeth Griffin Hill, *A Splendid Piece of Work*, 10.

9. "Women Organize to Conserve Food," *Arkansas Gazette*, July 3, 1917.

10. "Defines Relation of Two Governmental Organizations," *Arkansas Gazette*, August 12, 1917.

11. "Defines Relation of Two Governmental Organizations," *Arkansas Gazette*.

12. Report of the Arkansas Woman's Committee, "Report of County Councils," Arkansas State Archives ("ASA/LR").

13. Letter, Woman's Committee, Council of National Defense, to chairmen, state councils of defense, June 22, 1917, file 234, Council of Defense Records, ASA/LR; "Call for Heads of Women's Societies, *Arkansas Gazette*, June 24, 1917; "Women Organize to Save Food," *Arkansas Gazette*, July 8, 1917.

14. Letter, Ida Frauenthal to Wallace Townsend, Chairman, State Council of National Defense, August 16, 1917, folder 234, Council of Defense Records, ASA/LR; "Week of Campaign for Conservation," *Arkansas Gazette*, October 6, 1917; Report of the Arkansas Woman's Committee, 15, ASA/LR.

15. "Gives Object Lessons in Conservation of Wheat," *Arkansas Gazette*, November 1, 1917; "Prepare Breakfast Food at Home, Save More Wheat," *Arkansas Gazette*, December 30, 1917.

16. "Prepare Breakfast Food at Home, Save More Wheat."

17. "Camouflaging the Cottage Cheese," *Arkansas Gazette*, May 16, 1918.

18. "War Menus, Meatless Meals, Wheat Flour Substitutes," *Arkansas Gazette*, December 9, 1917; U.S. Department of Agriculture, *Cottage Cheese Dishes* (U.S. Printing Office, 1919). 1918 Annual Narrative Report, State Home Demonstration Agent (HDA), Record Group (RG) 33, National Archives and Administration (NARA), Fort Worth, TX.

19. Circular 109, *Cottage Cheese Dishes* (U.S. Government Printing Office, 1918).

20. "Best Methods of Cooking Soy Beans," *Arkansas Gazette*, July 28, 1918.

21. "War Menus, Meatless Meals, Wheat Flour Substitutes," *Arkansas Gazette*, December 9, 1917.

22. "Certificates for Buyers of Sugar," *Arkansas Gazette*, July 28, 1918; "A Demonstration of the Preservation of Fruit Juices and Jams Without the Use of Sugar," *Arkansas Gazette*, July 14, 1918; "To Increase the Yield of Jelly," *Arkansas Gazette*, August 11, 1918; "Eat the Prunes and Save the Pits," *Arkansas Gazette*, August 29, 1918 ("Free the pit of the pulp and dry thoroughly either by means of the sun or the oven. Place the pits in the containers provided for them in the downtown stores, etc. Two hundred pits or seven pounds of nut shells will make enough carbon for one gas mask, which may save the life of a soldier.")

23. "To Make Candy Without Sugar," *Arkansas Gazette*, September 22, 1918.

24. Newspapers usually placed the term "the boys" in quotation marks when referring to U.S. troops.

25. "Women in 1,200,000 Homes to Do Nation a Service by Eliminating Garbage Pail," *Arkansas Gazette*, June 20, 1917.

26. "Economy Not a Fad, but a Necessity," *Arkansas Gazette*, October 28, 1917.

27. "Substitutes for Wheat, Their Use," *Arkansas Gazette*, March 31, 1918.

28. "Are You a Woman Slacker?" *Arkansas Gazette*, July 14, 1918.

29. Report of the Arkansas Woman's Committee, "Reports of County Councils," ASA/LR.

30. "Defines Relation of Two Governmental Organizations," *Arkansas Gazette*, August 12, 1917.

31. Ida Clyde Clarke, *American Women and the World War* (New York:

D. Appleton and Company, 1918): 138. Online at http://net.lib.byu.edu/estu
/wwi/comment/Clarke/Clarke00TC.htm (accessed November 30, 2018).

32. Clarke, 140–41.

33. Clarke, Chapter XI, "The Red Cross."

34. "To Rush Knitting for the Soldiers," *Arkansas Gazette*, August 26, 1917.

35. "Local Red Cross has Rush Order," *Arkansas Gazette,* December 5, 1917.

36. "Woman 88 Years Old Works for Red Cross," *Arkansas Gazette*,
September 23, 1917.

37. Report of the Arkansas Woman's Committee, "Reports of County
Councils," ASA/LR.

38. "Colored People Rally to Cause of Red Cross," *Pine Bluff Daily Graphic*,
June 20, 1917.

39. "Women to Register for War Service," *Arkansas Gazette*, January 6, 1918.

40. "Registrars to Be Given Quiz Today," *Arkansas Gazette*, February 2, 1918;
"Women Registration Instruction School," *Pine Bluff Daily Graphic*, February
5, 1918. "For Colored Registration," *The Southern Standard* (Arkadelphia, AR),
February 14, 1918.

41. Report of the Arkansas Woman's Committee, "Reports of County
Councils," ASA/LR.

42. Report of the Arkansas Woman's Committee.

43. Report of the Arkansas Woman's Committee, 12–13, ASA/LR.

44. Report of the Arkansas Woman's Committee.

45. Report of the Arkansas Woman's Committee, "Reports of County
Councils," ASA/LR.

46. Carl H. Moneyhon, *Arkansas and the New South, 1874–1929* (Fayetteville:
University of Arkansas Press, 1997), 126–128.

47. "Wage Campaign for School Attendance," *Educational News Bulletin*,
published by the Arkansas Department of Education, March 1918 (found in the
Arkansas Council of Defense Records, ASA/LR).

48. Report of the Arkansas Woman's Committee, "Reports of County
Councils," ASA/LR.

49. Memorandum from Dr. Jessica B. Poixette, Chief, Child Conservation
Section, Council of National Defense, "Child Welfare Back-to-School Drive,"
to the State Chairmen of Child Welfare, dated November 13, 1918. Folder 19,
Arkansas Council of Defense Records, ASA/LR.

50. Degler, *At Odds*, 155.

51. Report of the Arkansas Woman's Committee, 16–17, ASA/LR.

52. Report of the Arkansas Woman's Committee.

53. Although telephone operators in Pine Bluff also went on strike, their situation was not included in this study.

54. "A Statement from Discharged Telephone Operators," *Arkansas
Gazette*, October 7, 1917; "Fort Smith Strike Finally Settled," *Arkansas Gazette*,
December 27, 1917.

55. Philip S. Foner, *Women and the American Labor Movement: From
World War I to the Present* (New York: The Free Press, a Division of MacMillan
Publishing, Inc., 1980), 91.

56. "A Statement of Facts to the Public" (paid advertisement by Southwestern
Bell Telephone Company), *Arkansas Gazette*, October 11, 1917.

57. "Some More Facts" (paid advertisement by striking telephone operators), *Arkansas Gazette*, October 12, 1917.

58. "Facts about the Wages and Working Conditions of the Little Rock Operators" (paid advertisement by Southwestern Bell Telephone Company), *Arkansas Gazette*, November 14, 1917.

59. "Phone Company to Seek Injunction," *Arkansas Gazette*, November 14, 1917; "Hope of Settling Telephone Strike," *Arkansas Gazette*, November 12, 1917.

60. "No Settlement Yet," *Arkansas Gazette*, November 25, 1917.

61. "No Settlement Yet," *Arkansas Gazette*.

62. "No Action on Strike," *Arkansas Gazette*, January 4, 1918.

63. "General Strike at Fort Smith Is On," *Arkansas Gazette*, December 9, 1917.

64. "Mediators Take Up Telephone Walkout," *Arkansas Democrat*, December 15, 1917.

65. "Fort Smith Strike Finally Settled," *Arkansas Gazette*, December 27, 1917.

66. "Dunaway Meeting," *Arkansas Gazette*, May 25, 1918.

67. According to author Elizabeth Haiken, between two-thirds and three-fourths of the laundry workers were African American women.

68. Three military establishments sent their laundry into Little Rock: Camp Pike across the Arkansas River and just west of Argenta/North Little Rock, housed 50,000 to 60,000 men toward the end of the war; Fort Roots, on a bluff across the river also, housed 10,000; and the Picric Acid Plant, just east of Little Rock, employed 3,000 to 4,000.

69. Elizabeth Haiken, "'The Lord Helps Those Who Help Themselves': Black Laundresses in Little Rock, Arkansas, 1917–1921," *Arkansas Historical Quarterly* 49, no. 1 (Spring 1990): 20–50.

70. Haiken, 22.

71. Haiken, 22.

72. Haiken, 20–21.

73. Haiken, 50.

74. J. Blake Perkins, "Persuading Arkansas for War: Propaganda and Homefront Mobilization during the First World War," in Polston and Lancaster, eds., *To Can the Kaiser*, 52.

75. "An Appeal to the State Suffragists," *Arkansas Gazette*, December 9, 1917.

76. "Camp Pike Gazette," *Arkansas Gazette*, September 26, 1918.

77. "Red Cross to Make Influenza Masks," *Arkansas Gazette*, October 6, 1918.

78. Report of the Arkansas Woman's Committee, 9, ASA/LR.

79. Report of the Arkansas Woman's Committee; 1918 Annual Narrative Report, State HDA, RG 33, NARA/Fort Worth, Texas.

80. Report of the Arkansas Woman's Committee, "Reports of County Councils," ASA/LR.

81. Report of the Arkansas Woman's Committee.

82. Report of the Arkansas Woman's Committee, "Reports of County Councils," ASA/LR.

83. "History of the Pulaski County Chapter of the Red Cross" (1963 presentation script), American Red Cross Collection, BC.MSS.16.36, Box 2, File 1, Butler Center for Arkansas Studies, Central Arkansas Library System, ("BC/CALS").

84. Moneyhon, *Arkansas and the New South*, 135–138.

85. 1927 Annual Narrative Report, Saline County HDA, RG 33, NARA, Fort Worth, Texas.

86. 1928 Annual Narrative Report, Phillips County HDA, RG 33, NARA, Fort Worth, Texas.

87. 1928 Annual Narrative Report, Phillips County HDA, RG 33, NARA, Fort Worth, Texas.

88. Frances Hanger and Clara B. Eno, "The Story of the AFWC 1897–1934," Federation of Women's Clubs, UALR.MS.0056, Box 6, File 8, Center for Arkansas History and Culture, University of Arkansas at Little Rock.

89. To combat elevated mortality rates among mothers and newborns, the Sheppard–Towner Maternity and Infancy Act provided $1 million annually in federal aid (for a five-year period) to state programs for mothers and babies, particularly prenatal and newborn care facilities in rural states. http://history.house.gov /HistoricalHighlight/Detail/36084 (accessed November 30, 2018). The act became law on November 23, 1921.

90. Hanger and Eno, "The Story of the AFWC 1897–1934," Federation of Women's Clubs, UALR.MS.0056, Box 6, File 8, Center for Arkansas History and Culture, University of Arkansas at Little Rock.

91. U.S. Census Bureau, Statistical Abstracts for 1916 and 1924, http://www .census.gov/library/publications/time-series/statistical_abstracts.html (accessed November 30, 2018).

92. Moneyhon, *Arkansas and the New South*, 145.

93. Moneyhon, *Arkansas and the New South*, 106. Consolidation of Arkansas's rural school districts continues to be covered by statewide news outlets even at the end of the second decade of the twenty-first century.

94. 1928 and 1929 Annual Narrative Reports, State HDA, NARA/Fort Worth, Texas.

95. Degler, *At Odds*, 413.

96. Degler, *At Odds*, 413.

97. "History of the Pulaski County Chapter of the Red Cross" (1963 presentation script), American Red Cross Collection, BC.MSS.16.36, Box 2, File 1, BC/ CALS.

98. "History of the Pulaski County Chapter of the Red Cross."

99. 1927 Annual Narrative Report, Phillips County Local Home Demonstration Agent, RG 33, NARA/Fort Worth.

100. 1934 Annual Narrative Report, State HDA, RG 33, NARA/Fort Worth, Texas.

101. "History of the Pulaski County Chapter of the Red Cross" (1963 presentation script), American Red Cross Collection, BC.MSS.16.36, Box 2, File 1, BC/ CALS.

Chapter 3

1. B. H. Liddell Hart, *The War in Outline, 1914–1918* (New York: Random House, 1936).

2. Paul A. C. Koistinen, *The Military-Industrial Complex: A Historical Perspective* (New York: Praeger, 1980).

3. Iron Trade Review, "Men Who Will Direct Our Industrial Mobilization," *Iron Trade Review* (April 20, 1916): 883.

4. Koistinen, *The Military-Industrial Complex*, 23.

5. "Advisory Board on Defense Is Named," *Arkansas Democrat*, October 12, 1916; "Advisory Board on Defense Is Named," *Batesville Daily Guard*, October 13, 1916; "National Defense Commission Named," *Daily Arkansas Gazette*, October 12, 1916.

6. Koistinen, *The Military-Industrial Complex*.

7. Arkansas State Council of Defense, *Report of the Arkansas State Council of Defense*, 1919.

8. Hart, *The War in Outline, 1914–1918*.

9. Carl H. Moneyhon, *Arkansas and the New South: 1874–1929*, Histories of Arkansas (Fayetteville: University of Arkansas Press, 1997), 98–100.

10. Arkansas State Council of Defense, *Report of the Arkansas State Council of Defense*.

11. U.S. Census Bureau, *Fourteenth Census of the United States, Taken in the Year 1920: Volume X, Manufactures: 1919; Reports for Selected Industries* (Washington DC: Government Printing Office, 1923).

12. U.S. Census Bureau, *Fourteenth Census of the United States, Taken in the Year 1920: Volume IX, Manufactures, 1919: Reports for States with Statistics for Principal Cities* (Washington, DC: Government Printing Office, 1919); U.S. Census Bureau; U.S. Census Bureau, *Fourteenth Census of the United States, Taken in the Year 1920: Volume X, Manufactures: 1919; Reports for Selected Industries*.

13. Arkansas State Council of Defense, *Report of the Arkansas State Council of Defense*, 39.

14. U.S. Census Bureau, *Fourteenth Census of the United States, Taken in the Year 1920: Volume IX, Manufactures, 1919: Reports for States with Statistics for Principal Cities*.

15. Moneyhon, Arkansas *and the New South: 1874-1929*.

16. "Warren Mills Buy 1,500 Bales Cotton Linters," *Arkansas Democrat*, March 23, 1916; "First Trainload of Cotton Linters Shipped from City," *Pine Bluff Daily Graphic*, July 6, 1916.

17. U.S. Census Bureau, *Fourteenth Census of the United States, Taken in the Year 1920: Volume XI, Mines and Quarries, 1919: General Report and Analytical Tables and Selected Industries* (Washington DC: Government Printing Office, 1919).

18. "New Mining Company," *Daily Arkansas Gazette*, August 22, 1917; "Mining News Notes," *Mountain Echo*, January 19, 1917; "To Mine Arkansas Iron," *Daily Arkansas Gazette*, July 3, 1917; "Copper Ore Found," *Daily Arkansas Gazette*, June 8, 1917.

19. U.S. Census Bureau, *Fourteenth Census of the United States, Taken in the Year 1920: Volume X, Manufactures: 1919; Reports for Selected Industries*, 40.

20. U.S. Census Bureau, *Manufactures, 1909, Reports for Principal Industries* (Washington, DC: Government Printing Office, 1913), 731.

21. Arkansas State Council of Defense, *Report of the Arkansas State Council of Defense*, 18–19; "Endorses Ark. Stock Conservation Plans," *Arkansas Democrat*, September 28, 1918.

22. U.S. Census Bureau, Fourteenth *Census of the United States: 1920 - Population* (Washington DC: U.S. Department of Commerce, 1920).

23. Arkansas State Council of Defense, *Report of the Arkansas State Council of Defense*.

24. Arkansas State Council of Defense.

25. Hermann Sprengel, *The Discovery of Picric Acid (Melinite, Lyddite) as a Powerful Explosive and of Cumulative Detonation with Its Bearing on Wet Guncotton*, 2nd Edition (London: Eyre & Spottiswoode, 1903).

26. Charles E. Heller, *Chemical Warfare in World War I: The American Experience, 1917–1918*, Leavenworth Papers 10 (Fort Leavenworth, KS: U.S. Army Command and General Staff College, 1984); Timothy T. Marrs, Robert L. Maynard, and Frederick Sidell, *Chemical Warfare Agents: Toxicology and Treatment* (John Wiley & Sons, 2007).

27. "Explosive Chemicals Removed from Schools," *Courier News*, April 18, 1979.

28. Benedict Crowell, *America's Munitions, 1917–1918: Report of Benedict Crowell, The Assistant Secretary of War, Director of Munitions* (Washington DC: Government Printing Office, 1919), 116.

29. "Three Cities Put Forth Claims for Picric Acid Plant," *Courier Journal*, May 18, 1918.

30. "Another Industrial Victory for Little Rock," *Arkansas Democrat*, May 22, 1918.

31. "Location of Picric Acid Plant Here Met with Enthusiasm," *Arkansas Democrat*, May 21, 1918.

32. "Material for Acid Plant Is Ordered," *Daily Arkansas Gazette*, May 29, 1918.

33. "Skilled Men Only to Stay at Picron," *Daily Arkansas Gazette*, December 11, 1918.

34. Sanborn Fire Insurance Company, *Sanborn Fire Insurance Map of Little Rock*, 100 ft. to 1 inch (Sanborn Fire Insurance Company, 1921).

35. Sprengel, *The Discovery of Picric Acid*.

36. Crowell, *America's Munitions, 1917–1918*.

37. Alexander Murray, "The Manufacture of Picric Acid," *Color Trade Journal* 4, no. 1 (1919): 5–8.

38. "Sink Wells for Picric Acid Plant," *Daily Arkansas Gazette*, June 7, 1918.

39. Murray, "The Manufacture of Picric Acid."

40. Leslie C. Stewart-Abernathy, "Urban Farmsteads: Household Responsibilities in the City," *Historical Archaeology* 20, no. 2 (1986): 5–15.

41. Rafael Marchán, "Rafael Marchán Statement" (Washington DC, 1918).

42. "Non-Essential Industries Here Are Designated," *Arkansas Democrat*, September 30, 1918.

43. "Porto Ricans Shy Only $40,000 Worth Clothes," *Daily Arkansas Gazette*, October 31, 1918.

44. U.S. House of Representatives, *Hearings Before the Select Committee on Expenditures in the War Department: Serial 1 - Volume 3, Reports of the Committee* (Washington, DC: Government Printing Office, 1921), 53.

45. Elizabeth Haiken, "'The Lord Helps Those Who Help Themselves': Black Laundresses in Little Rock, Arkansas, 1917–1921," *The Arkansas Historical Quarterly* 49, no. 1 (1990): 20–50.

46. "Jailed for Sedition," *Daily Arkansas Gazette*, October 1, 1918.

47. Marchán, "Rafael Marchán Statement."

48. GovernmentContractsWon.com, "Arkansas Defense Contractor Lists by City United States Government Contracts," 2017, https://www.government contractswon.com/department/defense/arkansas_cities.asp (accessed November 25, 2018).

49. U.S. House of Representatives, *Hearings Before the Select Committee on Expenditures in the War Department: Serial 1 - Volume 3, Reports of the Committee*, 35.

Chapter 4

1. Frank Lincoln Mather, ed., *Who's Who of the Colored Race: A General Biographical Dictionary of Men and Women of African Descent, Volume One* (Memento Edition, Half-Century Anniversary of Negro Freedom in U.S., Chicago, 1915), 227. Ray had also studied vocational education and dairying at Kansas Agricultural College in Manhattan and was the director of agriculture at Langston University in Oklahoma until he moved to Little Rock, Arkansas. See also the *Kansas State Agricultural College Catalogue, Fifty-First Session, 1913–1914* (Topeka: Kansas State Printing Office, 1914), 354.

2. Gloria Ray Karlmark is his daughter by his second wife, Julia. His first wife, Mary Lee McCrary Ray, was the first African American home demonstration agent hired in Arkansas in 1918. She died in 1934.

3. "5200 Registered for War Service from Little Rock," *Arkansas Democrat*, June 6, 1917, pg. 1.

4. Randy Finley, "Black Arkansans and World War One," *Arkansas Historical Quarterly* 49, no. 3 (Autumn 1990): 260. Emmett Jay Scott, *Scott's Official History of the American Negro in the World War* (Chicago: Homewood Press, 1919), 67.

5. "Ministers Will Explain Draft in Their Sermons," *Pine Bluff Daily Graphic*, June 1, 1917, 5.

6. Finley, "Black Arkansans and World War One," 257.

7. Thomas E. Patterson, *History of the Arkansas Teachers Association* (Washington, D.C.: National Education Association, 1981), 26.

8. "Says Negroes Are Loyal," *Arkansas Gazette*, April 9, 1917, 4; Finley, "Black Arkansans and World War One," 257.

9. "Branch to Train Negro Soldiers," *Arkansas Democrat*, September 2, 1918, 6.

10. Scott, *Scott's Official History*, 330.

11. "Program for Negro Soldiers," *Arkansas Democrat*, August 22, 1918, 7.

12. Scott, *Scott's Official History*, 104; "Bar Association Asks Light Penalty for Capt. Rowan," *Vardaman's Weekly*, Jackson, Mississippi, May 9, 1918, 6; "Would Not Order His Men to Fall in With Negroes," *Gaffney Ledger*, Gaffney, South Carolina, July 2, 1918, 1.

13. "Negro Sailor to Talk," *Daily Arkansas Gazette*, July 7, 1918, 10; Danny Groshong, "Taborian Hall," Central Arkansas Library System Encyclopedia of Arkansas, https://encyclopediaofarkansas.net/entries/taborian-hall-6984/ (accessed November 30, 2018).

14. "Negro Sailor to Talk," *Daily Arkansas Gazette*.

15. Scott, *Scott's Official History*, 471.

16. Scott, *Scott's Official History*, 472–473.

17. Finley, "Black Arkansans and World War One," 257.

18. "Negro Soldier Is Used for Mosquito Bait," *Arkansas Democrat*, July 18, 1918, 12.

19. Kerry L. Haynie and Candis S. Watts, "Blacks and the Democratic Party: A Resilient Coalition," in Jeffrey M. Stonecash, ed., *New Directions in American Political Parties* (New York: Routledge, 2010), 95.

20. "Lily Whites Bar 'Man and Brother,'" *Daily Arkansas Gazette*, June 30, 1914, 1.

21. "Negroes Are Told to Stay in Background," *Arkansas Democrat*, July 15, 1914, 1. The Mosaic Templars of America was founded in 1882.

22. "G.O.P. in a Split at Russellville," *Daily Arkansas Gazette*, April 22, 1920, 9.

23. "G.O.P. in a Split at Russellville," *Daily Arkansas Gazette*.

24. "Negro Women to Help," *Daily Arkansas Gazette*, April 27, 1917, 10.

25. See Elizabeth Griffin Hill, *Faithful to Our Tasks: Arkansas's Women and the Great War* (Little Rock: Butler Center Books, 2017). This book and an essay by Hill in this volume also discuss the activism and WWI work or the state's African American women.

26. "New Negro Federation Organized," *Daily Arkansas Gazette*, December 30, 1905, 7.

27. Charles Harris Wesley, *The History of the National Association of Colored Women's Clubs, A Legacy of Service* (Washington DC: National Association of Colored Women's Clubs, Inc., 1984), 486; Cherisse Jones-Branch, "Arkansas Association of Colored Women," Central Arkansas Library System Encyclopedia of Arkansas, https://encyclopediaofarkansas.net/entries/arkansas-association-of-colored-women-8201/ (accessed November 30, 2018).

28. "Donate Site for School," *Arkansas Gazette*, January 31, 1917, 8.

29. "Provision for Negro Boys," *Arkansas Gazette*, December 22, 1918, 11.

30. "Oppose 'Birth of a Nation,'" *Arkansas Gazette*, November 6, 1917, 8.

31. Finley, "Black Arkansans and World War One," 258.

32. "Register Negro Women," *Daily Arkansas Gazette*, February 19, 1918, 12.

33. "1000 Women Register," *Arkansas Democrat*, March 1, 1918, 2; "Hope to Induce Cooks to Conserve Food," *Arkansas Democrat*, July 25, 1917, 2.

34. "Negro Women Register," *Daily Arkansas Gazette*, March 2, 1918, 2; Hill, *Faithful to Our Tasks*, 13.

35. "Colored Patriots of Arkansas, Attention!," *Arkansas Democrat*, November 2, 1918, 9; "Little Rock is the Home of the Mosaic Templars of America," *Arkansas Democrat*, August 31, 1918, 67.

36. "Colored Patriots of Arkansas, Attention!," *Arkansas Democrat*.

37. "Employing Negro Women," *Batesville Guard*, Batesville, Arkansas, December 7, 1917, 3.

38. "Employing Negro Women," *Batesville Guard*.

39. "Women Employed as Laborers in Shops," *Arkansas Democrat*, October 4, 1918, 17.

40. "Women Do Men's Work: Negresses, Clad in Overalls, Employed in Lake Village Mills," *Daily Arkansas Gazette*, July 3, 1918, 9.

41. "Laundry Workers Given a Hearing, National War Labor Board Examiners Heard Their Complaints," *Daily Arkansas Gazette*, September 4, 1918, 8.

42. "Laundry Workers Given a Hearing," *Daily Arkansas Gazette*.

43. "To Help in Farm Work," *Arkansas Democrat*, June 10, 1918, 2.

44. "Around the City," *Arkansas Democrat*, September 13, 1918, 10.

45. Nan Woodruff, *American Congo: The African American Freedom Struggle in the Delta* (Cambridge, MA: Harvard University Press, 2003), 59–60.

46. "To Make Women Work or Fight," *Daily Arkansas Gazette*, September 22, 1918, 21.

47. Elizabeth Griffin Hill, *Faithful to Our Tasks*, 13.

48. Hill, *Faithful to Our Tasks*, 51.

49. "Negroes Help Red Cross," *Arkansas Democrat*, April 18, 1918, 4.

50. "Negro Women to Sew for the Red Cross," *Arkansas Democrat*, July 12, 1917, 1.

51. "Here and There in Arkansas," *Daily Arkansas Gazette*, June 10, 1918, 4.

52. Hill, *Faithful to Our Tasks*, 83.

53. Hill, *Faithful to Our Tasks*, 91.

54. "Recruit Negro Nurses," *Daily Arkansas Gazette*, August 5, 1918, 5.

55. Judith Anne Still, "Carrie Still Shepperson: The Hollows of Her Footsteps," *Arkansas Historical Quarterly* 42 no. 1 (Spring 1983): 40, 46.

56. "Acid Plant Here Met With Enthusiasm," *Arkansas Democrat*, May 21, 1918, 1.

57. "Late Locals," *Arkansas Democrat*, November 6, 1918, 8; "Picron, A Lively Suburb," *Arkansas Democrat*, November 13, 1918, 11, and "Ten Million Dollar Picric Acid Plant Is Awarded This City by War Department," *Arkansas Democrat*, May 21, 1918, 1.

58. "Raise Funds for Negro Soldiers," *Arkansas Democrat*, November 12, 1917, 9.

59. "Negro Ministers Meet," *Daily Arkansas Gazette*, July 3, 1918, 5.

60. "Negro Women Buy Bond," *Osceola Times*, May 3, 1918, 5.

61. "War Savings Campaign," *Daily Arkansas Gazette*, March 16, 1918, 2; "War Savings Club in Newport Grows," *Arkansas Democrat*, April 13, 1918, 2; See also Jajuan Johnson, "Pickens Black," Central Arkansas Library System Encyclopedia of Arkansas, https://encyclopediaofarkansas.net/entries/pickens-w-black-sr-5396/ (accessed November 30, 2018).

62. "Negro Women to Aid," *Hot Springs New Era*, September 17, 1918, 8. See also the "Report of the National Women's Liberty Loan Committee for the Fourth Liberty Loan Campaign, September 28th thru October 19th, 1918," entire document on hathitrust.org.

63. "Loan Leaders to Address Negroes," *Arkansas Democrat*, September 24, 1918, 4.

64. "Negro Women Organize," *Daily Arkansas Gazette*, September 25, 1918, 2.

65. "Negroes Impressed by Liberty Bond Address," *Arkansas Democrat*, April 23, 1918, 3.

66. "Negroes Impressed by Liberty Bond Address," *Arkansas Democrat*.

67. "Negro Soldiers Get Great Welcome Home," *Hot Springs New Era*, August 4, 1919, 2.

68. "Conway," *Daily Arkansas Gazette*, August 16, 1919, 11.

69. "Would Prohibit Negro Soldiers," *The Monticellonian*, Monticello, Arkansas, August 8, 1919, 2.

70. "To Keep Negroes Out of the Army," *Daily Arkansas Gazette*, August 1, 1919, 1.

71. "Race Troubles Near Star City Are Not Feared," *Pine Bluff Daily Graphic*, September 4, 1919, 1.

72. Woodruff, *American Congo*, 84.

73. Jeannie M. Whayne, "Low Villains and Wickedness in High Places: Race and Class in the Elaine Riots," *Arkansas Historical Quarterly* 58, no. 3 (Autumn 1999): 287.

74. Edward Passailaigue, Captain, Infantry, 3rd Ammunition Train to Assistant Chief of Staff, G-2, 3rd Division, October 7, 1919, Casefile 10218-372: Investigation of Race Riot, Elaine, Arkansas, 1919, folder 001360021-0766, *Federal Surveillance of Afro-Americans (1917-1925): The First World War, the Red Scare, and the Garvey Movement*, University Publications of America, 1985; Richard C. Cortner, *A Mob Intent on Death: The Arkansas Riot Cases* (Middletown, CT: Wesleyan University Press, 1988), 21.

75. David A. Joliffe, et al., *The Arkansas Delta Oral History Project: Culture, Place, and Authenticity* (Syracuse: Syracuse University Press, 2016), 171.

Chapter 5

1. Diary of J. H. Atkinson, June 25, 1918. J. H. Atkinson Papers, Arkansas State Archives, Little Rock, Arkansas.

2. Diary of J. H. Atkinson.

3. Unpublished document, Arkansas National Guard Museum, Camp Joseph T. Robinson, Little Rock, Arkansas.

4. "Camp Pike Exhibit," Arkansas National Guard Museum.

5. *Arkansas Gazette*, April 17, 1917, 1.

6. "Camp Pike Exhibit."

7. David Sesser, "World War I Training in Arkansas," in *To Can the Kaiser: Arkansas and the Great War*, ed. Michael D. Polston and Guy Lancaster (Little Rock: Butler Center Books, 2015), 23.

8. *Arkansas Gazette*, May 8, 1917, p. 1.

9. Ray Hanley, *Camp Robinson and the Military on the North Shore* (Charleston, SC: Arcadia, 2014), 9.

10. "Camp Pike Exhibit."

11. *Arkansas Gazette*, April 17, 1917, 1.

12. *Arkansas Gazette*, May 5, 1917, 1.

13. *Arkansas Gazette*, May 6, 1917, 1.

14. *Arkansas Gazette*, May 24, 1917, 1.

15. "Camp Pike Exhibit."

16. *Arkansas Gazette*, May 24, 1917, 1.

17. *Arkansas Gazette*, May 27, 1917, 1.

18. *Arkansas Gazette*, May 28, 1917, 1.

19. *Arkansas Gazette*, June 2, 1917, 1.

20. *Arkansas Gazette*, June 2, 1917, 1.

21. *Arkansas Gazette*, June 4, 1917, 1.

22. *Arkansas Gazette*, June 5, 1917, 1.

23. *Arkansas Gazette*, June 6, 1917, 1.

24. *Arkansas Gazette*, June 10, 1917, 1.

25. *Arkansas Gazette*, June 12, 1917, 1.

26. Sesser, "World War I Training in Arkansas," 23.

27. *Arkansas Gazette*, June 12, 1917, 1–2.

28. Leonard P. Ayres, *The War With Germany: A Statistical Summary* (Washington DC: Government Printing Press, 1919), 28.

29. *Arkansas Gazette*, May 30, 1917, 3.

30. *Arkansas Gazette*, June 1, 1917, 1.

31. Ayres, *The War With Germany*, 29.

32. *Arkansas Gazette*, June 12, 1917, 1.

33. *Arkansas Gazette*, August 26, 1917, 5.

34. Sesser, "World War I Training in Arkansas," 23.

35. *Arkansas Gazette*, June 15, 1917, 1.

36. *Arkansas Gazette*, June 14, 1917, 1.

37. *Arkansas Gazette*, June 18, 1917, 1.

38. Judy Byrd Brittenum, "John Rison Fordyce," Central Arkansas Library System Encyclopedia of Arkansas, https://encyclopediaofarkansas.net/entries/john-rison-fordyce-3186/ (accessed December 2, 2018).

39. S. W. Fordyce to Major John R. Fordyce, July 18, 1917, Arkansas State Archives.

40. Form, "Permanent Biographical, Civil, and Military Record Card For All Officers Under the Command of the Chief of Engineers," for Major John Fordyce. Filled out February 24, 1919, Arkansas State Archives.

41. Maj. John R. Fordyce, Biographical Materials, John Fordyce Papers, Arkansas State Archives.

42. Brittenum, "John Rison Fordyce."

43. *Arkansas Gazette*, June 22, 1917, 1.

44. *Arkansas Gazette*, June 25, 1917, 1.

45. *Arkansas Gazette*, July 1, 1917, 1.

46. *Arkansas Gazette*, July 12, 1917, 1.

47. *Arkansas Gazette*, July 16, 1917, 1.

48. *Arkansas Gazette*, July 23, 1917, 1.

49. *Arkansas Gazette*, July 12, 1917, 1.

50. *Arkansas Gazette*, July 16, 1917, 1.

51. J. R. Fordyce, Completion Report of Camp Pike" [1918], p. 3, Arkansas National Guard Museum.

52. Diary of Construction, Twelfth Division Cantonment, Edgar A. Grove, July 12, 1917, Arkansas State Archives.

53. Diary of Construction, Twelfth Division Cantonment, E. B. Black, July 14, 1917, Arkansas State Archives.

54. Diary of Construction, Twelfth Division Cantonment, Captain A. P. Upshur, July 13, 1917, Arkansas State Archives.

55. Dairy of Construction, E. B. Black, July 11, 1917, Arkansas State Archives.

56. Diary of Construction, E. B. Black, July 13, 1917, Arkansas State Archives.

57. John F. Fordyce, Camp Pike Construction Projections, 1917.

58. Diary of Construction, A. P. Upshur, August 6, 1917, Arkansas State Archives.

59. Diary of Construction, Twelfth Division Cantonment, John J. McConnell, July 21, 1917, Arkansas State Archives.

60. "Completion Report of Camp Pike," 8–9, Arkansas State Archives.

61. *Arkansas Gazette*, July 17, 1917, 3; July 18, 1917, 3.

62. *Arkansas Gazette*, August 8, 1917, 3.

63. *Arkansas Gazette*, August 2, 1917, 2.

64. John R. Fordyce to S. [Sam] W. Fordyce, August 11, 1917.

65. John Fordyce to S. W. Fordyce, September 17, 1917.

66. *Arkansas Gazette*, August 10, 1917, 1.

67. "Completion Report of Camp Pike," 7.

68. *Arkansas Gazette*, August 29, 1917, 2.

69. John Fordyce to S. W. Fordyce, September 12, 1917.

70. "Completion Report of Camp Pike," 7.

71. John Fordyce to S. W. Fordyce, September 12, 1917.

72. Flyer, distributed by John Fordyce, Camp Pike, Arkansas, 1917.

73. *Arkansas Gazette*, July 6, 1917, 1.

74. Sesser, "World War I Training in Arkansas," 24.

75. John R. Fordyce to S. [Sam] W. Fordyce, Jr., August 13, 1917.

76. John R. Fordyce to Colonel S. W. Fordyce, August 21, 1917.

77. [John Fordyce] "Report of Unfinished Work on December 5, 1917, of the authorized work at Camp Pike," December 11, 1917.

78. Hanley, *Camp Robinson and the Military on the North Shore*, 33.

79. "Camp Pike Exhibit."

80. Sesser, "World War I Training in Arkansas," 25.

81. John Fordyce to S. W. Fordyce, September 21, 1917.

82. *Arkansas Gazette*, September 2, 1917, 3

83. *Arkansas Gazette*, September 2, 1917, 1.

84. "Camp Pike Exhibit."

85. Unpublished document, information derived from the U.S. Army Center of Military History.

86. Michael David Polston, "'Time does not count here': Letters of a Camp Pike Doughboy," *Arkansas Historical Quarterly* (Spring 1986): 57.

87. *Trench and Camp* [Camp Pike], January 7, 1918, 1.

88. *Trench and Camp*, January 14, 1918, 4.

89. *Trench and Camp*, January 28, 1918, 8.

90. *Trench and Camp*, October 8, 1917, 4.

91. *Trench and Camp*, November 5, 1917, 7.

92. *Trench and Camp*, February 18, 1918, 8.

93. *Trench and Camp*, June 4, 1918, 7.

94. *Trench and Camp*, May 6, 1918, 4.

95. *Trench and Camp*, May 21, 1918, 5.

96. *Trench and Camp*, July 30, 1918, 1, 5.

97. *Trench and Camp*, December 3, 1917, 1.

98. *Trench and Camp*, March 18, 1917, 1

99. "Camp Pike Exhibit."

100. Unpublished document, information derived from the U.S. Army Center of Military History.

101. *Trench and Camp*, July 21, 1918, 4.

102. *Trench and Camp*, April 29, 1918, 1.

103. "Arkansas and the Great War: Camp Pike," Documentary, Butler Center for Arkansas Studies, 2016.

104. *Indian School Journal – About Indians*, November 1918, 110. Note: The Chilocco Indian School was located in northern Oklahoma near the Kansas border. It operated between 1885 and 1980.

105. *The Tomahawk*, January 31, 1918, 1.

106. American Battle Monuments Commission, www.fold3.com/title/853 /american-battle-monuments-commission (accessed December 2, 2018).

107. Sesser, "World War I Training in Arkansas," 24.

108. Diary of Construction, Twelfth Division Cantonment, A. P. Upshur, Captain, Medical Corps, August 2, 1917.

109. *Arkansas Gazette*, August 22, 1917, 3.

110. *Arkansas Gazette*, November 19, 1917, 5.

111. *Arkansas Gazette*, November 26, 1917, 4.

112. *Arkansas Gazette*, December 10, 1917, 1.

113. *Arkansas Gazette*, February 4, 1918, 8.

114. Kim Allen Scott, "Plague on the Homefront: Arkansas and the Great Influenza Epidemic of 1918," *Arkansas Historical Quarterly* (Winter 1988): 323–324.

115. Scott, "Plague on the Homefront," 329.

116. Camp Pike Exhibit.

117. Desmond Walls Allen, "1918 Camp Pike, Arkansas, Index to Soldiers' Naturalizations," 1988, 3.

118. Unpublished document, information derived from the U.S. Army Center of Military History.

119. Ayres, *The War With Germany*, 25.

120. "Camp Pike Exhibit."

121. Hanley, *Camp Robinson and the Military on the North Shore*, 32.

122. Nathan L. Barlow, "Camp Robinson's Role During World War II," *Arkansas Military Journal* (Fall 1994): 1.

123. E. W. Horner to E. M. Kirby, Chief Radio Branch, Washington DC, February 10, 1942.

124. Clyde F. Gay, "Beginning of the First World War: 1917 May–June, July, August." Notes by first civilian employee of the 6th Army Engineers, January 27, 1980. Unpublished document, Arkansas State Archives.

125. Unpublished document, information derived from the U.S. Army Center of Military History.

Chapter 6

1. Richard C. Cortner, *A Mob Intent on Death: The NAACP and the Arkansas Riot Cases* (Middletown: Wesleyan University Press, 1988); Grif Stockley, *Blood in Their Eyes: The Elaine Race Massacres of 1919* (Fayetteville: University of Arkansas Press, 2004); Robert Whitaker, *On the Laps of Gods: The Red Summer and the Struggle for Justice That Remade a Nation* (New York: Crown Publishers, 2008).

2. Nan Elizabeth Woodruff, *American Congo: The African American Freedom Struggle in the Delta* (Cambridge and London: Harvard University Press, 2003),

75–76; Randy Finley, "Black Arkansans and World War One," *Arkansas Historical Quarterly* 49, no. 3 (1990): 277.

3. Investigative Case Files of the Bureau of Investigation 1908–1922, Old German Files 1909–1921, RG65, NARA, M1085, C. M. Walser & C. R. Maxey report dated October 10, 1919, p. 5; Joey McCarty, "The Red Scare in Arkansas: A Southern State and National Hysteria," *Arkansas Historical Quarterly* 37, no. 3 (1978): 276–277; M. Langley Biegert, "Legacy of Resistance: Uncovering the History of Collective Action by Black Agricultural Workers in Central East Arkansas from the 1860s to the 1930s," *Journal of Social History* 32, no. 1 (1998): 85–87.

4. Cortner, *A Mob Intent on Death: The NAACP and the Arkansas Riot Cases*, 8; Stockley, *Blood in Their Eyes*, xxiii–xxiv; Whitaker, *On the Laps of Gods*, 78–80.

5. "Officer Comes for Negroes Charged with Inciting Riot," *New Orleans States Item*, November 10, 1919, 3; "Local Police Say They Have Caught Negro Ringleader," *Times-Picayune*, November 10, 1919, 1, 3.

6. Military Intelligence Division—Negro Subversion, RG 165, NARA M1440, Special Orders No. 264, 10218–372.

7. Advance Order from First Lieutenant T. A. Breen, Headquarters Third Division, Camp Pike, dated October 1, 1919, File 370.6, Elaine, Records of the Adjutant General's Office, RG407, NARA.

8. "Again on the Firing Line," *The Guardian*, October 11, 1919, 3; "Hats off to the Chaplain," *The Guardian*, October 11, 1919, 6.

9. Images of the deployment believed to be taken by Father Edward J. Sliney were found in the Arkansas State Archives (Charles Hillman Brough Collection: The Elaine Riot Scrapbook).

10. Report, Jenks to Sturgis, October 14, 1919, hereafter cited as Jenks Report, Records of the Adjutant General's Office, RG407, File 370.6, Elaine, NARA.

11. Jenks Report.

12. Ida B. Wells-Barnett, *The Arkansas Race Riot* (Chicago: Ida B. Wells-Barnett, 1920), 21.

13. Jenks Report; Guy Lancaster, ed., *The Elaine Massacre and Arkansas: A Century of Atrocity and Resistance, 1819–1919* (Little Rock: Butler Center Books, 2018), 237; Investigative Case Files of the Bureau of Investigation 1908–1922, Old German Files 1909–1921, NARA, M1085, C. M. Walser report titled: In RE: Negro Insurrection at Hoop Spur and Elaine in Phillips County, Arkansas, dated November 12, 1919, p. 3; J. W. Butts and Dorothy James, "The Underlying Causes of the Elaine Riot of 1919," *Arkansas Historical Quarterly* 20, no. 1 (1961): 95–104.

14. Jenks Report; Investigative Case Files of the Bureau of Investigation 1908–1922, Old German Files 1909–1921, NARA, M1085, C. M. Walser report titled: In RE: Negro Insurrection at Hoop Spur and Elaine in Phillips County, Arkansas, dated November 12, 1919, p. 2.

15. Jenks Report; Woodruff, *American Congo*, 78–79.

16. Wells-Barnett, *The Arkansas Race Riot*, 23; Jenks Report, Woodruff, *American Congo*, 78–79.

17. Woodruff, *American Congo*, 87–88; Gerald B. Lambert, *All Out of Step: A Personal Chronicle* (New York: Doubleday, 1956), 76–78.

18. Louis Sharpe Dunaway, *What a Preacher Saw through a Keyhole in Arkansas* (Little Rock: Parke-Harper Publishing, 1925), 102–109.

19. Jenks Report.

20. Military Intelligence Division - Negro Subversion, RG 165, NARA M1440, Report of Captain Edward P. Passailaigue dated October 7, 1919; Ralph H. Desmarais, "Military Intelligence Reports on Arkansas Riots: 1919–1920." *Arkansas Historical Quarterly* 33, no. 2 (1974): 175–191.

21. "Military Intelligence Reports on Arkansas Riots," *Arkansas Historical Quarterly*; Jenks Report.

22. "Blacks Prepared by Military Training for Arkansas Riots," *El Paso Herald*, November 6, 1919, 1.

23. Jenks Report; "Blacks Prepared by Military Training for Arkansas Riots," *El Paso Herald*.

24. Lancaster, *The Elaine Massacre and Arkansas*, 209, 211–212.

25. *Coffeyville Daily Journal*, "Posse Nabs Riot Leaders," January 22, 1920, 1

26. *Topeka Plaindealer*, "Plainsdealings," October 28, 1921.

27. Lancaster, *The Elaine Massacre and Arkansas*, 203–211

28. Dermott Board of Trade Bulletin dated March 26, 1920, Governor Henry Allen Collection, Correspondence Files 1919–1923, Kansas Historical Society.

29. Dunaway, *What a Preacher Saw through a Keyhole in Arkansas*, 102–109; Stockley, *Blood in Their Eyes*; Whitaker, *On the Laps of Gods*; *New Orleans States Item*, "Officer Comes for Negroes Charged with Inciting Riot," November 10, 1919, 1, 3.

30. Grif Stockley and Jeannie M. Whayne, "Federal Troops and the Elaine Massacres: A Colloquy," *Arkansas Historical Quarterly* 61, no. 3 (2002): 272–283.

31. Stockley and Whayne, "Federal Troops and the Elaine Massacres."

Chapter 7

1. John Barry, *The Great Influenza: The Epic Story of the Deadliest Plague in History* (New York: Viking Press, 2004), 93; Gavin Francis, "The Untreatable," a review of *Pale Rider: The Spanish Flu of 1918 and How It Changed the World* by Laura Spinney, *London Review of Books*, June 2017.

2. Francis, "The Untreatable"; Barry, *The Great Influenza*, 93–95.

3. Barry, *The Great Influenza*, 171; Francis, "The Untreatable."

4. Laura Spinney, *Pale Rider: The Spanish Flu of 1918 and How It Changed the World* (Public Affairs, 2017), 136.

5. Alfred Crosby, *America's Forgotten Pandemic: The Influenza of 1918* (Cambridge University Press, 2003); Barry, *The Great Influenza*; Francis, "The Untreatable."

6. Barry, *The Great Influenza*, 95.

7. Barry, *The Great Influenza*, 95–97.

8. Barry, *The Great Influenza*, 96.

9. Raymond Screws, Director at the Arkansas National Guard Museum, Camp Robinson, North Little Rock, Arkansas, interview with the author, August 21, 2018; Kim Allen Scott, "Plague on the Homefront: Arkansas and the Great Influenza Epidemic of 1918." *Arkansas Historical Quarterly* 47, no. 4 (Winter 1988): 323–324.

10. Scott, "Plague on the Homefront," 323–324, 329–330, 332.

11. *Arkansas Gazette*, October 13, 1918, quoted in Scott, "Plague on the Homefront," 331.

12. James Moshinskie, *Early Arkansas Undertakers* (Hot Springs: 1978), quoted in Scott, "Plague on the Homefront," 331–332.

13. "The 1918 Influenza Epidemic," a digital exhibit at the Arkansas National Guard Museum, Camp Robinson, Arkansas, http://arngmuseum.com/exhibits/exhibit-1918-influenza (accessed December 3, 2018).

14. Chantel Jennings, "A Season of Influenza and Influence: How World War I and a Pandemic in 1918 Changed College Football Forever." *The Athletic*, August 14, 2018.

15. Dorothy Ann Petit, "A Cruel Wind: America Experiences the Pandemic Influenza, 1918–1920, A Social History," PhD diss., University of New Hampshire, 1976. Quoted in Barry, *The Great Influenza*, 336.

16. Scott, "Plague on the Homefront," 323–324, 329, 332.

17. Eugene L. Opie, Allen W. Freeman, Francis G. Blake, James C. Small, and Thomas M. Rivers, *Pneumonia Following Influenza (at Camp Pike, Ark.)* (Chicago: The American Medical Association, 1919), 3. Reprinted from *The Journal of the American Medical Association*, February 22, 1919. The study indicated that 12,393 men at the camp contracted the flu and another 1,499 contracted pneumonia. However, the study lists only two persons as dying from the flu directly while another 466 are listed as dying of pneumonia. The researcher was an intern named Erik Brun.

18. Barry, *The Great Influenza*, 182.

19. Scott, "Plague on the Homefront," 321.

20. *Arkansas Gazette*, September 20, 1918, October 4, 1918.

21. *Arkansas Gazette*, October 5, 1918, October 6, 1918, October 8, 1918, quoted in Scott, "Plague on the Homefront," 320–321, 323.

22. *Nashville News*, October 16, 1918, October 23, 1918.

23. Scott, "Plague on the Homefront," 332.

24. Scott, "Plague on the Homefront," 336.

25. *Arkansas Gazette*, October 24, 1918.

26. Scott, "Plague on the Homefront," 321–322.

27. Marion Prather, letter to Brooks Hays, October 3, 1918. Lawrence Brooks Hays Papers, Special Collections, University of Arkansas Libraries, Fayetteville. Quoted in Scott, "Plague on the Homefront," 322.

28. Scott, "Plague on the Homefront," 326, 328; Brooks Hays, "The Campus Years," *Arkansas Historical Quarterly* 35 (Autumn 1976): 223–224, 227.

29. *The Courier* (Russellville), October 10, 1918.

30. James F. Willis, *Southern Arkansas University: The Mulerider School's Centennial History, 1909–2009* (Magnolia: Southern Arkansas University Foundation, 2009), 68.

31. *Arkansas Gazette*, October 24, 1918.

32. *Arkansas Democrat*, October 21, 1918.

33. Randi Knight, "The Influenza Epidemic of 1918 in Conway, Arkansas," University of Central Arkansas Archives, Small Manuscripts Collection 1452, 6–7; *Log Cabin Democrat* (Conway), October 7, 1918, October 8, 1918, November 4, 1918; *Troubadour* (Hendrix College Yearbook), "Calendar," 123.

34. *Log Cabin Democrat* (Conway), October 19, 1918, December 4, 1918; Knight, "The Influenza Epidemic of 1918 in Conway, Arkansas," 9.

35. *Fayetteville Daily Democrat*, October 23, 1918.

36. *Nashville News*, October 9, 1918, October 16, 1918, October 23, 1918; *Arkansas Gazette*, October 14, 1918.

37. *Nashville News*, October 9, 1918, October 14, 1918.

38. Information supplied by Frank Puryear, August 13, 2018.

39. *Arkansas Gazette*, October 24, 1918.

40. *Arkansas Gazette*, October 14, 1918.

41. *Arkansas Gazette*, October 14, 1918.

42. *Arkansas Gazette*, October 14, 1918.

43. Quoted in Francis, "The Untreatable."

44. *Arkansas Gazette*, October 24, 1918.

45. *Washington Telegraph*, October 25, 1918.

46. Scott, "Plague on the Homefront," 340–341.

47. *Pine Bluff Graphic*, December 15, 1918.

48. *Arkansas Gazette*, December 25, 1918.

49. Scott, "Plague on the Homefront," 340–342.

50. Scott, "Plague on the Homefront," 334.

51. Richard Collier, *The Plague of the Spanish Lady: The Influenza Pandemic of 1918-1919* (New York: Atheneum, 1974), 105. *Arkansas Gazette*, 22 October 1918. Dr. Geiger went on to a distinguished career as a researcher, professor, and public health official. He died at age ninety-five. For a brief account of Geiger's life, see Celia Storey, "Remembering (the extraordinary) Dr. Geiger," *Arkansas Gazette*, 24 September 2018.

52. Willis, *Southern Arkansas University*, 68.

53. Information supplied by Nan Snow, August 21, 2018.

54. Information supplied by Nan Snow, August 21, 2018.

55. *Pine Bluff Graphic*, December 3, 1918.

56. *Arkansas Democrat*, October 22, 1918.

57. *Pine Bluff Graphic*, November 12, 1918.

58. *Pine Bluff Graphic*, November 12, 1918.

59. *Arkansas Democrat Gazette*, December 7, 1918.

60. *Arkansas Democrat Gazette*, December 7, 1918.

61. *Dallas Morning News*, December 8. 1918. Reprinted in *Influenza Encyclopedia*, produced by the University of Michigan Center for the History of Medicine and Michigan Publishing, University of Michigan Library. Found at https://quod.lib.umich.edu/cgi/t/text/idx/f/flu/0050flu.0003.500/1/--theory -advanced?rgn=full+text;view=image;q1=Subject+--+theory+regarding +origin+of+influenza (accessed December 3, 2018).

62. Spinney, *Pale Rider*, 8.

63. Francis, "The Untreatable."

64. Thomas A. Garrett, "Economic Effects of the 1918 Influenza Pandemic: Implications for a Modern-Day Pandemic," Federal Reserve Bank of St. Louis (November 2007): 19. Cited in Nancy Hendricks, "PLAGUE!: The 1918 Influenza Epidemic in Arkansas," in *To Can the Kaiser: Arkansas and the Great War*, ed. Michael D. Polston and Guy Lancaster (Little Rock: Butler Center Books, 2015), 142.

65. Garrett cited in Hendricks, "PLAGUE," 142–143.

Chapter 8

1. Susan R. Grayzel, *Women and the First World War* (Essex, England: Pearson Education Limited, 2002), 104. According to Grayzel, one cannot ignore the "influence on women's disfranchisement" and lists countries that passed at least partial enfranchisement measures during or after the war: Austria, Belgium, Britain, Canada, Czechoslovakia, Denmark, Estonia, Germany, Hungary, Iceland, Latvia, Lithuania, Luxembourg, Poland, Sweden, and the United States, among others.

2. A substantial scholarship exists on the woman suffrage movement. For an overview, see Jean H. Baker, ed., *Votes for Women: The Struggle for Suffrage Revisited* (Oxford: Oxford University Press, 2002). For an overview of the struggle in the South, see Anne Firor Scott's *The Southern Lady: From Pedestal to Politics, 1830–1930* (Charlottesville: University of Virginia Press, 1970) and Marjorie Spruill Wheeler, *New Women of the New South: The Leaders of the Woman Suffrage Movement in the Southern States* (Oxford University Press, 1993), 102–113, 130–132. For an interesting new book that situates Midwestern suffragists in the national debate over woman suffrage, see Sara Egge, *Woman Suffrage and Citizenship, 1870–1920* (Iowa City: University of Iowa Press, 2018).

3. A. Elizabeth Taylor, "The Woman Suffrage Movement in Arkansas," *Arkansas Historical Quarterly* 15 (Spring 1956): 38–39.

4. My thanks to Michael Pierce for bringing this to my attention. See Freda Hogan to Mamey [Alice Hogan Wiley], July 9, 1917, Box 3, Folder 11, Oscar and Freda Ameringer Papers, Oklahoma Historical Society, Oklahoma City.

5. A. Elizabeth Taylor, "The Woman Suffrage Movement in Arkansas," *Arkansas Historical Quarterly* 15 (Spring 1956): 38–39; Paul Kyzer Taylor, "Women's Suffrage Movement," Central Arkansas Library System Encyclopedia of Arkansas, https://encyclopediaofarkansas.net/entries/womens-suffrage -movement-4252/ (accessed December 7, 2018).

6. Wheeler, *New Women of the New South*, 5; A. Elizabeth Taylor, "The Woman Suffrage Movement in Arkansas," 17–18. See also Jeanne Norton Rollberg, "Political Equality League," Central Arkansas Library System Encyclopedia of Arkansas, https://encyclopediaofarkansas.net/entries/political -equality-league-7834/ (accessed December 7, 2018); and Bernadette Cahill, *Arkansas Women and the Right to Vote, 1868–1920* (Little Rock: Butler Center Books, 2015), 34–35. For the antebellum South, see Stephanie McCurry, *Masters of Small Worlds: Yeomen Households & the Political Culture of the Antebellum South Carolina Low Country* (Oxford and New York: Oxford University Press, 1995). For Langley's Republican credentials, see Eugene Feistman, "Radical Disfranchisement in Arkansas, 1867–1868," *Arkansas Historical Quarterly* 12 (Summer 1953): 150 and Paul Palmer, "Miscegenation as an Issue in the Arkansas Constitutional Convention of 1868," *Arkansas Historical Quarterly* 24 (Summer 1965): 116, as well as John Williams Graves, *Town and Country: Race Relations in an Urban-Rural Context, Arkansas, 1865–1905* (Fayetteville: University of Arkansas Press, 1990), 21.

7. Rollberg, "Political Equality League."

8. A. Elizabeth Taylor, "The Woman Suffrage Movement in Arkansas," 19–20. Taylor identifies the organization meeting Fyler attended in 1884 as the National American Woman Suffrage Association (NAWSA), but since that organization was not founded until 1890, it is likely one of two other organizations:

The National Woman Suffrage Association or the American Woman Suffrage Association. The two organizations merged in 1890 to form NAWSA.

9. As cited in A. Elizabeth Taylor, "The Woman Suffrage Movement in Arkansas," 25.

10. A. Elizabeth Taylor, "The Woman Suffrage Movement in Arkansas," 28–29; Bernadette Cahill, "Clara Alma Cox McDiarmid (1847–1899)," Central Arkansas Library System Encyclopedia of Arkansas, https://encyclopediaof arkansas.net/entries/clara-alma-cox-mcdiarmid-8425/ (accessed December 7, 2018).

11. Cahill, *Arkansas Woman and the Right to Vote*, 27–28; A. Elizabeth Taylor, "The Woman Suffrage Movement in Arkansas," 24–29.

12. On book and literary clubs see Frances Mitchell Ross, "The New Woman as Club Woman and Social Activist in Turn of the Century Arkansas," *Arkansas Historical Quarterly* 50 (Winter 1991): 317–351 and Julianne H. Sallee, "General Federation of Women's Clubs in Arkansas," Central Arkansas Library System Encyclopedia of Arkansas, https://encyclopediaofarkansas.net/entries/general -federation-of-womens-clubs-of-arkansas-162/ (accessed December 7, 2018). For WCTU activities, see George H. Hunt, "A History of the Prohibition Movement in Arkansas" (MA thesis, University of Arkansas, 1933); Ben Johnson III, *John Barleycorn Must Die: The War against Drink in Arkansas* (Fayetteville: University of Arkansas Press, 2005), 38–42, 44–45, 56, 630–664, 67–69; Jeannie Whayne, "Caging the Blind Tiger: Race, Class, and Family in the Battle for Prohibition in Small Town Arkansas," *Arkansas Historical Quarterly* 71 (Spring 2012): 40–60 and Jane Ann Wilkerson, "Little Rock's Woman's Christian Temperance Union, 1888–1903" (MA thesis, University of Arkansas at Little Rock, 2009). See also Brent E. Riffel, "Prohibition," Central Arkansas Library System Encyclopedia of Arkansas, https://encyclopediaofarkansas.net/entries/prohibition-3002/ (accessed December 7, 2018).

13. A. Elizabeth Taylor, "The Woman Suffrage Movement in Arkansas," 28; Paula Kyzer Taylor, "Women's Suffrage Movement.". See also Rollberg, "Political Equality League" and Cahill, *Arkansas Women and the Right to Vote*, 44–45.

14. Michael Pierce, "Freda Hogan (1892–1988)," in *Arkansas Women: Their Lives and Times*, ed. Cherisse Jones-Branch and Gary T. Edwards (Athens: University of Georgia Press, 2018), 101–102.

15. Not to be confused with the defunct American Woman Suffrage Association (AWSA) under Stone/Howe which merged with the National Woman Suffrage Association (NWSA) under Stanton/Anthony in 1890 to become the National American Woman Suffrage Association (NAWSA)

16. Paula Kyzer Taylor, "Women's Suffrage Movement."

17. Cahill, *Arkansas Women and the Right to Vote*, 93

18. Paula Kyler Taylor, "Women's Suffrage Movement."

19. Lessie Stringfellow Read Papers, Special Collections, University of Arkansas Libraries, Fayetteville, Arkansas, MS R22, 233-B, Series 1, Folder 2, Box 2, newspaper clipping, May 16, 1915. Although the clipping did not identify the newspaper, it was almost certainly the *Northwest Arkansas Times*, for which Read worked.

20. Paula Kyzer Taylor, "Women's Suffrage Movement."

21. Paula Kyzer Taylor, "Women's Suffrage Movement."

22. Lea Flowers Baker, "Women," Central Arkansas Library System Encyclopedia of Arkansas, https://encyclopediaofarkansas.net/entries/women-400/ (accessed December 7, 2018); See also Cahill, *Arkansas Women and the Right to Vote*, 89–90.

23. A. Elizabeth Taylor, "Woman Suffrage in Arkansas," 42; Paula Kyzer Taylor, "Women's Suffrage Movement"; Freeman, *Arkansas Women*, 112. On John Riggs, see Elizabeth Riggs Brandon, "John Andrew Riggs (1867–1936)," Central Arkansas Library System Encyclopedia of Arkansas, https://encyclopediaof arkansas.net/entries/john-andrew-riggs-5509/ (accessed December 7, 2018). On the "boodling" charge, see James F. Willis, "Lewis Rhoton and the "Boodlers": Political Corruption and Reform during Arkansas's Progressive Era," *Arkansas Historical Quarterly* (Summer 2017): 123.

24. As cited in Lorraine Gates Schuyler, *The Weight of Their Votes: Southern Women and Political Leverage in the 1920s* (Chapel Hill: University of North Carolina Press, 2006), 27–28.

25. J. Morgan Kousser, *The Shaping of Southern Politics: Suffrage Restriction and the Establishment of the One-Party South, 1880–1910* (New Haven and London: Yale University Press, 1974), 127–129.

26. Graves, *Town and Country*, 194–195; John Kirk, "Civil Rights and Social Change," Central Arkansas Library System Encyclopedia of Arkansas, https:// encyclopediaofarkansas.net/entries/civil-rights-and-social-change-4564/ (accessed December 7, 2018).

27. Wheeler, *New Women of the New South*, 102–113, 130–132.

28. Cherisse Jones-Branch, "Mame Stewart Josenberger (ca. 1868–1964)," Arkansas Women's Suffrage Centennial Project, https://ualrexhibits.org/suffrage /mame-stewart-josenberger-ca-1868–1964/ (accessed December 7, 2018). And my thanks to Cherisse Jones-Branch for sharing this newspaper clipping with me on the meeting of the African American Eastern Star: "Negro O.E.S. Meets," *Arkansas Gazette*, July 3, 1919, 2.

29. Barney R. McLaughlin, "Men's and Women's Perspectives: The Woman Suffrage Debate in Arkansas, 1915–1919," *Ozark Historical Review* 21 (Spring 1993): 36–37.

30. Elizabeth Hill, "A Service that Could Not Be Purchased," in *To Can the Kaiser: Arkansas and the Great War*, ed. Michael D. Polston and Guy Lancaster, 51–52. (She cites Report of the Arkansas Women's Committee 68, ASA/LR).

31. Grayzel, *Women and the First World War*, 85.

32. Hill, "A Service that Could Not Be Purchased," 90.

33. Ida Clyde Clarke, *American Women and the World War* (New York and London: D. Appleton & Company, 1918), online at https://net.lib.byu.edu/estu /wwi/comment/Clarke/Clarke00TC.htm (accessed December 7, 2018). In addition to Rutherford-Fuller, Mrs. J. E. Andres Harrison, also of Little Rock, served as treasurer. Serving as heads of departments were: a Mrs. Schoenfeldt, Registration; Mrs. Byrd Tatum, Food Production; Mrs. G. W. Garrison, Child Welfare; Mrs. Frank Peel, Maintenance of Existing Social Agencies; Mrs. C. H. (Anne) Brough, Education; Mrs. E. O. Ellington, Liberty Loan; and a Mrs. Markwell, Health and Recreation. Except for Frauenthal, Peel, and Tatum, all the women were from Little Rock. Peel was from Bentonville and Tatum from Morrilton.

34. Hill, "A Service that Could Not Be Purchased," 90–91.

35. Report of the Arkansas Women's Committee, 9, Arkansas History Commission, Little Rock, as cited in Hill, "A Service that Could Not Be Purchased," p. 96.

36. J. Blake Perkins, "Persuading Arkansas for War: Propaganda and Homefront Mobilization during the First World War," in *To Can the Kaiser*, 68. See Elizabeth Hill for more on the contribution of the Home Demonstration Program, Hill, "A Service that Could Not Be Purchased," 93.

37. Hill, "A Service that Could Not Be Purchased," 92.

38. My thanks to Elizabeth Hill for bringing this to my attention. Cited in Hill, "A Service that Could Not Be Purchased," 96 and in Elizabeth Griffin Hill, *Faithful to Our Tasks: Arkansas's Women and the Great War* (Little Rock: Butler Center Books, 2017), 132.

39. Steven Teske, "Arming Arkansas: Putting the State on a War Footing," *To Can the Kaiser*, 16–17.

40. J. Blake Perkins, "Persuading Arkansas for War: Propaganda and Homefront Mobilization during the First World War," *To Can the Kaiser*, 67.

41. Hill, "A Service that Could Not Be Purchased," 95.

42. As quoted in J. Blake Perkins, "Persuading Arkansas for War," 68.

43. Cahill, *Arkansas Women and the Right to Vote*, 24–25.

44. Bernadette Cahill, "Stepping Outside the Bounds of Convention: Adolphine Fletcher Terry and the Radical Suffragism in Little Rock, 1911–1920," *Pulaski County Historical Review* 60 (Winter 2012): 124–126; Cahill, *Arkansas Women and the Right to Vote*, 48.

45. Cahill, "Stepping Outside the Bounds of Convention," 126.

46. Andrew Glass, "Woodrow Wilson Endorses Women's Suffrage on Sept. 30, 1918," *Politico*, September 30, 2007, https://www.politico.com/story/2007/09/woodrow-wilson-endorses-womens-suffrage-on-sept-30–1918–006071 (accessed December 7, 2018); Nancy Hendricks, "PLAGUE!: The 1918 Influenza Epidemic in Arkansas," *To Can the Kaiser*, 143.

47. "Present Qualifications of Electors Will Continue in Operation and Apply to Women Under the Federal Suffrage Amendment," Joseph T. Robinson Papers, Special Collections, University of Arkansas Libraries, Fayetteville, Arkansas, MS R 563, Series 7:1, Box/folder: 56: 2.

48. League of Women Voters of Arkansas, "History of the League," http://www.lwv-arkansas.org/history.html (accessed December 7, 2018). See also Paula Kyzer, "Promoting Political Responsibility: The League of Women Voters of Pulaski County," *Pulaski County Historical Review* 390 (Spring 1991): 53.

49. Sarah Wilkerson Freeman: "A Southern Stealth Feminist and Enigmatic Liberal (1878–1950)," in *Arkansas Women: Their Lives and Times*, 112.

50. Schuyler, *The Weight of their Votes*, 78.

51. Freeman, "A Southern Stealth Feminist and Enigmatic Liberal," 112.

52. Schuyler, *The Weight of their Votes*, 204.

53. Schuyler, *The Weight of their Votes*, 79; for the lily-white struggle within Arkansas in that year, see Todd E. Lewis, "Elias Camp Morris (1855–1922), Central Arkansas Library System Encyclopedia of Arkansas, https://encyclopedia ofarkansas.net/entries/elias-camp-morris-433/ (accessed December 7, 2018).

54. Velda Brotherton, "Virginia Maud Dunlap Duncan (1873–1958)," Central Arkansas Library System Encyclopedia of Arkansas, https://encyclopedia

ofarkansas.net/entries/virginia-maud-dunlap-duncan-1633/ (accessed December 7, 2018); Jefferson M. (Mrs. W. T.) Dorough, "The First Woman Legislator in Arkansas: A Tribute to Miss Erle Chambers," *Pulaski County Historical Review* 64 (Fall 2016); and Arkansas Senate, "More Women Than Ever Now Serving in the Arkansas Legislature," http://www.arkansas.gov/senate/newsroom/index .php?do:newsDetail=1&news_id=220 (accessed December 7, 2018).

55. Schuyler, *The Weight of their Votes*, 82; Julienne Crawford, "Hattie Ophelia Wyatt Caraway (1878–1950)," Central Arkansas Library System Encyclopedia of Arkansas, https://encyclopediaofarkansas.net/entries/hattie-ophelia-wyatt-caraway -1278/ (accessed December 7, 2018); David Malone, *Hattie and Huey: An Arkansas Tour* (Fayetteville: University of Arkansas Press, 1989): 1–3.

56. League of Women Voters of Washington County, Proceedings and Scrapbooks, LOC 1445, Series 1, Vol. 1, 1920–21. See minutes for April 1, May 6, June 10, July 8 and 9, and December 9, 1920; and February 10 and 15, March 10, May 12 and 17, June 9, and October 21, 1921.

57. J. Stanley Lemons, "The Sheppard-Towner Act: Progressivism in the 1920s," *Journal of American History* 55 (March 1969): 776.

58. Schuyler, *The Weight of their Votes*, 169.

59. Diane Kincaid (Blair) to Jane Mansbridge, October 2, 1987, Diane Blair Papers, Special Collections, University of Arkansas Libraries, Fayetteville, Arkansas, Series II, Subseries 1, Box 8, File 21.

60. Mary Jordan, "Record number of women heading to Congress," Washington Post, Nov. 8, 2018, https://www.washingtonpost.com/politics /record-number-of-women-appear-headed-for-congress/2018/11/06/76a9e 60a-e1eb-11e8–8f5f-a55347f48762_story.html?utm_term=.09b15b98df89 (accessed December 20, 2018).

Chapter 9

1. "Carnival Crowds Write 'Peace Day' in City Annals," *Arkansas Gazette*, November 12, 1918.

2. "Carnival Crowds Write 'Peace Day' in City Annals," *Arkansas Gazette*, November 12, 1918.

3. There have been some remarkably valuable recent works in World War I historiography. Among the best are: Heather Jones, "As the Centenary Approaches: The Regeneration of First World War Historiography, *The Historical Journal* 56 (2013): 857–878; Akira Iriye, "The Historiographic Impact of the Great War," *Diplomatic History* 38 (2014): 751–762; and Jennifer Keene, "Remembering the 'Forgotten War': American Historiography on World War I," *The Historian* 78 (2016): 439–468.

4. While the figure of $33 billion is accurate and frequently cited amongst historians and scholars, technically Germany was only required to pay $12.5 billion of this without reservation, while the victorious Allies set the remaining $20.5 billion aside and subject to possible re-assessment.

5. Walter Lippmann, *U.S. War Aims* (Boston: Little Brown, 1944), 161–163.

6. Thomas Bailey, *Woodrow Wilson and the Lost Peace* (New York: MacMillan, 1944).

7. John Meynard Keynes, *The Economic Consequences of the Peace* (New York: Dover, 2004), 233–235.

8. John Meynard Keynes, *A Revision of the Treaty* (London: MacMillan and Co., 1922), 1.

9. Keynes, *A Revision of the Treaty*, 186, and Adolf Hitler, *Mein Kampf* (New York: Houghton Mifflin, 1999), 654–655.

10. William Langer, "Alliance System and League," from *Explorations in Crisis: Papers on International History* (Cambridge: Belknap, 1969), 201. This article was first published in 1936 in *Polity*.

11. William Langer, "The Revival of Imperialism," from *Explorations in Crisis: Papers on International History*, 211. This article was first published in 1937 in *Harvard Guardian*.

12. See William Langer and S. Everett Gleason, *The Challenge to Isolation: 1937–1940* (New York: Harpers Brothers, 1953), in particular, "Farewell to Appeasement," 52–90.

13. Alan Kramer, "Recent Historiography of the First World War" Part II, *Journal of Modern European History* 12 (2014): 72.

14. Martin Francis, "Attending to Ghosts: Some Reflections on the Disavowals of British Great War Historiography," *Twentieth Century British History* 25 (2014): 361.

15. Historiography is the study of how historians have analyzed, written about, and debated past events.

16. Fritz Fischer, *Griff Nach der Weltmacht* (Dusseldorf: Droste, 1967).

17. Annika Mombauer, "Introduction: The Fischer Controversy after 50 Years," *Journal of Contemporary History* 48 (2013): 231–240.

18. Klaus Schwabe, "World War I and the Rise of Hitler," *Diplomatic History* 38 (2014): 864.

19. John Tierney Jr., "For America, the War to End War Was Just the Beginning," *Brown Journal of World Affairs* 21 (2014): 219–229.

20. John A. Moses, "The War Guilt Question: A Note on Politics and Historiography in the Weimar Republic," *Australian Journal of Politics and History* 61 (2015): 128–134.

21. Moses, "The War Guilt Question," 129.

22. Anthony Linter, *Lloyd George, Woodrow Wilson, and the Guilt of Germany* (Baton Rouge: Louisiana State, 1984), xiii.

23. John Milton Cooper Jr. "The World War and American Memory," *Diplomatic History* 38 (2014): 732.

24. For more information about the colorful story of John Heiskell and the *Arkansas Gazette*, see John A. Thompson, "Gentleman Editor: Mr. Heiskell of the *Gazette*: The Early Years," MA thesis, University of Arkansas at Little Rock, 1983; John A. Thompson, "An Ambition Achieved: J. N. Heiskell Becomes Editor of the 'Arkansas Gazette,'" Arkansas Historical Quarterly 46 (1987): 156–166; and Donna Lampkin Stephens, "*Arkansas Gazette*," Encyclopedia of Arkansas, https://encyclopediaofarkansas.net/entries/arkansas-gazette-2344/ (accessed December 7, 2018).

25. This seems to be the perspective of John A. Thompson in his MA thesis about Heiskell (see note 22)..

26. Fred Allsopp, *History of the Arkansas Press for a Hundred Years and More* (Little Rock: Parke-Harper, 1922), 19.

27. Some other sources say 1923. The 1924 date can be found in Karl Meyer, ed., *Fulbright of Arkansas: The Public Positions of a Private Thinker* (Washington: Luce, 1963), xxi–xxii.

28. Nan Snow and Dorothy Stuck, "The Formidable Roberta Fulbright," *Arkansas Historical Quarterly* 57 (1998): 33–45, and Dorothy Stuck, "Roberta Waugh Fulbright," Central Arkansas Library System Encyclopedia of Arkansas, https://encyclopediaofarkansas.net/entries/roberta-waugh-fulbright-1653/ (accessed December 7, 2018).

29. See the introductory comments in Roberta Fulbright, *As I See It* (Fayetteville: Privately published, 1952). Just as in the case of her husband, some sources list a different year of death for Roberta, in this case 1953.

30. Allsopp, *History of the Arkansas Press*, 464.

31. Schwabe, "World War I and the Rise of Hitler," 879.

32. "PEACE," *Fayetteville Democrat*, November 7, 1918.

33. "Peace Terms," *Fayetteville Democrat*, November 11, 1918.

34. "Terms Granted Germany Most Drastic Ever Forced Upon a Fallen Foe," *Arkansas Gazette*, November 12, 1918.

35. Thompson "Gentleman Editor," 167–168.

36. "Rebuking Wilson," *Fayetteville Democrat*, November 11, 1918.

37. "Americanism—Not Politics," *Fayetteville Democrat*, November 12, 1918.

38. I readily include myself in that category.

39. "Democrats Await the Return of Wilson," *Arkansas Gazette*, June 28, 1919.

40. "Read the Covenant," *Fayetteville Democrat*, June 30, 1919.

41. "Peace Treaty Not Ratified; Is Laid Aside," *Arkansas Gazette*, November 20, 1919.

42. "Germany and the Present Emergency," *Arkansas Gazette*, January 13, 1923.

43. "What Forests Mean to Germany," *Arkansas Gazette*, January 18, 1923.

44. "Europe and America's Responsibility," *Arkansas Gazette*, January 29, 1923. A more sarcastic and caustic view of the crisis was expressed in "Yea, Let's See," *Arkansas Gazette*, January 29, 1923.

45. Associated Press, "German Fascisti Meet in Bavaria," *Arkansas Gazette*, January 29, 1923.

46. "Coal for Coal," *Fayetteville Democrat*, February 3, 1923.

47. "Reluctant Approval Expected in France," *Arkansas Gazette*, August 17, 1924.

48. "After German Trade," *Fayetteville Democrat*, August 26, 1924.

49. "France and Germany and Lasting Peace," *Arkansas Gazette*, October 17, 1925.

50. "Christmas, the Great Law of Love, and the Locarno Pact," *Fayetteville Democrat*, December 2, 1925.

51. "Signing the War Renunciation Pact at Paris," *Arkansas Gazette*, August 29, 1928.

52. "We're Not Going to War for Oil in Ethiopia," *Arkansas Gazette*, September 1, 1935.

53. "The Rhine and France and Germany," *Arkansas Gazette*, March 10, 1936.

54. "The Rhine and France and Germany," *Arkansas Gazette*, March 10, 1936.

55. "Europe and Armageddon," *Arkansas Gazette*, March 10, 1936.

56. "If No Search Were Made for Amelia Earhart," *Arkansas Gazette*, July 9, 1937.

57. I say "appear," in that my search methods were certainly less than perfect and among the hundreds of pages of microfilm I reviewed, my blurry eyes may have admittedly missed an editorial or two.

58. "Roosevelt and Hitler and the Fate of Europe," *Arkansas Gazette*, September 29, 1938.

59. "Isn't Hitler Looking Beyond the Sudetenland?," *Arkansas Gazette*, September 30, 1938.

60. It is this sort of thing that raises questions as to whether John Heiskell wrote all the *Gazette*'s editorials.

61. "Let Us Prepare," *Northwest Arkansas Times*, September 22, 1938.

62. Roberta Fulbright, "As I See It: A Column of Comment," *Northwest Arkansas Times*, September 28, 1938.

63. Roberta Fulbright, "As I See It: A Column of Comment," *Northwest Arkansas Times*, September 28, 1938.

64. "They Wouldn't Listen to Mr. Roosevelt's Warning," *Arkansas Gazette*, September 1, 1939.

65. "What of the United States?" *Arkansas Gazette*, September 2, 1939.

66. "The Tragedy of Munich in the Light of Today" *Arkansas Gazette*, September 4, 1939.

67. Roberta Fulbright, "As I See It: A Column of Comment," *Northwest Arkansas Times*, August 31, 1939.

68. "War!," *Northwest Arkansas Times*, September 1, 1939.

69. "Time for Thinking," *Northwest Arkansas Times*, September 4, 1939.

70. Roberta Fulbright, "As I See It: A Column of Comment," *Northwest Arkansas Times*, September 4, 1939.

71. "No Comfort for Dictators," *Arkansas Gazette*, March 13, 1941.

72. "Guarantee of Liberty," *Northwest Arkansas Times*, August 4, 1941.

73. "How Could America Avoid 'Foreign Entanglements?,'" *Arkansas Gazette*, December 5, 1941.

74. "Who Brought This Suffering upon Japan?," *Arkansas Gazette*, December 5, 1941.

75. "To the End and to the Death," *Arkansas Gazette*, December 8, 1941.

76. "We Will Do Our Duty," *Northwest Arkansas Times*, December 8, 1941.

77. "We Will Do Our Duty," *Northwest Arkansas Times*, December 8, 1941.

78. "It Adds Up," *Northwest Arkansas Times*, December 11, 1941.

79. "Of Course Hitler Didn't Want War With Us—Just Now," *Arkansas Gazette*, December 13, 1941.

80. "Nobody enjoys isolation more today than an isolationist," *Arkansas Gazette*, December 13, 1941.

81. Roberta Fulbright, "As I See It: A Column of Comment," *Northwest Arkansas Times*, December 12, 1941.

BIBLIOGRAPHY

Archival Sources

Arkansas State Archives:
  Council of Defense Records
  J. H. Atkinson Papers
  John Fordyce Papers
  Report of the Arkansas Woman's Committee

Butler Center for Arkansas Studies, Central Arkansas Library System:
  American Red Cross Collection

Center for Arkansas History and Culture, University of Arkansas at Little Rock:
  Federation of Women's Clubs Records

National Archives and Records Administration:
  Annual Narrative Report, State Home Demonstration Agent, Record
    Group 33
  Records of the United States Senate; Record Group 46

Oklahoma Historical Society, Oklahoma City:
  Oscar and Freda Ameringer Papers

Special Collections, University of Arkansas Libraries, Fayetteville, Arkansas:
  Diane Blair Papers
  Joseph T. Robinson Papers
  Lawrence Brooks Hays Papers
  Lessie Stringfellow Read Papers

University of Central Arkansas Archives:
  Small Manuscripts Collection

Books

Baker, Jean H., ed. *Votes for Women: The Struggle for Suffrage Revisited*. Oxford:
  Oxford University Press, 2002.
Barnes, Kenneth C. *Anti-Catholicism in Arkansas: How Politicians, the Press, the
  Klan, and Religious Leaders Imagined an Enemy, 1910–1960*. Fayetteville:
  University of Arkansas Press, 2016.
Barry, John. *The Great Influenza: The Epic Story of the Deadliest Plague in History*.
  New York: Viking Press, 2004.
Blight, David W. *Race and Reunion: The Civil War in American Memory*. Cambridge,
  MA: Harvard University Press, 2001.

Cahill, Bernadette. *Arkansas Women and the Right to Vote, 1868–1920*. Little Rock: Butler Center Books, 2015.

Christ, Mark K., and Cathryn H. Slater. *Sentinels of History: Reflections on Arkansas Properties on the National Register of Historic Places*. Fayetteville: University of Arkansas Press, 2000.

Churchill, Winston. *The World Crisis, 1911–1918*. New York: Free Press, 2005.

Collier, Richard. *The Plague of the Spanish Lady: The Influenza Pandemic of 1918–1919*. New York: Atheneum, 1974.

Clarke, Ida Clyde. *American Women and the World War*. New York: D. Appleton and Company, 1918.

Congressional Medal of Honor and Distinguished Service Cross. United States War Department, 1919.

Cooper, John Milton. *Woodrow Wilson: A Biography*. New York: Vintage Books, 2011.

Cortner, Richard C. *A Mob Intent on Death: The Arkansas Riot Cases*. Middletown, CT: Wesleyan University Press, 1988.

Crosby, Alfred. *America's Forgotten Pandemic: The Influenza of 1918*. Cambridge University Press, 2003.

Crowell, Benedict. *America's Munitions, 1917–1918: Report of Benedict Crowell, The Assistant Secretary of War, Director of Munitions*. Washington DC: Government Printing Office, 1919.

D'Amore, Laura Mattoon, and Jeffrey Meriwether. *We Are What We Remember: The American Past through Commemoration*. Cambridge Scholars Publishing, 2012.

Davenport, Matthew J. *First Over There: The Attack on Cantigny, America's First Battle of World War I*. New York: St. Thomas Press, 2015.

Degler, Carl N. *At Odds: Women and the Family in America from the Revolution to the Present*. New York: Oxford University Press, 1980.

Dunaway, Louis Sharpe. *What a Preacher Saw through a Keyhole in Arkansas*. Little Rock: Parke-Harper Publishing, 1925.

Egge, Sara. *Woman Suffrage and Citizenship, 1870–1920*. Iowa City: University of Iowa Press, 2018.

Faulkner, Richard. *Pershing's Crusaders: The American Soldier in World War I*. Lawrence: University Press of Kansas.

Federal Surveillance of Afro-Americans (1917–1925): The First World War, the Red Scare, and the Garvey Movement. Lanham, MD: University Publications of America, 1985.

Foner, Philip S. *Women and the American Labor Movement: From World War I to the Present*. New York: The Free Press, a Division of Macmillan Publishing, Inc., 1980.

Fussell, Paul. *Great War and Modern Memory*. Oxford: Oxford University Press, 2013.

Gladden, Washington. *Christianity and Socialism*. New York: Eaton & Mains, 1905.

Graves, John Williams. *Town and Country: Race Relations in an Urban-Rural Context, Arkansas, 1865–1905*. Fayetteville: University of Arkansas Press, 1990.

Grayzel, Susan R. *Women and the First World War*. Essex, England: Pearson Education Limited, 2002.

Gutiérrez, Edward A. *Doughboys on the Great War: How American Soldiers Viewed Their Military Experience*. Lawrence: University Press of Kansas, 2014.

Hanley, Ray. *Camp Robinson and the Military on the North Shore*. Charleston, SC: Arcadia, 2014.

Hart, B. H. Liddell. *The War in Outline, 1914–1918*. New York: Random House, 1936.

Heller, Charles E. *Chemical Warfare in World War I: The American Experience, 1917–1918*, Leavenworth Papers 10. Fort Leavenworth, KS: U.S. Army Command and General Staff College, 1984.

Hill, Elizabeth Griffin. *A Splendid Piece of Work 1912–2012: One Hundred Years of Arkansas's Home Demonstration and Extension Homemakers Clubs*. CreateSpace: 2012.

Hill, Elizabeth Griffin, *Faithful to Our Tasks: Arkansas's Women and the Great War*. Little Rock: Butler Center Books, 2018.

House, Roger. *Blue Smoke: The Recorded Journey of Big Bill Broonzy*. Baton Rouge: Louisiana State University Press, 2010.

Johnson, Ben, III. *John Barleycorn Must Die: The War against Drink in Arkansas*. Fayetteville: University of Arkansas Press, 2005.

Joliffe, David A., et al. *The Arkansas Delta Oral History Project: Culture, Place, and Authenticity*. Syracuse: Syracuse University Press, 2016.

Jones-Branch, Cherisse, and Gary T. Edwards, eds. *Arkansas Women: Their Lives and Times*. Athens: University of Georgia Press, 2018.

Keegan, John. *First World War*. New York: A. Knopf, 1999.

Koistinen, Paul A. C. *The Military-Industrial Complex: A Historical Perspective*. New York: Praeger, 1980.

Kousser, J. Morgan. *The Shaping of Southern Politics: Suffrage Restriction and the Establishment of the One-Party South, 1880–1910*. New Haven and London: Yale University Press, 1974.

Lambert, Gerald B. *All Out of Step: A Personal Chronicle*. New York: Doubleday, 1956.

Lancaster, Guy. *The Elaine Massacre and Arkansas: A Century of Atrocity and Resistance, 1819–1919*. Little Rock: Butler Center Books, 2018.

Laurie, Clayton David, and Ronald H. Cole. *The Role of Federal Military Forces in Domestic Disorders, 1877–1945*. Washington DC: Center of Military History, 1997.

Lisenby, Foy. *Charles Hillman Brough: a Biography*. Fayetteville: University of Arkansas Press, 1996.

Malone, David. *Hattie and Huey: An Arkansas Tour*. Fayetteville: University of Arkansas Press, 1989.

Marrs, Timothy T., Robert L. Maynard, and Frederick Sidell. *Chemical Warfare Agents: Toxicology and Treatment*. John Wiley & Sons, 2007.

Mather, Frank Lincoln, ed. *Who's Who of the Colored Race: A General Biographical Dictionary of Men and Women of African Descent, Volume One*. Memento Edition, Half-Century Anniversary of Negro Freedom in U.S., Chicago: 1915.

McCurry, Stephanie. *Masters of Small Worlds: Yeoman Households, Gender Relations, & the Political Culture of the Antebellum South Carolina Low Country* (Oxford and New York: Oxford University Press, 1995).

McWhirter, Cameron. *Red Summer: The Summer of 1919 and the Awakening of Black America*. New York: Henry Holt, 2011.

Moneyhon, Carl. *Arkansas and the New South, 1874–1929*. Fayetteville: Arkansas University Press, 1997.

Murray, Jennifer M. *On a Great Battlefield: The Making, Management, and Memory of Gettysburg National Military Park, 1933–2013*. Knoxville: University of Tennessee Press, 2016.

Opie, Eugene L., Allen W. Freeman, Francis G. Blake, James C. Small, and Thomas M. Rivers. *Pneumonia Following Influenza (at Camp Pike, Ark.)*. Chicago: The American Medical Association, 1919.

Patterson, Thomas E. *History of the Arkansas Teachers Association*. Washington DC: National Education Association, 1981.

Polston, Michael D., and Guy Lancaster, *To Can the Kaiser: Arkansas and the Great War*. Little Rock: Butler Center Books, 2015.

Schuyler, Lorraine Gates. *The Weight of Their Votes: Southern Women and Political Leverage in the 1920s*. Chapel Hill: University of North Carolina Press, 2006.

Scott, Anne Firor. *The Southern Lady: From Pedestal to Politics, 1830–1930*. Charlottesville: University of Virginia Press, 1970.

Scott, Emmett Jay. *Scott's Official History of the American Negro in the World War*. Chicago: Homewood Press, 1919.

Spinney, Laura. *Pale Rider: The Spanish Flu of 1918 and How It Changed the World*. New York: PublicAffairs, 2017.

Sprengel, Hermann. *The Discovery of Picric Acid (Melinite, Lyddite) as a Powerful Explosive and of Cumulative Detonation with Its Bearing on Wet Guncotton*, 2nd Ed. London: Eyre & Spottiswoode, 1903.

Stockley, Grif. *Blood in Their Eyes: The Elaine Race Massacre of 1919*. Fayetteville: University of Arkansas Press, 2004.

Stonecash, Jeffrey M., ed., *New Directions in American Political Parties*. New York: Routledge, 2010.

United Daughters of the Confederacy. *Minutes of the Annual Convention*, Vol. 24, 1918.

Wells-Barnett, Ida B. *The Arkansas Race Riot*. Chicago: Ida B. Wells-Barnett, 1920.

Wesley, Charles Harris. *The History of the National Association of Colored Women's Clubs, A Legacy of Service*. Washington DC: National Association of Colored Women's Clubs, Inc., 1984.

Wheeler, Marjorie Spruill. *New Women of the New South: The Leaders of the Woman Suffrage Movement in the Southern States*. Oxford University Press, 1993.

Whitaker, Robert. *On the Laps of Gods: The Red Summer and the Struggle for Justice That Remade a Nation*. New York: Crown Publishers, 2008.

Willis, James F. *Southern Arkansas University: The Mulerider School's Centennial History, 1909–2009*. Magnolia: Southern Arkansas University Foundation, 2009.

Woodruff, Nan. *American Congo: The African American Freedom Struggle in the Delta*. Cambridge, MA: Harvard University Press, 2003.

Articles

Barlow, Nathan L. "Camp Robinson's Role During World War II." *Arkansas Military Journal* (Fall 1994).

Butts, J. W., and Dorothy James. "The Underlying Causes of the Elaine Riot of 1919." *Arkansas Historical Quarterly* 20 (Spring 1961).

Cahill, Bernadette. "Stepping Outside the Bounds of Convention: Adolphine Fletcher Terry and the Radical Suffragism in Little Rock, 1911–1920." *Pulaski County Historical Review* 60 (Winter 2012).

Davis, David A. "Not Only War Is Hell: World War I and African American Lynching Narratives." *African American Review* 42, no. 3/4 (2008).

Desmarais, Ralph H. "Military Intelligence Reports on Arkansas Riots: 1919–1920." *Arkansas Historical Quarterly* 33 (Summer 1974).

Dorough, Jefferson M. (Mrs. W. T.). "The First Woman Legislator in Arkansas: A Tribute to Miss Erle Chambers." *Pulaski County Historical Review* 64 (Fall 2016).

Feistman, Eugene. "Radical Disfranchisement in Arkansas, 1867–1868." *Arkansas Historical Quarterly* 12 (Summer 1953).

Finley, Randy. "Black Arkansans and World War One." *Arkansas Historical Quarterly* 49, no. 3 (Autumn 1990).

Francis, Gavin. "The Untreatable," a review of *Pale Rider: The Spanish Flu of 1918 and How It Changed the World* by Laura Spinney, *London Review of Books* (June 2017).

Haiken, Elizabeth. "'The Lord Helps Those Who Help Themselves': Black Laundresses in Little Rock, Arkansas, 1917–1921." *Arkansas Historical Quarterly* 49, no. 1 (Spring 1990).

Jennings, Chantel. "A Season of Influenza and Influence: How World War I and a Pandemic in 1918 Changed College Football Forever." *The Athletic*, August 14, 2018.

Kyzer, Paula. "Promoting Political Responsibility: The League of Women Voters of Pulaski County." *Pulaski County Historical Review* 390 (Spring 1991).

Lemons, J. Stanley. "The Sheppard-Towner Act: Progressivism in the 1920s." *Journal of American History* 55 (March 1969).

Lewis, Todd E. "Mob Justice in the "American Congo": "Judge Lynch" in Arkansas during the Decade after World War I." *Arkansas Historical Quarterly* 52 (Summer 1993).

McCarty, Joey. "The Red Scare in Arkansas: A Southern State and National Hysteria." *Arkansas Historical Quarterly* 37 (Autumn 1978).

McLaughlin, Barney R. "Men's and Women's Perspectives: The Woman Suffrage Debate in Arkansas, 1915–1919." *Ozark Historical Review* 21 (Spring 1993).

Murray, Alexander. "The Manufacture of Picric Acid." *Color Trade Journal* 4, no. 1 (1919).

Palmer, Paul. "Miscegenation as an Issue in the Arkansas Constitutional Convention of 1868." *Arkansas Historical Quarterly* 24 (Summer 1965).

Rogers, O. A. "The Elaine Race Riots of 1919." *Arkansas Historical Quarterly* 19 (Summer 1960).

Ross, Frances Mitchell. "The New Woman as Club Woman and Social Activist in

Turn of the Century Arkansas." *Arkansas Historical Quarterly* 50 (Winter 1991).

Sanborn Fire Insurance Company. *Sanborn Fire Insurance Map of Little Rock.* Sanborn Fire Insurance Company, 1921.

Scott, Kim Allen. "Plague on the Homefront: Arkansas and the Great Influenza Epidemic of 1918." *Arkansas Historical Quarterly* 47 (1988).

Stewart-Abernathy, Leslie C. "Urban Farmsteads: Household Responsibilities in the City." *Historical Archaeology* 20, no. 2 (1986).

Still, Judith Anne. "Carrie Still Shepperson: The Hollows of Her Footsteps." *Arkansas Historical Quarterly* 42, no. 1 (Spring 1983).

Stockley, Grif, and Jeannie M. Whayne. "Federal Troops and the Elaine Massacres: A Colloquy." *Arkansas Historical Quarterly* 61 (Autumn 2002).

Taylor, A. Elizabeth. "The Woman Suffrage Movement in Arkansas." *Arkansas Historical Quarterly* 15 (Spring 1956).

Taylor, Kieran. "'We Have Just Begun': Black Organizing and White Response in the Arkansas Delta, 1919." *Arkansas Historical Quarterly* 58 (Autumn 1999).

Whayne, Jeannie M. "Caging the Blind Tiger: Race, Class, and Family in the Battle for Prohibition in Small Town Arkansas." *Arkansas Historical Quarterly* 71 (Spring 2012).

———."Low Villains and Wickedness in High Places: Race and Class in the Elaine Riots." *Arkansas Historical Quarterly* 58 (Autumn 1999).

Willis, James F. "Lewis Rhoton and the 'Boodlers': Political Corruption and Reform during Arkansas's Progressive Era." *Arkansas Historical Quarterly* (Summer 2017).

Government Documents

Kansas State Agricultural College Catalogue, Fifty-First Session, 1913–1914 (Topeka: Kansas State Printing Office, 1914).

Summary of Casualties Among Members of the American Expeditionary Forces (United States. War Department, 1919).

U.S. Census Bureau Records.

U.S. Department of Agriculture. *Cottage Cheese Dishes* (U.S. Printing Office, 1919).

U.S. House of Representatives, *Hearings Before the Select Committee on Expenditures in the War Department: Serial 1, Volume 3, Reports of the Committee* (Washington DC: Government Printing Office, 1921).

The War with Germany: A Statistical Summary (United States War Department, 1919).

Newspapers and Periodicals

Arkansas Democrat
Arkansas Gazette
Batesville Guard
Coffeyville Daily Journal
Confederate Veteran
Courier Journal
Courier News

Daily Arkansas Gazette
El Paso Herald
Fayetteville Daily Democrat
Gaffney Ledger
Guardian
Hot Springs New Era
Indian School Journal
Iron Trade Review
Log Cabin Democrat
Monticellonian
Mountain Echo
Nashville News
New Orleans States Item
Osceola Times
Pine Bluff Daily Graphic
Southern Standard
Time Picayune
Tomahawk
Topeka Plaindealer
Trench and Camp
Vardaman's Weekly
Washington Post

Online

"America's Wars." https://www.va.gov/opa/publications/factsheets/fs_americas
    _wars.pdf
The Arkansas Great War Letter Project. https://chsarkansasgreatwar.weebly.com
Awards and Decorations: World War I Statistics. https://history.army.mil
    /documents/wwi/23awd.htm
Baker, Lea Flowers. "Women." Central Arkansas Library System Encyclopedia of
    Arkansas, https://encyclopediaofarkansas.net/entries/women-400/
Brandon, Elizabeth Riggs. "John Andrew Riggs (1867–1936)." Central Arkansas
    Library System Encyclopedia of Arkansas, https://encyclopediaofarkansas
    .net/entries/john-andrew-riggs-5509/
Brittenum, Judy Byrd. "John Rison Fordyce." Central Arkansas Library System
    Encyclopedia of Arkansas, https://encyclopediaofarkansas.net/entries/
    john-rison-fordyce-3186/
Brotherton, Velda. "Virginia Maud Dunlap Duncan (1873–1958)." Central
    Arkansas Library System Encyclopedia of Arkansas, https://encyclopedia
    ofarkansas.net/entries/virginia-maud-dunlap-duncan-1633/
Cahill, Bernadette. "Clara Alma Cox McDiarmid (1847–1899)." Central Arkansas
    Library System Encyclopedia of Arkansas, https://encyclopediaofarkansas
    .net/entries/clara-alma-cox-mcdiarmid-8425/
Crawford, Julienne. "Hattie Ophelia Wyatt Caraway (1878–1950)." Central
    Arkansas Library System Encyclopedia of Arkansas, https://encyclopedia
    ofarkansas.net/entries/hattie-ophelia-wyatt-caraway-1278/

Gilbert, James L. "World War I and the Origins of U.S. Military Intelligence."
    http://www.firstworldwar.com/features/propaganda.htm

Glass, Andrew. "Woodrow Wilson Endorses Women's Suffrage on Sept. 30, 1918."
    Politico, September 30, 2007. https://www.politico.com/story/2007/09
    /woodrow-wilson-endorses-womens-suffrage-on-sept-30–1918–006071

GovernmentContractsWon.com. "Arkansas Defense Contractor Lists by City
    United States Government Contracts," 2017. https://www.government
    contractswon.com/department/defense/arkansas_cities.asp

Groshong, Danny. "Taborian Hall." Central Arkansas Library System Encyclopedia
    of Arkansas, https://encyclopediaofarkansas.net/entries/taborian-hall-6984/

Johnson, Jajuan. "Pickens Black." Central Arkansas Library System Encyclopedia
    of Arkansas, https://encyclopediaofarkansas.net/entries/pickens-w-black
    -sr-5396/

Jones-Branch, Cherisse. "Arkansas Association of Colored Women." Central
    Arkansas Library System Encyclopedia of Arkansas, https://encyclopedia
    ofarkansas.net/entries/arkansas-association-of-colored-women-8201/

———. "Segregation and Desegregation." Central Arkansas Library System
    Encyclopedia of Arkansas, https://encyclopediaofarkansas.net/entries/
    segregation-and-desegregation-3079/

Kirk, John. "Civil Rights and Social Change." Central Arkansas Library System
    Encyclopedia of Arkansas, https://encyclopediaofarkansas.net/entries/
    civil-rights-and-social-change-4564/

Lewis, Todd E. "Elias Camp Morris (1855–1922). Central Arkansas Library
    System Encyclopedia of Arkansas, https://encyclopediaofarkansas.net/
    entries/elias-camp-morris-433/

McDaniel, Jim. "William Jayson (Bill) Waggoner." Central Arkansas Library
    System Encyclopedia of Arkansas, https://encyclopediaofarkansas.net/
    entries/william-jayson-2991/

Riffel, Brent E. "Prohibition." Central Arkansas Library System Encyclopedia of
    Arkansas, https://encyclopediaofarkansas.net/entries/prohibition-3002/

Rollberg, Jeanne Norton. "Political Equality League." Central Arkansas Library
    System Encyclopedia of Arkansas, https://encyclopediaofarkansas.net/
    entries/political-equality-league-7834/

Sallee, Julianne H. "General Federation of Women's Clubs in Arkansas." Central
    Arkansas Library System Encyclopedia of Arkansas, https://encyclopedia
    ofarkansas.net/entries/general-federation-of-womens-clubs-of-arkansas
    -162/

Taylor, Paul Kyzer. "Women's Suffrage Movement." Central Arkansas Library
    System Encyclopedia of Arkansas, https://encyclopediaofarkansas.net/
    entries/womens-suffrage-movement-4252/

U.S. Army Center of Military History. https://history.army.mil/index.html

CONTRIBUTORS

MARK K. CHRIST, editor, is the head of adult programming for the Central Arkansas Library System in Little Rock. He previously worked for nearly thirty years at the Arkansas Historic Preservation Program. While there, he served as the Department of Arkansas Heritage's representative on the Arkansas World War I Centennial Commemoration Committee. An award-winning preservationist and author, he has written, edited, and coedited a number of books, primarily on Arkansas and the Civil War, and serves as president of the Arkansas Historical Association.

THOMAS A. DEBLACK, recently retired as professor of history at Arkansas Tech University in Russellville, received his bachelor's degree at Southern Methodist University, his master's degree at Ouachita Baptist University, and his doctorate at the University of Arkansas in Fayetteville. Winner of a 2015 Lifetime Achievement Award from the Arkansas Historical Association, he is the author of *With Fire and Sword: Arkansas, 1861–1874*; coauthor of *Arkansas: A Narrative History*; and coeditor of *The Southern Elite and Social Change: Essays in Honor of Willard B. Gatewood Jr.*

CARL G. DREXLER runs the Arkansas Archeological Survey's research station at Southern Arkansas University in Magnolia. He is a specialist in conflict archaeology, having worked on Civil War, Revolutionary War, Indian Wars, and World War I sites across the country. A native of Bethlehem, Pennsylvania, he earned his doctorate at the College of William & Mary, in Virginia.

SHAWN FISHER is an assistant professor of history at Harding University in Searcy. He earned his doctorate at the University of Memphis, where he was the recipient of the Ruth and Harry Woodbury Fellowship in Southern History and the Major L. Wilson Graduate Paper Prize. He has spoken at conferences in England and Ireland, at the Society for Military History's national conference, and at the annual Conference of Tennessee Historians. He was the keynote speaker at the Phi Alpha

Theta regional conference and at the forty-first annual conference of the Arkansas Political Science Association. The Arkansas Historical Association awarded him the 2013 James L. Foster and Billy W. Beason Award for his dissertation on the Little Rock Central High Crisis titled "The Battle of Little Rock."

ELIZABETH GRIFFIN HILL returned to college following her retirement from a federal human resources position, receiving her master's degree from the Department of Rhetoric and Writing of the University of Arkansas at Little Rock in 2013. Midway through the program, Hill accepted the opportunity to do extensive research at the National Archives at Fort Worth, Texas, going on to write the book *A Splendid Piece of Work—1912–2012: One Hundred Years of Arkansas's Home Demonstration and Extension Homemakers Clubs.* She also is the author of *Faithful to Our Tasks: Arkansas's Women and the Great War.*

CHERISSE JONES-BRANCH is an associate professor of history at Arkansas State University in Jonesboro, where she teaches courses in U.S. history, women's history, civil rights and African American history, and heritage studies. She received her bachelor's and master's degrees from the College of Charleston, South Carolina, and a doctorate in history from Ohio State University in Columbus. She is the author of numerous published works on women's civil rights activism. In 2014, she published *Crossing the Line: Women and Interracial Activism in South Carolina during and after World War II* with the University Press of Florida and is the coeditor of *Arkansas Women: Their Lives and Times,* published by the University of Georgia Press in 2018. She is also working on a second monograph, *Better Living by Their Own Bootstraps: Rural Black Women's Activism in Arkansas,* which is under contract with the University of Arkansas Press.

BRIAN K. MITCHELL teaches in the Department of History at the University of Arkansas at Little Rock. His interests include African American antebellum history, free black communities, and urban history. He is currently working on several digital projects that pertain to free blacks in the antebellum South and commemoration of the 1919 Elaine Massacre.

RAYMOND D. SCREWS is the director of the Arkansas National Guard Museum at Camp Robinson in North Little Rock, a position he has held since 2014. He received a BS in history from the College of the Ozarks in Missouri in 1985 and earned his MA in American history in 1991 from Pittsburg State University in Kansas. He earned his PhD in American history at the University of Nebraska in 2003. He previously served as assistant history professor and assistant coordinator of the master's program in public history at the University of Arkansas at Little Rock and was a visiting professor in history at Minot State University in North Dakota.

JEANNIE M. WHAYNE is university professor of history at the University of Arkansas and author of two award-winning books, *Delta Empire: Lee Wilson and the Transformation of Agriculture in the New South* (2011) and *A New Plantation South: Land, Labor, and Federal Favor* (1996), both of which won the Arkansas Library Association's Arkansiana prize. *Delta Empire* won the Arkansas Historical Association's Ragsdale Award. She is the editor or coauthor of nine other books, including *The Ongoing Burden of Southern History: Politics and Identity in the Twenty-First-Century South* (2012). She is coauthor of a college-level textbook on Arkansas history: *Arkansas: A Narrative History*. Whayne is a distinguished lecturer with the Organization of American Historians, a fellow of the Agricultural History Society, and winner of the Arkansas Historical Association's Lifetime Achievement Award. Whayne, who served as president of the Agricultural History Society (2013–2014), was awarded the society's Gladys Baker Lifetime Achievement Award in 2017.

ROGER PAULY is an associate professor of history at the University of Central Arkansas in Conway. He attended St. Olaf College and the University of Aberdeen, Scotland for his undergraduate degree, awarded in 1988, and earned a PhD in history at the University of Delaware in 2000. He is an eclectic writer who has explored historical subjects from Marcus Garvey to the Mau Mau rebellion of Kenya to the pop-culture significance of *Miami Vice*. His most noteworthy book is *Firearms: The Life Story of a Technology* (Johns Hopkins University Press), which has led to other projects relating to the history of guns, such as the 2010 PBS television series *Ground War*. Most recently, he appeared extensively in Millcreek Entertainment's new documentary series *American Guns*, which premiered on Amazon Prime in 2017.

INDEX

126th Infantry Regiment, 19
142nd Field Artillery, 128
148th Aero Squadron, 7
153rd Infantry Regiment, 128
162nd Depot Brigade, 87
312th Signal Corps, 119
369th Infantry Regiment. *See* Harlem
   Hellfighters

A

Adkins, Dave, 143
Adkins, W. A., 131
Aitken, Geo. L., 143
Alabama Great Southern Railroad, 108
Alabama, 71, 107, 119, 124, 125, 186
Alexandria, Louisiana, 105
Allen, Henry J., 140
America's Forgotten Pandemic: The
   Influenza of 1918 (book), 148
American Chemical Society, 56
American Expeditionary Force (AEF),
   6, 7, 17, 23
American Federation of Labor
   (AFL), 78
American Institute of Electrical
   Engineers, 56
American Institute of Mining
   Engineers, 56
American Legion Hall, 131
American Legion Post 41, 139, 140,
   143–44
American Legion, 137, 138, 139
American Red Cross. *See* Red Cross
American Society of Civil Engineers, 56
American Society of Mechanical
   Engineers, 56
American Women and the World War
   (book), 35
American Women's Suffrage

Association (AWSA), 169, 171, 180,
   181, 235n
Anderson, Mrs. H. C., 37
Anthony, Susan B., 169, 170, 171
Anti-Catholicism, 16
Anti-Saloon League, 171
Archduke Franz Ferdinand, 3
Argenta, Arkansas, 71, 105, 112, 114
Arizona, 78
Arkadelphia, Arkansas, 154
Arkansas Agricultural Cooperative
   Extension Service, 26, 54, 84, 182
Arkansas Association of Colored
   Women (AACW), 90, 92, 94, 180
Arkansas Democrat (newspaper), 69, 89,
   93, 154, 161
Arkansas Echo (newspaper), 16
Arkansas Equal Suffrage Association,
   170, 180
Arkansas Equal Suffrage Central
   Committee, 48, 180
Arkansas Federation of Women's Clubs
   (AFWC), 25, 52, 92, 174, 190
Arkansas Gazette (newspaper), 26, 29, 31,
   32, 45, 49, 69, 90, 92, 107, 108, 109,
   110, 115, 136, 150, 151, 154, 156,
   157, 160, 164, 178, 180, 185, 191,
   196–212 passim
Arkansas League of Women Voters,
   186, 187, 188
Arkansas National Guard Museum, 150
Arkansas Power and Light Company,
   71, 76, 80
Arkansas Race Riot, The (book), 134
Arkansas State Board of Health, 151,
   152, 153, 158
Arkansas State Constitutional
   Convention, 19
Arkansas State Normal School, 154

Brun, Erik, 232n
Brunson's Famous Prescription, 162–3
Brunswick, Georgia, 70, 74, 76, 80
Bryan, William Jennings, 126
Bunceton, Missouri, 83
Burgess, J. C., 180
Burkes, E. L., 143
Burn, Harry, 186
Bush, A. E., 94
Bush, John E., 90, 91, 94
Butts, J. B., 143
Byerly, E. F., 143
Byrd, Newt, 162

C

C. P. Wilson stave mill, 95
Cahill, Bernadette, 171, 174
Calico Rock, Arkansas, 158
Callen, N. E., 134
Callery, Ida, 172
Calvary Cemetery, 75, 77
Camden, Arkansas, 158
Camp Beauregard, Louisiana, 21
Camp Dodge, Iowa, 88, 102
Camp Funston, Kansas, 148
Camp Grant, Illinois, 88
Camp Jackson, South Carolina, 22
Camp Merritt, New Jersey, 21
Camp Pike College, 126
Camp Pike, Arkansas, 17, 23, 43, 46, 49,
    67, 75, 78, 87–9, 99, 101, 103, 105,
    114–128 passim, 132, 137, 148–51,
    182, 219n
Camp Robinson, Arkansas, 105,
    127–8, 150
Campau, Harry, 143
Capital Hotel, 174
Capitol Hill School, 98
Capper, Arthur, 210
Caraway, Hattie, , 187
Caraway, Thaddeus, 100, 187
Carolina, Henrietta E., 94
Carpenters Union, 115
Carroll, Fred, 79
Carville, E. B., 143
casualties (WWI), 6–7
Catt, Carrie Chapman, 168, 169,
    176, 186

Cavein, Milton, 143
Center for Infectious Disease Research
    and Policy, 150
Center, Arkansas, 159
Central [Baptist] College, 154
Central Trades Council, 45
Chamberlain, Austen, 203
Chamberlain, Neville, 206
Chaney, Mitchell, 85
Chautauqua, 14
Chavey, W. C., 143
Cherry Acres, 73
Chicago Medial Society, 163
Chicago, Illinois, 24, 91, 163, 186
Chicot County, Arkansas, 163
Children's Bureau of the U.S.
    Department of Labor, 40
Chilocco Indian School, 122, 229n
China, 124, 204, 205, 209, 210
Chippewas, 122
Choctaws, 122, 127
Christianity and Socialism (book), 5
Christmas, Lugenia, 30
Churchill, Winston, 5, 194
Citizens Co-operative Laundry, 48
Clancy, Frank D., 143
Clansman, The (book), 93
Clarendon, Arkansas, 22
Clark County, Arkansas, 37,
    38, 50
Clark, Clement G., 118
Clarke, Ida Clyde, 35
Clarke, James P., , 171
Clarke, William H., 88
Clayton, J. H., 107
Cleburne, Patrick R., 13, 22
Cleveland County, Arkansas, 100
Coal Hill, Arkansas, 157
Cohn, Millard, 143
Cold War, 57, 80
Cole, Glenn, 21, 22
Cole, M. L., 21
Coleman, Ed, 139
College Station, Arkansas, 73
Collegeville, Arkansas, 16
Collins, "Kidd", 130–1
Columbia County, Arkansas, 80
Columbia, South Carolina, 109